NAVIGATING ARGUMENT
A Guidebook to Academic Writing

NAVIGATING ARGUMENT
A Guidebook to Academic Writing

Written and Illustrated by Sheila Morton

Tusculum College

Greeneville, TN
2014

For My Students

Copyright © 2014 by Sheila Morton

All rights reserved. This book or any portion thereof may not be reproduced or used in any manner whatsoever without the express written permission of the publisher except for the use of brief quotations in a book review, scholarly journal, or other scholarly endeavor.

First Printing: 2014

ISBN 978-1-312-25384-1

Tusculum College
50 Shiloh Rd.
Greeneville, TN 37743

www.tusculum.edu

Contents

Part One: Navigating The Writing Process 9

Chapter One: Getting Ready for the Journey: Pre-writing 10
    Brainstorming 11
    Mapping 12
    Sketching 14
    Freewriting 16
    Focused Freewriting 18
    Ghost Writing 19
    New Writing 20
    Round-Robin Writing 20

Chapter Two: Beginning Your Journey: Drafting 24
    Outlining an Argument 25
    Supporting with Evidence 35
    Introducing & Concluding 40

Chapter Three: The Final Trek: Revising 52
    Revising Globally 54
    Revising Locally 62

Part Two: Navigating English 110 68

Chapter Four: Learning the Ways: The Rhetorical Analysis 73
    Choosing & Deconstructing Your Text 74
    Analyzing Claims & Subclaims 75
    Evaluating Evidence 77
    Categorizing Audience 78
    Appealing to Readers (Ethos, Pathos, & Logos) 80
    Avoiding Fallacies 87
    Recognizing Figures of Speech 99
    Sample Rhetorical Analysis 105

Chapter Five: Taking the Lead: The Argument Paper 111
    Starting with Curiosity 112

> Considering Audience   114
> Choosing Your Evidence   116
> Organizing the Essay (Argument Styles)   124
> Developing Style & Voice   131
> Sample Argument Paper   133

PART THREE: NAVIGATING ENGLISH 111   144

> Chapter Six: Choosing Your Conversation: The Research Proposal   149
>> Navigating the Research Process   150
>> Finding Your Topic   151
>> Formulating a Research Question   155
>> Drafting the Proposal   158
>> Sample Research Proposals   160
>
> Chapter Seven: Listening to Others: The Annotated Bibliography   171
>> Selecting & Analyzing Sources   173
>> Writing Summaries   181
>> Sample Bibliographies   185
>
> Chapter Eight: Joining the Conversation: The Research Paper   190
>> Organizing the Essay   191
>> Paraphrasing, Summarizing, & Quoting   193
>> Avoiding Plagiarism   197
>> Retaining Rhetorical Authority   199
>> Addressing Counter Claims   204
>> Revising a Research Paper   207
>> Sample Research Papers   211

APPENDICES   239

> Appendix A: Formatting a Paper in APA & MLA   241
>
> Appendix B: In-Text Citation   247
>
> Appendix C: Bibliographic Formatting   256

INTRODUCTION

How to use this book

I recently went to South America, visiting famous sites across Peru and Equador, and taking a brief trek through the jungle. I was a little nervous about my first jungle excursion. After all, I was an inexperienced trekker, with no knowledge of the jungles of South America. As I followed my guide through the unknown, it occurred to me that this was likely how my students often felt. Like me, they were entering a place they'd never been (college), and being asked to perform tasks for which they'd had little preparation. Being asked to write a college-level paper was often quite intimidating to many of them. Like me, they were on a journey, one potentially fraught with pitfalls and obstacles for which they might not be prepared. And so I decided to offer them a guide book, helping them in the best way I knew how to navigate the difficulties of college-level writing. The result is this book you are holding.

This guidebook is divided into three sections. The first section will help you when you are assigned any paper for any class. This section guides you through the "writing process," giving you ideas on how to formulate a topic, how to organize a topic into a draft, and how to revise that draft to make it ready for submission. I hope that you will return to this section often in your future courses at the College. I hope that you will find it useful even after college, when you find yourself needing to write something but stymied about how to begin.

The second and third sections are specific to the two required composition courses at Tusculum. Section two will introduce you to the two major papers you will write in English 110: the rhetorical analysis paper, and the argument paper. The third section will guide you through the writing of the three major assignments in English 111: the proposal, the annotated bibliography, and the research paper. Your instructor will guide you through these sections and help you to understand these projects.

Finally, at the end of the book, I have included a guide to writing in APA and MLA styles, including both how to format in-text citations and how to compose the bibliography. These sections, included in the Appendices, will be invaluable to you as you move through your coursework at the College. Please learn to use these guides and consult them any time you are assigned a paper.

I know that learning to explore the paths of academic writing can be a challenging, sometimes even daunting task. So in addition to the advice I have provided, I have also included advice from students, past and present, of Tusculum's composition courses. Throughout each section, you will see dialogue boxes featuring this advice, and I hope that these will help you as well.

I and all of the writing instructors here at the college wish you a happy and successful journey as you learn to explore the complex environment of academic writing and navigate your way to good writing habits.

I. Navigating the Writing Process

CHAPTER 1: PREWRITING
Getting Ready for the Journey

Before I left for my jungle excursion, I wanted to make sure that I had packed properly. I researched weather conditions and read recommendations on what kinds of clothing to plan for. I packed my suitcase carefully with sun screen, bug spray, canvas pants, cotton socks, and hiking boots. I knew it would be important to be well prepared for an environment I had no experience with. I certainly would not have thrown just any old clothes in a suitcase and gone without adequate preparation.

In the same way that you would never depart for an important trip without first preparing, you should never embark on a writing assignment without similar and adequate preparation. Over the course of your studies here at Tusculum, you are going to embark on many different kinds of new and unfamiliar writing adventures. In some cases, your professors will assign you specific writing topics. In others, you will be left to design your own topic. In either case, you will need to adequately prepare for your journey before you sit down at your computer to begin composing the actual writing project. That's why the first stage in the writing process is *"**prewriting**."* Prewriting is the general term used to describe all of those activities that come before the actual drafting and that help us to either 1) Generate topics for writing, or 2) Generate material in support of a given topic. The following pages detail several different approaches to prewriting, and you should consult these pages *first* whenever you are given a new writing assignment.

BRAINSTORMING

Most of you have probably been asked to brainstorm on a writing topic before, but for those of you who have not, brainstorming is a powerful way to come up with ideas for writing. You use this technique to generate topic ideas for a paper by simply writing down everything that comes to mind that might interest you. Don't worry about dissecting these ideas yet. Write down the ugly and the beautiful. Most of them probably won't make good writing topics, but writing them down might lead you to think of similar and better topics. As Peter Elbow (one of the most important writing theorists in the country) claims, "You can't get the good ones [topic ideas] and the fruitful interaction among the odd ones unless you welcome the terrible ones" (8). So don't be shy about writing down whatever ideas come to you.

Moreover, brainstorming will help you avoid one of the biggest pitfalls that young writers/explorers often make—latching onto the first idea that occurs to them. In fact, Frank L. Cioffi (a writing professor at Princeton and author of *The Imaginative Argument*) claims that you should throw away at least the first *five* ideas that occur to you, as these will be the ones that occur first to *most* people and are thus likely the most obvious. Brainstorming, then, will lead you from those topics that most immediately occur to you and down a chain of connections into more original and interesting ideas worthy of writing about.

In my own writing classes, students and I brainstorm topics together for the first several days of any writing assignment. Each class has a theme, structured around a set of readings, and from this theme, we brainstorm a variety of possible writing topics. Each day, I ask students to meet together in small groups and come up with a list of four or five possible writing topics. Then we share these as a class, and I compile them into a single document. The following is an example of one of these brainstorms created by students in English 111. The students had just finished reading Walter Dean Myers' novel, *Monster*, about a young black teenager from Harlem on trial for murder. The protagonist of the novel, Steven, is also an aspiring filmmaker, and the novel is written as if it were a screenplay that Steven is developing to help him cope with his experiences in prison. Students used the novel's themes to generate topic ideas for a research paper. As you can see, some of these ideas are quite strong, others less so. But even the weaker ideas led to better ideas, and in the end, all of the students found topics they were interested in and able to write well about.

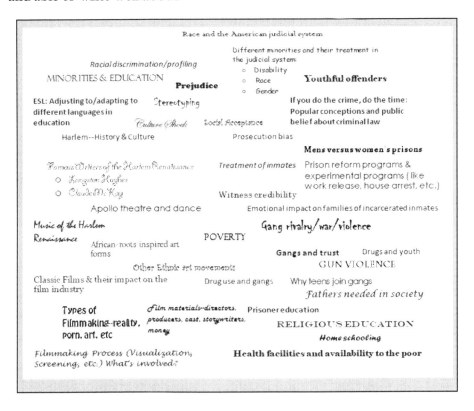

Figure 1.1: Brainstorming

MAPPING

Sometimes called clustering or bubble mapping, this technique offers you a way to visually depict your ideas and allow those visuals to guide you to new ideas. You can use this as a discovery strategy to narrow down topic ideas, or you can use it as a way to generate ideas for subtopics once you have chosen the primary topic of your essay. You

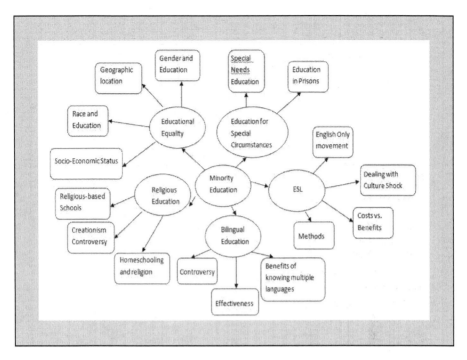

Figure 1.2: Mapping

begin by writing down either ONE idea for an essay's primary topic, or THE idea (if a specific topic has been assigned or already decided upon). Then, think of as many related ideas as you can. Don't worry if this chain of ideas leads you off on some kind of tangent—these side roads can sometimes be very productive and lead you to truly interesting and unique topics. Jot these ideas down surrounding the main idea, and connect them via lines or arrows. Then do the same for each of *those* ideas, in an expanding web. The example in figure 1.2 is from a group mapping exercise in English 111. The group of students involved knew that they wanted to write their papers on a topic related to minority education but had not yet chosen their specific topics. The bubble map helped them to explore some possible topics related to minority education.

SKETCHING

Another way to visually represent ideas on paper is sketching. For those of you who may be visual-spatial learners, this can be a particularly productive way to think through a topic, to explore connected ideas, implications, and arguments. Even if you aren't a great artist, sketching allows you to access other parts of your brain that writing does not typically tap into, thus allowing new ideas to emerge. Patricia Dunn (a writing professor at The State University of New York at Stonybrook and author of *Talking, Sketching, Moving: Multiple Literacies in the Teaching of Writing*) advocates sketching as a method of discovery for *all* writers, even those who don't typically think of themselves as artistic: "Sketching, drawing, or graphing developing ideas gives students who can visualize images an opportunity to use that talent productively." By contrast, she explains, "it forces those comfortable with *words* to see their text through a different perspective" (66, italics added). Regardless of your drawing skills, sketching can help you to think outside the boundaries of your normal writing routine and potentially discover some intriguing new ideas for writing.

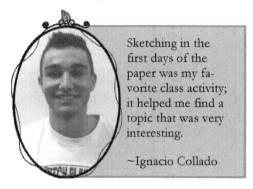

Sketching in the first days of the paper was my favorite class activity; it helped me find a topic that was very interesting.

~Ignacio Collado

The sketch in Figure 1.3 is by Bo, a previous student in English 111. Students had read Chaim Potok's novel, *The Chosen*, and began developing possible writing topics from that novel. One of the prompts I gave students to think about was how parental goals for our lives often differ from our own goals. On the left side of the sketch, Bo depicts his parents' desire for his happiness but also some of their hopes for his future, including his becoming a successful businessman with a college degree, a family, and a home near them in Ohio. In the sketch of his own hopes for his future (right side), a desire to live near his family in Ohio is still present, but much smaller, and his parents' aspiration that he be a businessman is here dwarfed by his desire to make a difference in the world (though the money symbol still indicates that pecuniary interests are not lacking!). Bo's sketch helped him begin thinking about what could happen if parental goals for a child's future were in serious conflict with the child's own goals. Through other research and discussion, he later became interested in the topic of arranged marriage. However, because he had begun his process by thinking about parents' real hopes for their children, he didn't simply write a paper condemning the practice, but instead approached the issue with the assumption that parental expectations are usually a result of love. Consequently, he wrote an excellent research paper that was sensitive to the complexity of the issue. While his sketch is then only tangentially relevant to his final research topic, beginning with this sketch helped him to start from a place of sensitivity and respect, and he was then able to write an A-level paper!

Figure 1.3: Sketching

FREEWRITING

Many of you have probably been asked to do freewriting at some point in the past, and that's because many of us who teach writing find freewriting one of the most effective methods for developing writing skills at *any* stage of the writing process. Peter Elbow, who developed the method and coined the phrase, describes freewriting as the process of writing without editing and without self-critique, and most importantly **without stopping**! That means that even if you can't think of anything profound to write, you write anyway. Even if what you're writing goes off topic and becomes completely disconnected, you write anyway. And even if you think what you are writing is utter garbage, *you write anyway*. In fact, "garbage writing" is good, Elbow argues, because our heads are full of garbage and we can't write anything decent until we get the garbage out. By freewriting, we can clear our minds of mundane, obvious, *garbage* ideas, which will leave our heads clearer for better, more innovative ideas. The more you write, Elbow says, the more chance you will discover a pearl amidst the muck.

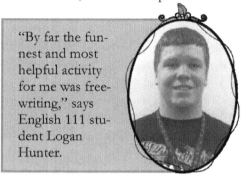

"By far the funnest and most helpful activity for me was freewriting," says English 111 student Logan Hunter.

Freewriting also frees us from the constant editor and critic in our head. True innovation can be halted, even frozen by this inner critic, so the aim of freewriting is to shut this critic up and allow the ideas to flow: "It's an unnecessary burden to try to think of words and also worry at the same time whether they're the right words," writes Elbow (5). A freewrite is never graded writing and shouldn't be critiqued even by you. It's simply a way to get ideas out on paper.

Elbow recommends freewriting for 10 minutes every day to keep your mind free from muck and your writing muscles nimble. Many of you will be asked to do this in your writing classes, but feel free to do so on your own time as well. Remember, the more you write, the more chance you'll find that pearl!

The following two freewrites come from students in an English 110 class. They were given no guides or prompts, just asked to write for 10 minutes. From these two examples, you can see that sometimes freewrites are generative of topic ideas, and sometimes they aren't. Rebecca, who was having a very rough day, used the freewrite to vent some of her frustration. But that venting eventually opened the door to a good paper topic: the benefits of being a commuter student. Of course, not all freewrites are going to generate good ideas. But even if, like Chae, all you can think to write is how you can't think of anything to write, at least you'll be clearing your head!

> Yesterday I got a parking ticket. I was parked outside of Welty-Craig in apparently a spot where I wasn't supposed to park. It had already been a bad week and class didn't make it any better, then I come outside and find a parking ticket on my car. What the heck? I was so mad. I called my dad and was going off because I don't understand why you pay a buttload of money to come here and then you have to freaking pay for a parking ticket. It's ridiculous! I hate having to park in a certain space and for commuters its hard to find a place to park. The different colored lines for different people to park is STUPID cause I don't pay attention to what color lines are, if I see a parking spot empty then I'm going to park there. I can't believe how much sleep I have lost either. I stay up late working on homework and don't go to bed. Then I have to get up early the next morning to go class. That means there is way too much homework. Homework sucks! We even have homework on the weekends. The only thing bad about commuting is the money. You have to pay money for gas to get you back and forth and after a while it gets old. The only good thing about commuting is that I get to see my family everyday. And work study, work study is so stupid. You're supposed to be working to help pay off your college expenses but in my work study, we don't do anything but sit there because she never has anything for us to do. Drinking on campus, I think that that is one reason most kids go away to college, is to get drunk and party all the time. Well they are crazy. One day it will eventually catch up with them and they will realize what they did. The computer labs that are here on campus. . .

Figure 1.4: Rebecca's Freewrite

> Umm ten minutes. WOW that's a lot of writing to do about nothing. So. . . I don't know. She said write whatever is on our minds. Im hella tired right now. I didn't get bed til a little after two. I don't know what I was doing. Maybe I just couldn't sleep. Besides that I had to get up at 9:00 to get ready for work. Hunter just stopped writing. I didn't know we could take a break. I wonder if Dr. Morton saw him. I like Dr. Morton. She teaches good. I actually understand everything she talks about! I hope I have her again. . . We got 5 minutes left and hunter has stopped two times already. I need a break. LOL. Seriously. My hand is starting to hurt. I can't wait to get out of class. Imma eat and go straight to sleep. I don't know where I wanna go for dinner b/c I don't eat the caf food all lik that. Time is about to be up. . . Horray! :)

Figure 1.5: Chae's Freewrite

FOCUSED FREEWRITING

Like freewriting, focused freewriting requires that you write continually for 10 minutes. However, in a *focused* freewrite, your professor will give you a general topic on which to write. In the following focused freewrite, Chelsea responds to her professor's prompt: "Think of an experience in your life that has made you feel a strong emotion. It doesn't have to be a major life event, just a memory to which you attach a great deal of feeling." Chelsea chose to write her focused freewrite on a memorable basketball game from her high school years.

> My junior year of high school in the state playoffs we had the dream team throughout regular season we lost one game and went 20 games undefeated before we lost one. We were very confident going into the state playoffs. We had won the conference and thought we could wind it all we beat the first 3 teams we played no problem. It was the 4th round and we were playing at home which gave us another advantage. The team we were playing only had one more loss than we did. It was sure to be a good game. The game started and how we started the game playing did not match our egos. We were down by 18 points in the first at the end of the first quarter. Needless to say we went to the locker room at half time down by four. The game was nerve racking the lead went back in fourth numerous times. At the end of the 4th quarter we were tied. We went into overtime in the last minute of the game we were down by 3 we put our best shooter in and she tied it up. But they went down and scored they were now up to. I took it cost to coast to score to tie the game once more there were ten seconds on the clock and they came down shot a long 3 to win. I had never felt so devastated. I felt like nothing worse could have happened at that point. It was the hardest game I had ever lost in my basketball career. If there was a year to win a state championship it would have been that year.

Figure 1.6: Chelsea's Focused Freewrite

GHOST WRITING

Freewriting is very successful for many of my students. However, there are some who simply can't turn off the editor-within, and freewriting is then anything but "free." Instead, they write, edit, revise, rethink, add, delete, etc. All of which negates the purpose of freewriting. If this describes you, you may want to try a "ghostwrite." Like a freewrite, a ghostwrite is 10 minutes of continual writing without stopping and without editing or revising. However, ghostwrites are done on the computer with either the computer screen off (if you have a desktop) or a piece of paper covering your screen (if you have a laptop). In a ghostwrite, you should type continually for ten minutes, and force yourself not to peek at the screen. Personally, I love ghostwriting. I feel as if I'm sending my words out into the darkness of cyberspace where they will eventually, *possibly*, coalesce into coherent ideas; but they are sent out there, apart from me, free. My students concur; most of them find ghostwriting the most freeing way to freewrite.

New Writing

Frank Cioffi, in his book *The Imaginative Argument*, describes an activity he calls "the newrite" or "new-write." Like the freewrite, the new-write requires you to write as much as you can think of in the space of 10 minutes. The difference, however, is that the new-write is a space for creativity, even craziness, to reign. Think of something wacky to write, Cioffi says. Or try writing in a crazy way—like only using words without the letter "a." Write about something silly that you know wouldn't fit the assignment but is fun or even funny to you. The importance here is to *play* with your writing. Moreover, Cioffi says, you needn't worry about *continuously* writing; feel free to pause, think, and begin again.

One example of a new-write was given me by a previous student, Ryan. The writing assignment was to think of a problem on campus and offer a solution. Ryan did a new-write on the scratchy toilet-paper in the campus bathrooms and proposed that all bathrooms be supplied with Charmin, arguing that this would help students relax and focus on their school work. The paper was fun and funny; he enjoyed writing it, and I enjoyed reading it. It was obviously not going to make a very good *academic* paper, but that wasn't the point. Ryan was writing, getting ideas out, playing, having fun, and a good writing topic eventually emerged from all of this play.

Round-Robin Writing

Round-Robin writes allow you to generate additional ideas and support for a topic you have already selected by taking advantage of the ideas and experiences of your peers. Later in this book, you will read about the different kinds of evidence that a writer might offer in support of her arguments. One of these types of evidence is personal experience;

another is the experience had by friends and acquaintances. Round-robin writes allow to you to gather the latter type of evidence and, with your friends' permission, use it to support your arguments.

> My favorite activity was Round-robin Writes. I was able to choose an interesting topic and get feedback from my peers.
>
> ~Lukas Winkelmann

Another benefit to round-robin writes is that you might potentially discover alternate points of view. You will read later in this book about the importance of including counter-arguments in your essay. It is vital to making a good argument that you acknowledge—and show that you understand—these opposing views. Round-robin writing allows you to gather the opinions of those who might not agree with you so that you can *respectfully* address those dissenting voices in your paper.

In a round-robin exercise, you will begin by putting your topic at the top of a piece of paper and then writing about your topic for approximately 8-10 minutes. Explain what you hope to argue in your paper; share some of your own experiences and opinions about the topic; even outline some of the major arguments you intend to make. After you've finished, trade this paper with a friend (or, if you are doing this activity in a computer lab, stand up and move to your peer's computer). Read what your peer has written about his or her topic, and then spend 8-10 minutes sharing *your* opinions and experiences about that topic. Do this again with another peer, and another, until you feel you have enough information to support your claims.

Figure 1.7 shows an example of a round-robin write done in class by a group of English 110 students. The author of the paper, Jamie, wanted to write about college students working. Notice that not all of her classmates agreed with her initial claim, and their ideas and experiences helped her to modify her central argument to include their counter-claims, giving her a much more rounded and well-considered argument.

Topic: Should College students work part-time jobs?

CENTRAL CLAIM: College student should not work part-time jobs because 1. College students cannot focus wholly on school like they need to if they work a part-time job. 2. It is almost impossible to balance working and going to school. 3. If students work a part-timejob, they cannot commit to college fully like they need to. 4. Working a part-time job takes away from much needed studying, resting, and sleeping.

- Cecily—I don't completely agree with this statement. I have a part time job, but I only work on the weekends, so I can focus on my school during the week. I think that college students can have jobs as along as they don't let their job get in the way of their school work. I feel like as long as a student can be responsible with their work, they can have a job if they want, they just need to have their priorities straight.
- Megan—I would have to disagree. I personally have always worked while in school and am working while in college; even working part time I still do better work that the people who don't have jobs. I think it that it is about how much effort you're willing to put into your job and school work. If you are willing to do your work and do it well, you shouldn't have a problem with working a part time job while in school. This just being my own personal experience.
- Deanna—I agree, I actually do not have a job but I do however teach a Sunday school class and I am in a band, these things take away from your time that should be devoted to homework and it also adds onto the level of stress. I would not encourage students to quit their job or their ministry because this may take away from much needed school work break time. All students need to focus on school work however; students should continue to have a break of some sort from book work. That way students are less likely to go insane with all the stress caused from homework.
- Bree—I agree whole heartedly with this statement, right now I am just working 2 hours with work study and I work in the pool but when I am down there I cannot do my work like you are supposed to be able to with work STUDY because they do not get internet service down there and it makes me so behind on my studies when I get home so I am often staying up till about 3:30 every night catching up

Figure 1.7: Round-Robin Write

Outlining

Outlining is a kind of prewriting activity that allows you to organize your thoughts into a set of assertions to support your main argument. Although outlining is technically a form of prewriting, we are going to address it later in this book under the section on "drafting."

Researching

For many types of writing assignments, conducting research is also a vital step in the prewriting process. But because this is covered extensively in English 111, we're going to talk more about the process of academic research in that section, found later in this book.

CHAPTER 2: DRAFTING
Beginning Your Journey

Once you've gathered your thoughts and materials, packed your bags and strapped on your boots, it's time to depart. This is potentially the most treacherous part of your journey because this is the stage during which you will begin generating the product that will eventually be graded. However, if you have adequately prepared for your journey, the drafting process need not be either as dangerous or laborious as it would without that preparation.

And just as you would never begin a literal journey without knowing where you are going, you should not embark upon the drafting of a paper without thoroughly familiarizing yourself with your intended destination. For that reason, you should carefully read the paper assignment and make certain you understand what the requirements of the writing project are. If you are at all confused, meet with your professor. Think of your writing assignment as your map and your professor as your guide, and use these conscientiously to get where you need to go. Few things are more frustrating to professors than students who turn in papers that evidence no attention to the assignment sheet. You would never pilot a plane with such disregard for direction, and neither should you write a paper that way.

Once you thoroughly understand the assignment, it's time to start drafting. As we saw in the last chapter, if you've done some effective prewriting, you will approach the drafting stage with a solid set of ideas, arguments, counter-arguments, and evidence. Sometimes, in fact, you have so much material that it is difficult to know where to actually begin. For that reason, I want to begin our discussion of the drafting process by describing a kind of pre-writing/drafting hybrid activity: outlining.

OUTLINING AN ARGUMENT

Many of you have probably been asked to create an outline for a paper you wrote in the past. If you have not, then you are about to learn one of the most important tricks that good writers use to organize solid, cohesive arguments.

The first step to writing a good outline is to carefully read through your prewriting (including any research you may have conducted) and decide on the *main argument* you intend to make. Ask yourself the following question: "**When readers are finished with my paper, what do I want them to** *think, believe,* or *do*?" The answer to that question is your primary argument, and you will usually want to formulate this argument in the form of a **central claim.** (Please note: different instructors and different text books will use different terms for this guiding purpose. Your instructor may call it a ***thesis statement***, for example, or a ***purpose statement.*** For the rest of this book, however, I will call it a **central claim** for the arbitrary reason that that's the term I personally prefer.)

You must outline your paper by writing down what you're going to talk about in each paragraph. Make sure that your outline stays on topic
~Samantha Dykes

One final note, there are some forms of writing—even research writing—that work on a more exploratory basis. For these kinds of assignments, you won't be expected to know what your central claim is at the beginning of the paper; instead, the paper will serve as an exploration leading you eventually to a conclusion or claim. In this style of writing, you may have a ***guiding question***. A guiding question is an acceptable replacement for the central claim in some forms of writing, but be sure to check with your instructor for your particular assignment.

Formulating Your Central Claim

To begin, it's important to understand that a central claim, as the name suggests, makes some kind of *claim* or *assertion*. By doing so, it presupposes an ongoing conversation, even a debate, about the topic at hand. After all, you would never need to convince someone of something that everyone already knows. You convince readers to take a position on issues for which there can be *at least* two possible points of view, and likely more. So, "Many more Tusculum students own cars than bikes," cannot be a central claim, since you need not convince anyone to believe it; it simply *is*. But "Tusculum students should consider bringing bikes rather than cars to campus" is a claim which invites discussion since more than one side might be taken.

That brings me to the first rule of central claims:

1. **A central claim is never a declaration of *fact*, but is always an *opinion*.**

Now that word, "opinion," occasionally causes me some difficulty. Unfortunately, many people have somewhere gathered the erroneous belief that "opinion" is purely personal, and as such, is exempt from the demands of reason and logic. Not true. And this is perhaps the *most* important rule to keep in mind when drafting a good central claim: **All opinions are NOT created equal!** In fact, some opinions are even stupid opinions, and people shouldn't have them. "Men are smarter than women," may, technically, be an *opinion*, but it's a stupid opinion, and certainly not one backed up by either solid reasoning or good research.

And so we have rule number two for the creation of a solid central claim:

2. **A central claim expresses an opinion based on well-reasoned and carefully researched evidence.**

In the previous chapter we talked about ways to discover topics for writing that interest you, as your interest will almost always translate into a more well-written paper. And in general, topics interest us when we already know a little bit about them and have formed some sort of opinion in regards to them. I would caution you, however, to keep an open mind as you research your topic or as you talk to others about it in an attempt to learn more. As you delve more deeply into your topic, you may change your mind and switch sides. Or you may simply take your topic in a new direction revealed by your research. Keep yourself open to these changes, understanding that a really *good* central claim is only reached through the process of careful research, critical reasoning, and honest reflection.

I try to think of interesting claims that make the reader wonder and think about the content of that claim before they even start reading the paper.
~Kaleb Buffalo

This process of research and reflection will also reveal the depth of your topic, and you will often find that there is *much* more to write about than you initially thought.

This brings me to rule number three for good central claims:

3. **A central claim is narrow enough that you can offer sufficient evidence to convince a reader within the confines of the page limit.**

Rule number two then leads logically to rule three: as you *research* and *reason*, you will find ways to narrow your topic so that you can say something significant rather than offer your readers vague generalities. So while you may have begun with an interest in "phobias," you will inevitably need to narrow that topic (unless you intend to embark on a series of scholarly books), perhaps to something like "hydrophobia." And from there, you will need to narrow even further, keeping in mind rules one and two as well, to construct a paper that will assert a claim for "the best treatments for hydrophobia."

Your instructor will likely have lots of other advice for constructing your central claim; these rules are only the most basic guides. However, I wanted to offer one other general rule, this one based less on your reasoning as a writer, but important nonetheless if you want anyone to actually *read* your argument:

4. A central claim is worded carefully so as to *persuade* and not *alienate*.

Most of us, when we are in debates with our friends about a topic (and if we want to *remain* friends) try to state our opinions kindly by couching them in language calculated not to offend. For example, I have a friend who really likes a certain new movie (for the sake of discretion, we'll just call it *Movie X*). I hate this movie. I find it almost painful to watch. And yet, she's my friend, so telling her this as bluntly as I just told you might offend her. Consequently, we had a conversation that went something like this:

> "Didn't you just love the new *Movie X*?"
>
> In my head, I was screaming, '*Are you kidding? Like it? I HATED it! The dialogue was so bad I wanted to poke out my own eardrums to end the pain of listening to it!*' But what I *said* was, "Well, not really. It wasn't quite my cup of tea, I guess. I thought the writing could have been better."

And from there, we discussed. We debated. But at no point did I tell her that I thought her position was "stupid," or in any other way try to demean her position. Instead, we had a polite and reasoned debate. Had I said those harsh things, she would likely have been offended and our discussion (and possibly our friendship) would have ended. Likewise, when you are writing a paper, you want to *gently persuade* your audience to your position by choosing your words carefully and judiciously, particularly if the topic you have chosen is a controversial one.

There's another important reason that I didn't say those things to my friend: I respect her. I know that she is, in fact, a very intelligent person. Consequently, for her to hold the opinion she does, there must be good reasons, possibly reasons I am missing. And because I respect my friend, when I want to persuade her to my side on any issue, I do so from a position of respect. As a writer, you should hold a similar level of respect for your readers, as well as for those who hold a position opposite yours. Thus, we use judicious language out of both a desire to persuade and a genuine respect for the other scholars and thinkers involved in the academic conversation.

For example, *"Abortion is nothing short of murder and anyone who supports it is a sinner,"* is probably going to raise some "hallelujahs" from those already in your camp, but such a statement will do nothing but alienate those who don't already agree with you. And far from persuading them to see the merits of *your* argument, you will likely lose them as readers altogether, right from your first paragraph. If, however, you think of your readers as friends, people who may disagree with you but are ultimately people of intelligence and good will, you will write your central claim in such a way as to gently persuade them to see, if not agree, with the merits of your argument. *While I believe in the sanctity of a woman's right to control her own body and her own life, I also believe that abortion can be a damaging decision, not only in the most obvious sense of terminating a life, but equally importantly, in the emotional impact it has on those making the decision.* Pro-choice readers, then, may not initially agree with your statement, but at least this central claim persuades them to continue reading the paper with an open mind, sensing the writer's respect for *their* position.

> Make the thesis the heart of your paper... Be open to both sides of your argument; don't just stay with one opinion because your audience won't get the full effect of the situation.
> ~Brandon Evans

■   ■   ■   ■

Placement of the Central Claim

Readers naturally look to the introduction to give them a sense of the purpose of the essay; they expect to know early in the essay what the essay seeks to accomplish. Consequently, the most common place to find a central claim is in the paper's introduction. And by tradition, the most common place to locate a central claim is in the last sentence of the introduction, though this is by no means a hard and fast rule. Providing the readers can clearly identify the central claim (or the paper's central purpose), you should feel free to place it where it makes the most sense in the context of *your* writing style.

Moreover, if, as we mentioned earlier, you are writing an exploratory essay, you may simply explain your topic or even frame your topic as a question in the introduction, and save your actual central claim for the paper's conclusion. However, this unconventional placement will not suit all readers, and you should check with your professor before you begin about his or her expectations.

■   ■   ■   ■

Examples of Good Central Claims

The following are examples of good central claims. They are *argumentative*, *well-reasoned*, *sufficiently narrowed*, and *persuasively worded*.

> "There is no doubt that education is important. There is also no doubt that every person has the right to an education. However, not every person should attend college."
>
> From the article, "Is College for Everyone?"

In this central claim, the author finds common ground with his readers, acknowledging that they probably hold education in high regard and that this is a point on which he and his readers can agree: "There is no doubt that education is important. There is also no doubt that every person has the right to an education." Not until *after* he's established this common ground and demonstrated his respect for readers' (and potential opponents') opinions does he offer the claim that he will seek to convince them of: that despite his respect for education, he believes that not every person should attend college. This is a good example of a firmly held opinion couched in conciliatory but still decisive language.

Another good example:

> "Whatever we've been doing in our schools, it hasn't reduced educational inequality between children from upper- and lower-income families. Part of knowing what we should do about this is understanding how and why these educational disparities are growing."
>
> From Sean F. Reardon, "No Rich Child Left Behind"

Here, Reardon begins with a piece of general knowledge that most people can agree upon: that students from rich and poor families are not getting equal educational opportunities. This won't surprise many readers; it's a fact generally known. In this way, Reardon finds common ground with his readers. He then delivers his claim: We need to do something about this problem, but first, we need to understand why it is happening.

This implies a classical argument setup for the remainder of Reardon's article. He will first "establish the problem," providing evidence that there *is* a problem and establishing the causes of it. He will then spend the latter part of the argument providing solutions. Many argument papers take this form, and Reardon shows us that he is creating just such a classical structure right from his central claim.

Another good example:

> When I refer to integrity, I have something very specific in mind. Integrity, as I will use the term requires three steps: discerning what is right and what is wrong; acting on what you have discerned, even at personal cost; and saying openly that you are acting on your understanding of right and wrong.
> Stephen L. Carter, "The Insufficiency of Honesty"

Like the other good examples above, Carter expresses a firm and well-reasoned opinion in language designed not to alienate. And like Reardon's thesis, Carter's central claim implies his essay's organization. In fact, this is what we sometimes call a "roadmap thesis" because it lays out all of the major parts of the essay in miniature form, providing a "roadmap" to the rest of the essay. Carter then divides his paper into three major sections, the first illuminating what he means by "discerning what is right and what is wrong," the second illustrating his claim that integrity involves "acting on what you have discerned" and the third, showing that integrity demands "saying openly that you are acting on your understanding of right and wrong."

As a warning, some professors don't like roadmap theses. Too often, they are overly simplistic and derivative. But when done well, as Carter has done here, they provide clear and intelligent direction for the reading of the essay.

One final example:

> As people recognize the dangers of fossil fuel plants... nuclear power begins to look more attractive. But what about the waste—all that highly radioactive debris that will endure for thousands of years? Do we have the right to leave such a legacy to our children? (171)
> Richard A. Muller, *Physics for Future Presidents*

Notice that this "central claim" is really a guiding question. Through the first part of his chapter, Muller examines the pros and cons of nuclear fuel and whether or not the costs are too high. He thoroughly explores the claims of those who oppose nuclear fuel before then giving his own conclusion (this about midway through the article): that nuclear fuel is far less risky than many other problems we are currently faced with in the fuel crisis.

Here, Muller takes us on a small journey of discovery with him. He asks the guiding question that compelled his own research, explores (in a respectful way) the opinions of those who reached a different conclusion, then describes the conclusion he has come to after years of study, and finishes the chapter by laying out his own evidence.

I've presented here four very effective strategies for central claims. All four obey the rules established in the first part of this chapter: All are based on well-reasoned and well-researched opinions; all are narrowed and specific, avoiding large generalities and able to be argued in an essay-length work; and all use language that demonstrates awareness of and respect for opposing opinions.

In the next section, we will explore the drafting of "subclaims" or supporting points. As indicated above, sometimes your central claim implies your subclaims within it. Sometimes is does not. Either way, subclaims should feel like a natural outgrowth of the central claim.

■   ■   ■   ■

Constructing Subclaims

You may be the kind of writer who begins the drafting process with a central claim established, or you may be the kind who discovers that central claim as you go, but in either case, you need some **subclaims**, or subordinate arguments, that will help support your central claim. If you can convince your readers to accept these subclaims, it should then follow that they will be able to accept your central claim. It's often easiest to think of these

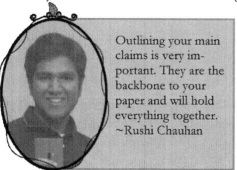

Outlining your main claims is very important. They are the backbone to your paper and will hold everything together.
~Rushi Chauhan

subclaims as *reasons* to believe in the primary claim. However, it is also important that you not formulate these as simple statements of fact. Subclaims, just as central claims, are *critically reasoned opinions*.

The **central claim** and the **subclaims** that support it make up a **claims structure**. (Alternatively, your instructor might call these the **thesis** or **purpose statement** and **topic sentences**, both of which form an **argument structure**.) Regardless of which set of terminology is employed in your class, a solid argument begins with a solid outline of claims and arguments.

The following example (figure 2.1) is from English major Sarah Holly. Her assignment was to analyze the metaphors in an essay by Tusculum professor and published essayist Desirae Matherly.

> Central Claim: Desirae Matherly's personal essay "Wagering Pressures" wields two symbols—weather and horses—in order to explain the innate wildness of the human spirit, that irrepressible shuttering of emotive ferocity, and how these sentiments might properly be conveyed: relentless and free or suppressed, though hopefully somewhere in between.
>
> Subclaim 1: Matherly deals with weather in much the same way she endures weather, atop the crest of an emotional wave, never quite plunging into its depths.
>
>> Evidence A: "I like my weather sublime, just on the edge of being truly life-threatening." Here, Matherly explains her position on storm watching, a parallel to inner turmoil (and later, mental breakdown), which in her view should exist at the cliff of reality where we are conscious of them, but constrain impulse just enough to prevent such a breakdown.
>>
>> Evidence B: She imagines a mental breakdown as the calm after a storm, a lapse in consciousness where one may be coddled and quieted, though the reality, she admits, "is far too damaging. A bit like those heavy spring rains which beat the flowers into pieces. . ."
>
> Subclaim 2: In the context of this essay, Matherly unveils a portrait of the domesticated horse as a suppressed and tamed creature, which once allowed an inkling of freedom, will run wild.

Evidence A: Speaking primarily of feminism in reference to the horses and women of the Victorian Age, Matherly describes a parallel between the two in terms of an internally manifesting ferocity, not quite smothered, but repressed by men and the culture of that period until they spin into violent mental hysteria, are committed, and in some cases lobotomized.

Evidence B: However, aside from the parallel, Matherly also consistently refers to the metaphorical "reins" of her life, which she is both in control of and controlled by, a sort of double-edged blade that perhaps stands in the place of modern cultural assumptions and values that she feels she must abide by.

Subclaim 3: Both symbols, that is weather and horses, are direct representatives of the extreme ends of the human spirit, dangerous and absolutely free to one edge, then constrained and yearning at the other.

Evidence A: "To 'let' one's self go is like letting the weather out, like moving into a full gallop and dropping the reins." And "We might as well let these storms free in one fell swoop, or we will be beaten to pieces by its . . . failed repression, the *sta-sta*-staccato stammering of pops and snaps that signal our breaking down."

Evidence B: "Is the irrational part of ourselves something to be commanded or controlled by expertise, as in those philosophies granting human beings indomitable wills? Or is it like weather: to be endured and borne, beyond our control, without order, absurdly impervious to skill and station?" And this, this is the real point of her entire essay, not only is there a decision to be made regarding one's treatment of emotion, but does one even have control of that decision? Matherly seems to think not.

Conclusion: The horse and the storm are conditions of the human spirit, perhaps interchanging levels that fluctuate at the pinprick of a comment, eye roll, or the sudden outburst of a woman stifled.

Figure 2.1: Claims Outline

You can see here the way that Sarah's subclaims clearly support her central claim. I tell my students to think of a claims structure as a kind of formula:

If x is true, then y is true.

In this formula, "x" represents the subclaims and "y" the central claim. In this example, you can see the way that subclaim 1 (Matherly's essay likens weather to emotion and demonstrates her desire to "ride" it safely) added to subclaim 2 (domesticated horses also act as symbols of the dangers of "running free"), finally combine with subclaim 3 (that both symbols demonstrate the dangers of the extreme ends of the human spirit—wild and constrained) to persuade readers to accept the truth of her central claim (that happiness lies somewhere in between).

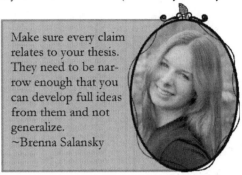

Make sure every claim relates to your thesis. They need to be narrow enough that you can develop full ideas from them and not generalize.
~Brenna Salansky

Supporting with Evidence

Each one of your subclaims must be supported with sufficient examples and evidence that your reader will feel that your conclusions are logical and well-warranted. If you fail to give your reader sufficient evidence, they will not accept your claims. And if they cannot accept your individual claims as true, then your argument as a whole is in danger.

On all of this rests, then, the evidence you provide. For that reason, it is crucial that you select the most compelling, most well-reasoned, and most carefully selected pieces of evidence to back up each claim.

Evidence can be of several types:

- *Personal Evidence* (including personal experiences & observations, as well as the experiences of friends and family members)

- *Expert Opinions*, gathered from either primary or secondary research
- *Statistics*, gathered either from primary or secondary research
- *Examples*
- *Analogies*

Let's briefly take a look at each type of evidence and the kind of writing assignment for which each is appropriate.

Personal Evidence

Personal stories and observations can be one of the most powerful kinds of evidence in argument writing, especially for young scholars like you. After all, you haven't yet had time to become an "expert" on a subject, and no matter what you are arguing for or against, there are probably other writers out there who have argued with greater expertise than you can currently claim. So why bother to write at all? What do *you* have to lend to the debate? The answer, of course, is that you have your own experiences, those that belong only to you and which allow you to offer a perspective that is unique and new to the topic. Jane Expert may know more about your writing topic, but you can lend support to her expertise by contributing your own story. For this reason, personal evidence will be emphasized heavily by your English 110 and 111 instructors as we encourage you to find your own voice and the consequent power in your writing. In English 110, this is the primary type of evidence you will use.

However, personal evidence is not appropriate for all disciplines, and some of your professors will not want you to include it. Many of the social sciences, for example, discourage the use of personal stories, emphasizing instead primary and secondary research. Because different disciplines at the college emphasize the worth of different kinds of evidence, make sure you read paper assignments carefully and, if in doubt, ask your professors how they feel about personal evidence in writing.

Expert Opinions

You may have observed as you've read this book that occasionally I draw on expert opinions to support some of my claims. Citing experts in a field lends credence (or *ethos*) to your text. Moreover, expert opinion is a kind of evidence used in every discipline on campus, though you will need to check with your professors on individual assignments. In English 111 you will learn more thoroughly how to choose these experts and how to cite them properly. One word of caution: while expert opinion is an excellent source of evidence to back up a claim, be careful not to let your own voice get lost in the shuffle. One of the biggest mistakes that young writers make is to cite expert after expert, with little or no explanation or commentary from the student's own perspective. Don't let the voices of experts drown out your own voice. Even in those disciplines where the use of first-person ("I") is prohibited, expert opinion needs to be balanced with your own explanations and defenses.

Statistics

Everyone loves statistics. And we are easily convinced by them. When I see a commercial telling me that "Lysol kills 99.9% of viruses and bacteria on commonly touched surfaces in your home," I feel a sort of compulsion to spray my house down with Lysol. When I hear that "9 out of 10 women saw a dramatic improvement in skin tone for flawless, younger-looking skin," I begin to think maybe I need to try Avon skin toner. Numbers are convincing; they have power. Perhaps this is because we continue to perpetuate the myth that numbers don't lie. Or perhaps it's because math was a difficult subject for many of us, so we endow numbers with exaggerated importance. Whatever the reason, it is true that you can offer fewer more convincing pieces of evidence than statistical evidence. However, please be aware of some of the pitfalls of statistical evidence as well.

If you are gathering data to create your own statistics, please read carefully through the guidelines in chapter five on creating and administering surveys and on conducting formal observations. If other methods of data collection are used (such as through formal experiments specific to your discipline), you should consult your advisor or faculty member to make sure you understand how to set up your study in such a way that your data will be accepted by that discipline.

If, however, you are seeking statistical data generated by others (as found in secondary sources), the following rules will help you to choose the most reliable and most credible evidence:

- Only use statistics from trustworthy sources (most of those you find in Tusculum's library will be trustworthy, and these should be trusted over statistics found on websites).
- Only use the most current, up-to-date statistics.
- Even if the first two rules are met, still take the time to carefully analyze the agenda and possible biases of the organization supplying the statistics.

In reality, statistics can be skewed in all kinds of ways in order to mislead, if not down-right trick, the unwary. While statistical evidence can be impressive, it can also be dangerous if not approached with an analytical and wary mind.

Examples

While you may be supplying evidentiary examples from your own life and experience, sometimes you simply don't have much experience with the topic you are writing about. In that case, you may want to turn to other kinds of anecdotal evidence from things you have read and seen. This is still a kind of secondary evidence gathered from research, but rather than experts or statistics, this kind of evidence emphasizes the stories of people who've had first-hand experience with the topic.

> When writing an argument paper, the most important advice I can give you is to have plenty of strong, credible evidence to back up your argument. If you have great evidence, a reader will be easily persuaded to believe your side of the argument.
> ~Tyler Bailey

This kind of evidence is usually gathered from primary sources such as interviews or observations, as well as from primary source documents like newspapers and personal diaries. Drawing on the experiences of others to support your claims can be a powerful way of showing the real-life impact of your topic.

Another type of exemplary evidence is the hypothetical example. Stephen Carter, in his essay "The Insufficiency of Honesty," uses primarily hypothetical examples as evidence to support his claims. "Consider an example," Carter writes in one paragraph, "A man who has been married for fifty years confesses to his wife on his deathbed that he was unfaithful thirty-five years earlier." Carter then goes on to explore this hypothetical example and why it is an example of honesty but not an example of integrity. Real life examples are often more credible and convincing than hypothetical examples, but if done well, a hypothetical example can serve to demonstrate the plausibility of your claims.

Analogies

One of the most difficult kinds of evidence to use *well* is analogical evidence. Analogies allow you to liken one thing to another and thus convince your reader that, if they believe the one, they should believe the other. Analogies can be powerful persuaders, but they are also difficult to use without straying into *false* analogies. For example, you may have heard pro-life advocates liken abortion to murder, and claim that, for that *reason*, abortion is wrong. In their view, then, abortion = murder. This is an example of analogical evidence. Unfortunately, this is an example of a *false* analogy, a type of *logical fallacy*. Your personal belief may dictate that abortion is murder, but *logically* the two are not analogous (they do not share all of the same characteristics and, in fact, are different in many—and obvious—ways). Using such an analogy in an argument essay will not advance your argument so much as bring it to a screeching halt as you alienate many of your readers and cause the more logical among them to question your credibility. Avoid inflammatory analogies, as well as those that claim to be too literal.

Analogies can be persuasive, on the other hand, if they help us to understand a difficult concept by framing it in terms of more familiar concepts. For example, this book attempts to explain the writing process by likening it to a jungle exploration. The analogy isn't meant to be literal, and readers all know this. Moreover, there is little to take offense at in the analogy. On the other hand, if it serves at all to clarify (or even make more enjoyable) the writing process, then it is a successful use of analogy.

• • • •

If you follow the outline you have now created, writing each subclaim as a separate paragraph or group of paragraphs, you will have composed the ***body*** of your paper. But while this is the largest part of your paper, you aren't finished yet. You still need to write the ***introductory*** and ***concluding*** paragraphs. The following section will offer tips on how to write these comparatively short—but very important—parts of your paper.

Introducing & Concluding

Many people find introductions and conclusions to be the most difficult part of a paper. This can be problematic because they are such important parts of your paper: the introduction is the first chance you have to make an impression on your readers and can either win them initially to your side, or else make them wary or even alienate them. Similarly, the conclusion is the last chance you have to make an impression and is often the thing readers remember most vividly.

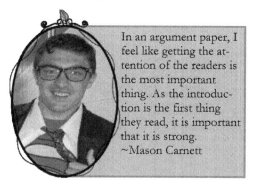

In an argument paper, I feel like getting the attention of the readers is the most important thing. As the introduction is the first thing they read, it is important that it is strong.
~Mason Carnett

Because these are such important parts of your paper, then, you should give them adequate attention and not simply write the first thing that occurs to you. In fact, many writers suggest composing the introduction and conclusion *last*, after the rest of the paper has been written. This allows you to give adequate time and attention to these important pieces of writing and to make certain they match the argument you have made.

• • • •

Using Introductory Techniques

Because the introduction is your first chance to make a good impression, you want it to sound interesting, to intrigue your readers and encourage them to read on. There are some common introductory techniques frequently employed by writers to catch readers' attention in this way:

Starting with a Story

One of the most common ways to begin an essay is with a story. Stories are effective as introductions because narrative has the potential to seize the imagination, to make readers feel as if they have experienced the topic. Here's an excellent example of an introduction that begins with a story.

> No one ever gave me directions like this on a golf course before: "Aim at either Microsoft or IBM." I was standing on the first tee at the KGA Golf Club in downtown Bangalore, in Southern India, when my playing partner pointed at two shiny glass-and-steel building off in the distance, just behind the first green. The Goldman Sachs building wasn't done yet; otherwise he could have pointed that out as well and made it a threesome. HP and Texas Instruments had their offices on the back nine, along the tenth hole. That wasn't all. The tee markers were from Epson, the printer company, and one of our caddies was wearing a hat from 3M. Outside, some of the traffic signs were also sponsored by Texas Instruments, and the Pizza Hut billboard on the way over showed a steaming pizza, under the headline "Gigabites of Taste!"

This story begins Thomas Friedman's important book *The World is Flat: A Brief History of the Twenty-first Century*, in which he examines the way that globalization affects us both economically and culturally, changing the ways in which we define ourselves and our place in the world. Beginning with a story captures readers' attention and also helps concretize the complex issues that Friedman is introducing.

Starting with a Historical Story or Background

Starting with a historical story accomplishes many of the same goals as beginning with a personal story, but in addition, it can serve to give background to your topic. Make certain, however, that the history you relate is interesting to readers, tells them something new and intriguing. Commonly known historical information is not a good way to begin, nor is vague or unsupported summaries of historical realities. Never begin, for example, with something as uninspiring as "Television was invented in the mid-twentieth century and has changed the way we view the world." Everyone already knows that and such an introduction will capture the imagination of exactly no one. This introduction from Neil Postman, however, shows how the relation of a historical story can effectively engage readers:

> There could not have been a safer bet when it began in 1969 than that *Sesame Street* would be embraced by children, parents,

and educators. Children loved it because they were raised on television commercials, which they intuitively knew were the most carefully crafted entertainments on television. To those who had not yet been to school, even to those who had just started, the idea of being *taught* by a series of commercials did not seem peculiar: And that television should entertain them was taken as a matter of course.

Parents embraced *Sesame Street* for several reasons, among them that it assuaged their guilt over the fact that they could not or would not restrict their children's access to television. *Sesame Street* appeared to justify allowing a four- or five-year-old to sit transfixed in front of a television screen for unnatural periods of time. Parents were eager to hope that television could teach their children something other than which breakfast cereal has the most crackle. At the same time, *Sesame Street* relieved them of the responsibility of teaching their pre-school children how to read—no small matter in a culture where children are apt to be considered a nuisance.

Postman's relation, and interpretation, of the historical reception of *Sesame Street* is anything but boring. It might have some readers nodding their heads and other shaking their fists, but it certainly engages readers' interest.

Starting with a Question or Series of Questions

Questions beg answers, and beginning an essay with a question leads readers to both mentally propose answers and to anticipate the answers that the author will give. For this reason, beginning with a question or series of questions can be a very effective technique. On the other hand, this is perhaps the most often abused and poorly used introductory technique. It's difficult to do well; consequently, these introductions are often cliché and sloppy. In fact, I've had colleagues that forbid their students from beginning essays with questions because they had despaired of teaching students to do it well. Only if the questions are interesting, well framed, and original will they truly engage readers' attention. If your questions are obvious or ordinary, they will simply distance readers. The following introduction to the essay "The Pleasures of Eating" by Wendell Berry, on the other hand, shows how this introductory technique can be used well:

> Many times, after I have finished a lecture on the decline of American farming and rural life, someone in the audience has asked, "What can city people do?"
>
> "Eat responsibly," I have usually answered. Of course, I have tried to explain what I meant, but afterward I have invariably felt that there was more to be said than I had been able to say. Now I would like to attempt a better explanation.

Beginning his essay with the question "What can city people do?" provokes the reader to reframe the question: "What can *I* do?" Berry then answers that question in brief: "Eat responsibly." But as readers, we don't really know what he means, and consequently, the curiosity roused by the opening question remains unfulfilled. His promise to then answer the question in greater detail throughout the essay thus makes us want to read on for the fuller answer to the question.

Starting with a Surprising Fact or Statistic

Another way to engage your readers is to begin your essay with a statement that will startle them. Surprising your reader right from the start makes them want to read more, to see the explanation behind the startling thing you have revealed. "Really?" they will ask. "Are you sure? Show me!" The following introduction is a good example of this kind of technique:

> Until the eighteenth century, Western philosophers and scientists thought that there was one sex and that women's internal genitalia were the inverse of men's external genitalia: the womb and vagina were the penis and scrotum turned inside out (Laqueur 1990). Current Western thinking sees women and men as so different physically as to sometimes seem two species. The bodies, which have been mapped inside and out for hundreds of years, have not changed. What has changed are the justifications for gender inequality. (Judith Lorber, "*Believing is Seeing: Biology as Ideology*).

"Wow! Really? Scientists and philosophers thought that women's bodies were just men's bodies turned inside-out? Tell me more!" That's the kind of response you want readers to have to this kind of introduction, engaging their attention and curiosity from the start and compelling them to read on.

Starting with a Quote

Another effective way to begin an introduction is to start with a quote. You will want to choose a quote that is well-phrased and catchy, and preferably by someone famous. This gives your paper *ethos* or authority right from the beginning and inspires your reader to trust you by showing them that your argument is aligned with well-known and important writers, scholars, and thinkers. Take, for example, this introduction to the essay "Cancer Alley: The Poisoning of the American South," written by Jason Berry and photographed by Richard Misrach:

> "Baton Rouge was clothed in flowers, like a bride—no, much more so; like a greenhouse. For we were in the absolute South now," wrote Mark Twain of the vistas from a riverboat in his 1883 classic *Life on the Mississippi*. "From Baton Rouge to New Orleans," he continued, "the great sugar-plantations border both sides of the river all the way, and stretch their league-wide levels back to the dim forest of bearded cypress in the rear. The broad river lying between the two rows becomes a sort of spacious street."
>
> Twain caught the ninety-mile river corridor between the old Capitol and New Orleans at a poignant moment.

However, Berry goes on to point out, the area Twain describes has been corrupted by the pollution of oil and petro-chemical producers, and the beauty of the Old South has been replaced with disease and death. Beginning with a quote from a writer as famous as Mark Twain allows Berry to draw on Twain's fame and authority to lend ethos to Berry's own writing. Moreover, the quote provides a striking contrast between the South of 100 years ago and the South of today, a contrast that should interest readers and compel them to read on.

Starting with a "Mind the Gap" Warning

In advanced academic discourse, a common way of beginning a paper or article is to review the current literature on the topic and point out to readers those gaps that still need addressing. The researcher then explains that she or he will be filling in one of those gaps with the current research project. This shows readers the significance of the research up-front and, at least for academic audiences, convinces them of the importance of the piece they are reading. In their book, *From Inquiry to Aca-*

demic Writing, Stuart Greene and April Lidinsky call this the "Mind the Gap" strategy, named for the warning issued every time a train approaches on the British Tube and Rail system. Just as commuters are warned explicitly to pay attention to the gap between the train and the platform, readers of this kind of introduction are warned to pay attention to the gaps in research on the current topic. The following is an excellent example of this kind of introduction:

> The events of September 11 have sent scholars and pundits alike scrambling to make sense of those seemingly senseless acts. While most analyses have focused on the political economy of globalization or the perversion of Islamic teachings by Al Qaeda, several commentators have raised gender issues.
>
> Some have reminded us that in our haste to lionize the heroes of the World Trade Center collapse, we ignored the many women firefighters, police officers, and rescue workers who also risked their lives. We've been asked to remember the Taliban's vicious policies toward women; indeed, even Laura Bush seems to be championing women's emancipation.
>
> A few have asked us to consider the other side of the gender coin: men. Some have rehearsed the rather tired old formulae about masculine bloodlust or the drive for domination and conquest, with no reference to the magnificent humanity displayed by so many on September 11. . .
>
> As for myself, I've been thinking lately about a letter to the editor of a small, upstate-New York newspaper, written in 1992 by an American GI after his return from service in the gulf War. . . That letter writer was Timothy McVeigh from Lockport, N.Y. Two years later, he blew up the Murrah federal building in Oklahoma City in what is now the second-worst act of terrorism ever committed on American soil.
>
> What's startling to me are the ways that McVeigh's complaints were echoed in some of the fragmentary evidence that we have seen about the terrorists of September 11, and especially in the portrait of Mohammed Atta, the suspected mastermind of the operation and the pilot of the first plane to hit the World Trade Center.

> Looking at these two men through the lens of gender may shed some light on both the method and the madness of the tragedies they wrought. (Michael S. Kimmel, "Gender, Class, and Terrorism").

This kind of introduction follows a pretty specific formula: "Some writers have said this. Others have said this. However, no one has yet considered this. And that is what I will be writing about." You can see the way that Kimmel followed this pattern in the excerpt provided above. This is a particularly academic kind of introduction and requires that you be very familiar with the current research on your topic. You probably won't be asked to try this kind of introduction in your lower-division courses (except, perhaps, in English 111), but you should be prepared to write this way for many of your upper-division courses as this kind of introduction shows your readiness to participate in the scholarship of your field.

■ ■ ■ ■

Concluding Techniques

As important as your introduction is in drawing in your readers, your conclusion is possibly *more* important since it is the final—and often most lasting—impression you make. It is the last opportunity you have to win readers over, and the final chance you have of convincing them of your knowledge and good will. That's a big job for a single paragraph to accomplish. It's not surprising, then, that writing conclusions is, for many of us, the most difficult part of a paper. Personally, I hate writing conclusions. I feel the pressure to write something memorable and convincing, something that will imprint permanently on the minds of my readers the importance of what I am saying, and I feel overwhelmed. I usually calm myself by reading over the conclusions of some of my favorite essays from some of my most-admired writers, and reminding myself that there are methods that can help make this process a little less arbitrary. Of

> The most difficult part of writing for me was the conclusion.... If I could do my paper again, I would work on the conclusion longer.
> ~ Chase Ward-McEwan

course, I still want my conclusion to sound fresh and original, not cookie-cutter and boring. But that's more a matter of tweaking the standard techniques than of inventing the entire process. So here, I give you the standard techniques of writing conclusions. Follow these standards, and then add your own special touch, to leave readers wowed at the end of your essay.

Echoing the Introduction

One very effective way of concluding an essay is to return readers full circle to your introduction. This "bookend" technique reminds readers why they wanted to read the essay in the first place and points out to them how much more they know about the topic now that they have finished. In his famous speech "A More Perfect Union," President Obama follows this concluding strategy. His introduction begins with a quote from The Declaration of Independence:

> "We the people, in order to form a more perfect union." Two hundred and twenty-one years ago, in a hall that still stands across the street, a group of men gathered and, with these simple words, launched America's improbable experiment in democracy. Farmers and scholars; statesmen and patriots who had traveled across an ocean to escape tyranny and persecution finally made real their declaration of independence at a Philadelphia convention that lasted through the spring of 1787.

Beginning with this quote, as famous as it is and as fundamental to our country's history, allies President Obama with the great statesmen of the past and gives him credibility. His conclusion then returns us to this reference:

> It is not enough to give health care to the sick, or jobs to the jobless, or education to our children.
>
> But it is where we start. It is where our union grows stronger. And as so many generations have come to realize over the course of the 221 years since a band of patriots signed that document in Philadelphia, that is where the perfection begins.

Returning readers to your introduction in this way gives a nice finished feeling to your piece; it's very tidy, and it gives readers a pleasing sense of balance.

Using Another Introductory Technique

While echoing your introduction can be a nice way to tie an essay together, you can also use one of the other (typically introductory) techniques to conclude your paper as a way to add interest. While the techniques discussed above are generally used for introductions, less often, you can also use them for conclusions. They serve the same purpose at the end of your paper that they do at the beginning. That is, they capture readers' attention, make them think, make them curious. This can be an effective way to move readers from the points you have made into consideration of the wider implications of your argument. Take this conclusion from David Buckingham's "Childhood in the Age of Global Media" as an example:

> And so I conclude with a series of questions. Is Kenichi Ohmae correct: Is global marketing really creating a common culture of childhood? Is it helping children to communicate across cultural differences—or is it simply eradicating those differences? And even if it is, is that something we should necessarily regret?

Buckingham's questions here propel readers forward into a consideration of the future implications of the argument he has just made about the way media is spreading across the globe and its consequent impact on children.

The other introductory techniques can do the same: ending with a narrative (either personal or historical), ending with a famous quote, or concluding with a startling fact or statistic. These all serve to propel readers forward from the argument you just made into a consideration of the future implications of accepting that argument.

Predicting the Future

In the example above, David Buckingham leaves his readers with a consideration of the future via a series of questions. Whether you do so through questions, or simply through statements, predicting the future is one of the most common—and most effective—kinds of conclusions. This kind of conclusion answers the question at the root of any argumentative essay, "So what? Why should I care?" By showing readers the future impact of your argument, you show them why your argument is important. In order to be relevant to your readers, your essay *must* do this at some point, and the conclusion is a natural place. Take as an example this conclusion from author Tamara Draut in her essay "The Growing College Gap":

> Without major new efforts by the federal and state governments and our nation's colleges to widen access to higher education, a new social inequality will emerge. We'll have a well-educated minority that is mostly white, and a swelling, undereducated majority that is mostly African American and Latino. As the college-age population grows swiftly, our nation's financial aid system will leave millions of college-ready students without the means to fulfill their dreams. The Advisory Committee on Student Financial Assistance projects that if current enrollment trends persist, over the next decade 4.4 million students from households with incomes below $50,000 will not attend a four-year college, and 2 million students will not attend college at all. And those are conservative estimates. Who knows how many scientists, nurses, teachers, and doctors we will lose as a result?
>
> The loss to both individuals and society is just too large to allow such social cleavages to develop.

Draught projects a bleak future for young Americans if something is not done to address the growing inequality in educational access. And this prediction, based on solid research and demonstrated by the preceding argument, reinforces the importance of the issue to Draught's readers.

Calling Readers to Action

As we mentioned earlier, an argument essay aims to convince readers to ***think, believe,*** or ***do*** something. If "do" is your objective, then concluding your essay with a call to action is an appropriate and effective choice. In his essay "Crack and the Box," Pete Hamill writes to convince readers that television is at least in part to blame for the US's growing drug problem. We learn in our youth, he argues, to enjoy the stupefaction and mindlessness that television provides, and in our adult years, seek this same mindless escape in the use of cocaine and heroin. He details the parallel development of the two phenomena in our country—television and the drug crisis—and links their common impetuses. He then concludes his essay with a call to action:

> What is to be done? Television is certainly not going away, but its addictive qualities can be controlled. It's a lot easier to "just say no" to television than to heroin or crack. As a beginning, parents must take immediate control of the sets, teaching children to watch specific television *programs*, not "television," to get out of the house and play with other kids. Elementary and high schools must begin teaching television as a subject, the way literature is taught, showing children how shows are made, how to distinguish between the true and the false, how to recognize cheap emotional manipulation. All Americans should spend more time reading. And thinking.
>
> For years, the defenders of television have argued that the networks are only giving the people what they want. That might be true. But so is the Medellín cartel.

This, too, is a very common concluding strategy and an effective one. Like a prediction of the future, a call to action lets readers know explicitly what the importance of your essay is and why they should care about the subject. Moreover, it has the added bonus of supplying them with some ideas about what they can do with this new knowledge.

Concluding with a Summary

Perhaps the easiest—and unfortunately often the dullest—kind of conclusion is one in which you end by summarizing the main points made throughout the paper. I would suggest you avoid this kind of conclusion for the most part. Only if the paper is particularly lengthy do you want to utilize this method. Writing a summary conclusion for a short paper (anything under ten pages) tells your readers that you do not trust them to hold all the points you have made in their heads long enough to make a decision about the argument. If you are writing a book-length piece, this may be true. But for most college-paper length essays, trust your reader to remember the points you have made and spare them the dullness of the summary conclusion. Here is an example of a summary conclusion to a longer piece of writing. Use this as a good example in those instances when this kind of conclusion may be appropriate.

After writing for 191 pages about the connection between brain chemistry and external circumstance, and postulating how these two combine to form our notions of morality and goodness, Sam Harris concludes his book *The Moral Landscape* with this paragraph, a basic summary of what he has written, but one that also serves to emphasize what his argument can teach us about ourselves and our future:

> If our well-being depends upon the interaction between events in our brains and events in the world, and there are better and worse ways to secure it, then some cultures will tend to produce lives that are more worth living than others; some political persuasions will be more enlightened than others; and some world views will be mistaken in ways that cause needless human misery. Whether or not we ever understand meaning, morality, and values in practice, I have attempted to show that there must be something to know about them in principle. And I am convinced that merely admitting this will transform the way we think about human happiness and the public good. (from *The Moral Landscape*)

• • • •

At this point, you have landed. Your drafting is complete; your journey is at an end. Right?

WRONG! It's true that you have navigated yourself safely to your destination, but there is a long path yet to travel. In the next chapter, we will talk about the important road to revision that will allow you to refine and perfect your argument

CHAPTER 3: REVISING
The Final Trek

As part of my trip to the Amazon, my husband and I visited Machu Pichu, one of the most sublime experiences of my life. There are many ways to get to Machu Pichu—we took the easy route, riding in an air-conditioned bus to the top of the mountain, which left only a short hike up a small hill. As we rounded the corner and saw the famous ruin laid out on the hillside before us, we had to stop for several minutes, trying to take in the wonder of the place. Our guide then led us around many of the sites, describing ancient Incan living conditions, military strategies, and religious ceremonies.

And then he said, "But we're not finished. The best view of Machu Pichu is from the Sun Gate." And then he pointed at a two-mile track snaking its way up the mountain side to a large stone gatehouse a thousand feet above us. "Your journey," he said, "has only begun."

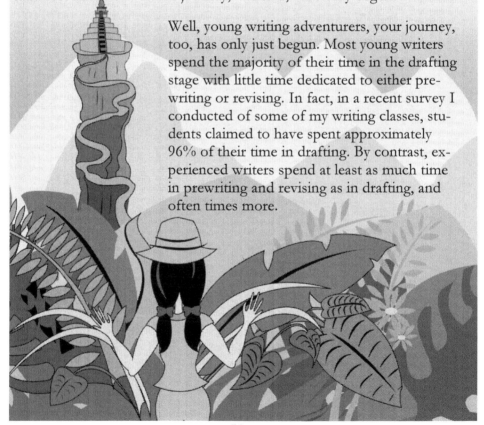

Well, young writing adventurers, your journey, too, has only just begun. Most young writers spend the majority of their time in the drafting stage with little time dedicated to either pre-writing or revising. In fact, in a recent survey I conducted of some of my writing classes, students claimed to have spent approximately 96% of their time in drafting. By contrast, experienced writers spend at least as much time in prewriting and revising as in drafting, and often times more.

The difference between beginning and experienced writers, however, is not only in the amount of time spent on different parts of the writing process, but also on the way that they conceive of the process itself. In her article "Revision Strategies of Student Writers and Experienced Adult Writers," Nancy Sommers describes a series of studies she conducted with student and professional writers, interviewing them as they wrote and rewrote different kinds of texts. Her article has been very important in composition studies, helping instructors to understand the different ways that experienced and inexperienced writers approach revision. "The students" Sommers explains, "understand the revision process as a rewording activity." Vocabulary was the primary concern of those student writers she interviewed, and they described their revision process in terms such as these:

> I read what I have written and I cross out a word and put another word in; a more decent word or a better word. Then, if there is somewhere to use a sentence that I have crossed out, I will put it there. (380)

Another wrote this:

> Reviewing means just using better words and eliminating words that are not needed. I go over and change words around. (381)

More experienced writers, on the other hand, conceive of the process of revision in much more *global* terms. That is, they see revision as a *part* of the actual writing of the paper, an essential part of structuring their argument, not simply fixing their sentences. Notice the difference between the responses above and those below:

> It is a matter of looking at the kernel of what I have written, the content, and then thinking about it, responding to it, making decisions, and actually restructuring it. (383)

And from another professional writer:

> It means taking apart what I have written and putting it back together again. I ask major theoretical questions of my ideas, respond to those questions, and think of proportion and structure, and try to find a controlling metaphor. I find out which ideas can be developed and which should be dropped. I am constantly chiseling and changing as I revise. (384)

Notice that for these experienced writers, revising is an essential part of the shaping of their argument. They aren't afraid to discard ideas, paragraphs, even whole drafts. One writer explained that he rarely trusts a first draft and usually discards the majority of it. For experienced writers, revision is an indispensable step in the formation of a tight and cohesive argument, and word selection is only a small part of that revision.

I have noticed similar trends in my own students' revising. I recently asked some of my classes about their revision strategies, and for the overwhelming majority, their focus was on the sentence level—changing words, correcting grammar, fixing sentences. If this describes your revision process, then you are missing out on the most important part of true revision—the "re-seeing" or "re-visioning" of your argument as a whole. This means you must be willing to *see* and then *make* big changes. Such revision requires not only the intelligence to reexamine and rewrite points you'd thought already "completed," but also the bravery to discard parts of your precious writing, and to change it in profound ways. It's hard. Most students don't want to put forth the effort. But the view from the Sun Gate is well worth it, I promise!

REVISING GLOBALLY

Have you ever visited an art museum and stood very close to a large painting? That's a good way to see the individual details of the painting, each brush stroke and line, but it hinders your ability to see the painting as a whole. Backing up, however, allows you to see the painting's entire structure, though you lose each individual detail.

Similarly, in writing, we gain as much from the distant perspective as we do the close-up. Experienced writers are accustomed to backing up, then walking forward for a closer look, then backing up, then walking forward. They notice the way that each individual paragraph contributes to the overall argument and are able to decide if each paragraph should stay, or go, or become something different. Then they close in, focusing on sentence structure and word choice. Then back out, to see how those choices affect the overall tenor of the argument.

It's a difficult skill and one that, as I can personally attest, takes a deal of practice. The following, however, are some practical strategies to help you to "back up" and see your essay more clearly as a whole argument before you get yourself lost in the details.

Try Waiting

This is difficult on the block system as we often ask you to write a draft, revise it, and turn in a new copy within just a couple of days. But you do usually have at least a couple of days, and if you've done your assignments in a timely manner, you should be able to wait at least overnight before reading through your draft again. This will allow you to approach your writing with fresh eyes and more easily spot inconsistencies or places where improvements are needed.

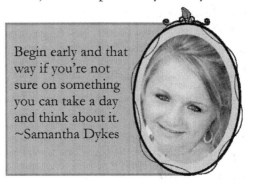

Begin early and that way if you're not sure on something you can take a day and think about it.
~Samantha Dykes

Try Reading Out Loud

Reading your draft out loud helps you to literally "hear" it and thus spot any mistakes or confusing language. It also allows you to recognize gaps that might need to be filled with additional evidence. You might even ask a friend to read it out loud to you so that you can hear how your words sound coming from someone else's voice. This gives you even more distance from your writing and might make it easier for you to spot places for improvement.

Try Writing a Post-Draft Outline

In the previous chapter, I advised you to outline before you started your essay as a way to organize your early thoughts into a coherent argument. You should now put that outline away, somewhere where you can't see it, and read through your essay as if you didn't know what that original outline contained. Now, on a separate sheet of paper, summarize each subclaim and under it, the kind of evidence you used to support that subclaim. Then, look over this "post-draft outline" and see if you've repeated any ideas, if there are ideas that are logically closer to others and should be moved nearer them, or if there are claims that are dependant on other claims and should be moved closer to them. Be brave and cross out any subclaims that just don't logically support the central claim. Try to be objective. You might also have a friend do this outline for you.

The value in this activity is that your claims structure changes as you write. The outline you began with is rarely the one you end up with. And while you may have started with a cohesive argument, often in writing it, you will have added new elements, gone down different paths, followed new hypotheses. Usually, then, the first draft of a paper has cohesion and logic problems, things that need to be moved, eliminated, changed, or elaborated on.

The following shows an outline of a student paper written for English 111. I created the outline after having read the student's first draft, and the following is my attempt to summarize, as accurately as possible, what Tyler intended to claim in each paragraph. Though I quite like Tyler's thesis, you can see that the overall organization of the claims is a bit chaotic:

I. Introduction.
Thesis: "While race still serves as a way for Americans to discriminate against one another, interracial friendships can help to build racial understanding and help deconstruct prejudice."
II. Parents influence their children's racial attitudes and this parental influence varies by race.
III. Interracial friendships are beneficial in eliminating prejudice and stereotypes.
IV. Interracial friendships not only help eliminate stereotypes, but also help build positive connections between racial groups.
V. Some people feel that interracial frienships can backfire, leading some to reinforce their negative racial stereotypes.
VI. People who come in contact with different races early tend to be more open minded later in life.
VII. One reason that people *don't* develop interracial friendships is discomfort
VIII. Another reason is the sometimes conscious, sometimes *un*conscious racism on the part of parents.

IX. A third reason is that students in schools form cliques and people are uncomforatable moving outside their circles.
X. Finally, the larger community makes racial differences, placing people in categories and even in neighborhoods.
XI. Teachers can help, however.

You can see from this outline that Tyler's essay, while it makes many interesting points, did not yet follow a logical development with each subclaim leading naturally into the next. He included reasons why people often don't form interracial friendships all mixed up with the benefits for doing so, and thrown in the middle, he's placed some counter-arguments. After working together, he and I came up with the following outline for his revised draft:

I. Introduction.
Thesis: "While race still serves as a way for Americans to discriminate against one another, interracial friendships can help to build racial understanding and help deconstruct prejudice."
II. Some people are nervous about forming interracial friendships and don't know how to cross racial barriers that have existed all their lives. (This corresponds roughly to section V. in Tyler's earlier draft, but is a much more realistic and representative counter-argument).
III. However, there are many benefits to crossing those barriers and forming friendships across races. For example, interracial friendships will eventually help us eliminate prejudice. (This corresponds with point III in the earlier draft but is now framed in such a way as to logically follow point II above).
IV. Interracial friendships build positive connections between groups and can help to eliminate social and financial inequities in our culture.
V. Interracial friendships can help us be more open minded and lead us to accept many other relationships that could enrich our lives.
VI. So, if there are so many benefits, why are we still so resistant? Parental influence is one reason. (Notice that here, Tyler combined two paragraphs, one from early in the original draft and one from much later—numbers II and VIII on the original outline).
VII. Classmate's influence also serves to keep us apart as we join social circles already constructed along racial lines.

VIII. Even our communities serve to preserve racial separation, with many neighborhoods, churches, and schools predominantly of a single race. (Notice that these three points are still much as they were in the original draft, but now the reader can see more explicitly the way that Tyler sees first home, then school, then community—from the personal to the public sphere—as culpable in perpetuating racial separation).
IX. But there are things we can do to help; teachers and students can both help.
X. Parents, too, need to examine their unconcious attitudes and behaviors and how they are affecting their children. (Notice that Tyler expanded his conclusion to include solutions that would address each of the problem areas he had earlier identified).

Notice that there were some sections of the outline that Tyler decided to eliminate. After we discussed the relevance of part of section II in his original outline, Tyler decided that it wasn't either relevant to his paper or judicious in a paper on racial stereotyping to claim that parents of specific races tended to be even more prejudiced and to transmit these values to their children. He eliminated that paragraph from his paper all together. However, he added new paragraphs to his "solutions" section, and moved many of his paragraphs around. In a similar way, outlining your own paper after it is finished can help you to see if the overall structure is logical and well-connected.

Try Peer Review

You're probably going to be asked to do peer review in class, but you might also want to seek out additional peer help on your own. Peer review can be empowering for you as a writer because you get recommendations not from your instructor, who will eventually be giving you a grade and whose comments, therefore, hold a great deal of weight, but from a peer who is at your same level, doing the same writing tasks as you, and who can help you to see your own writing more clearly without imposing his or her authority on it. Remember that you should always

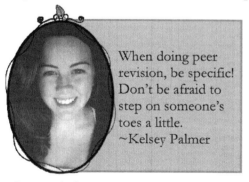

When doing peer revision, be specific! Don't be afraid to step on someone's toes a little.
~Kelsey Palmer

carefully consider your peers' suggestions, and then *decide for yourself* how to improve your writing.

There are a number of different ways to do peer response. The following are just a couple of possible types of peer response. Try them out and see which works best for you.

Peer Response Worksheet 1

1. After reading your peer's introductory paragraph, underline what you think is the central claim or thesis. Then, in the box below, fill in the following sentence, using your own words:

What I think you will be arguing in this paper is _____
_____
_____

2. Now read the first body paragraph and fill in the following sentences with your own words:

It seems to me that this paragraph is arguing _____
_____
_____.

In support of that argument, you provided this kind of evidence
_____
_____
_____.

If this were my paragraph, I would have _____
_____
_____.

3. Move on to the next paragraph and do the same:

It seems to me that this paragraph is arguing: _____
_____
_____.

In support of that argument, you provided this kind of evidence
_____
_____

> If this were my paragraph, I would have _____
> _____
> _____.
>
> 4. Continue until you've discussed each paragraph. Then, complete the following in your own words:
>
> What I especially liked about your paper was _____
> _____
> _____
>
> If this were my paper, the main thing I would work on would be
> _____
> _____
> _____.
>
> Note: You CANNOT write "nothing" for any of the statements above. Since you are NOT the writer of the paper, you would obviously have done things differently since no two people write exactly the same. So tell your peer what you would have done. It might give him or her some ideas for the next draft.

Figure 3.1: Peer Revision Example 1

Here's another example, this one from Dr. Nancy Thomas's English 110 class. She instructs students to answer the questions on a separate sheet of paper, and admonishes them to "Remember to write thorough answers with specific details and examples." This peer review sheet is considerably different from the previous one. I suggest you try them both out and see which works best for you. When done well, peer review can provide very valuable input for revision.

> Try to find some good things, too. This can really help the other person, because they can see what others like in their paper. That, in turn, allows them to write a better paper. I can speak from experience that it has greatly benefited me.
> ~Rushi Chauhan

Peer Response Worksheet 2

1. Is the title an effective hook?
2. Does the thesis meet all of the criteria of a proper thesis? Why or why not?
3. Does the paper support the thesis all the way through? Point out places where improvement is needed.
4. Has a clear outline been followed? Is the paper repetitive or redundant? Indicate problems.
5. Does each paragraph contain a topic sentence that states an idea that clearly and specifically relates the paragraph to the thesis or previous paragraph? Indicate topic sentences that do not "work."
6. Does each paragraph focus on and develop only one idea? Indicate paragraphs that lack focus.
7. Has adequate use been made of examples and person experience? Are they clearly explained, especially in terms of how they support a point?
8. Does the paper address counter-arguments and develop a rebuttal? Describe.
9. Are solutions for problems included and adequately developed? Mark examples where improvement is needed.
10. Do any words need to be defined? Do any concepts or ideas need explanation? If so, mark them.
11. Are effective transitions used? Mark examples of problem areas.
12. Does the final paragraph really conclude or is it simply a summary?
13. Does the paper fulfill the assignment? Why or why not?

Finally, please help the writer brainstorm ways to add depth to the paper, asking questions, addressing possible issues. Note the results of this brainstorm on the last page of the paper.

Figure 3.2: Peer Revision Example 2

Revising Locally (Editing)

After you've finished the long, windy road to revision, you have only those last stairs to climb as you clean up your sentences, fixing word choice and punctuation and, in general, tidying up your prose. In his famous "little book," *The Elements of Style*, William Strunk offers students 10 rules for clean prose, three of which I would like to summarize here.

First, Strunk advises writers to

"Use definite, specific, concrete language."

Avoid generalizations that simply fill up space. Choose words that make your readers feel like they are present in your writing. Here's an example from one of my past student papers. This student, writing about the difficulty of holding onto high school relationships in college wrote,

Everyone experiences love at some point in their lives.

Yawn. Not only does everyone already know that (so why bother taking my time to make me read it), but it's boring. It lacks specific, concrete language. How much better would the following sentence have been?

When I was 17, I fell in love with a handsome, red-haired senior.

In other words, remove all vague and general language and try to replace it with concrete, specific examples.

■ ■ ■ ■

The second "rule" I'd like to advise you on is to

"Use the active voice."

"The active voice," writes Strunk, "is usually more direct and vigorous than the passive." So instead of writing a sentence like this:

Daily exercise is regarded by most therapists as essential to mental health.

You should consider writing one like this:

Most therapists consider daily exercise essential to mental health.

You can recognize passive voice because it employs the following construction:

to-be verb (am, is, are, was, were, be, been) **+ a verb in the past participle** (usually ending with –ed).

Here are a few examples I've gathered from student papers:

Women *were oppressed* for centuries.

African-American's *have been denied* equal rights in our society.

Girls *are pressured* to be thin.

These are each examples of passive voice. But they are also examples of lazy writing. These sentences show an unwillingness on the part of the student to examine *who* is doing the oppressing, denying, and pressuring. Using the active voice in each of these cases would help to make both a stronger statement and a more lively writing voice.

Of course, there are occasions when the passive voice is appropriate: when, for example, the actual topic of your paper is the *object* of your sentence and you want to emphasize that object rather than the actor or actors. For example, consider the following sentence:

Alcohol abuse is considered by many to be one of the primary causes for student failure in the first year of college.

In this case, the writer wants to emphasize the object of the sentence, "alcohol abuse," rather than the actor, "many," because alcohol abuse is the topic of the argument. There may be other times when the actors are either unknown or unimportant (though you should be cautious of employing this excuse very often).

Moreover, in some disciplines such as the hard sciences and social sciences, passive voice is more acceptable because it helps writers avoid the first person "I." So rather than a sentence that emphasizes the actions of the writer/researcher, such as this:

I sampled 120 student responses

These disciplines would rather you write the more objective sounding sentence:

120 student responses were sampled.

In the majority of writing situations, however, active voice is better than passive. The key to revising passive voice is to ask yourself, "who is doing the action of this sentence?" Then move that person, group, or thing to the front of the sentence.

■ ■ ■ ■

"Omit needless words."

Strunk writes the following about using needless words:

> Vigorous writing is concise. A sentence should contain no unnecessary words, a paragraph no unnecessary sentences, for the same reason that a drawing should have no unnecessary lines and a machine no unnecessary parts. This requires not that the writer make all his sentences short, or that he avoid all detail and treat his subjects only in outline, but that every word *tell* (17, emphasis added).

You'll never make it to the top of the mountain with a pack weighted down with rocks, nor will your prose rise to the top with the weight of unnecessary words. So lighten your load by eliminating phrases like those in Table 3.1. Read your sentences carefully to see if you have any phrases like those on the left. If you do, replace them with phrases similar to those on the right.

Dead Weight Phrases	Replace with. . .
The question as to whether	Whether
There is no doubt but that	No doubt (or "doubtless")
Due to the fact that	Because
In spite of the fact that	Although
A small number of	Few
A large number of	Many
In my personal opinion	In my opinion
Ever since the time when	Since
Went on to say	Continued
We as human beings	We
In our day and time	Today
The fact of the matter	Truthfully
Each and every	Each
In the event that	If
One and the same	The same

Table 3.1: Needlessly Wordy Phrases

You should look not only for the phrases above, but for *all* unnecessary or overly complicated words, paring sentences down to their most basic meaning by using concrete language. Please note that this does *not* mean that you should only use elementary-level vocabulary. Please, develop and use a robust vocabulary. But do omit meaningless phrases like those above.

A few sample sentences from real student papers might help to illustrate what I'm talking about.

One student wrote the following:

> **Learning to live with a roommate is a key important factor in the development and growth as a student while at college.**

If we cross out unnecessary words and phrases, it might look like this:

> **Learning to live with a roommate is** ~~a key~~ **important** ~~factor~~ **in the** ~~development and~~ **growth** ~~as a~~ **student** ~~while at college~~**.**

Then we clean it up. This sentence sounds much better:

> **Learning to live with a roommate is important in the growth of a college student.**

We can even make it more concrete and active by beginning with the true actor of the sentence:

> **A college student can grow in important ways by learning to live with a roommate.**

Another example taken from a student paper further illustrates:

> **With Tusculum being a service school like it says it is in its mission statement, students expect the mission statement to be fulfilled in some way.**

If we cross out unnecessary words, we might get something like this:

> ~~With~~ **Tusculum** ~~being a~~ **service school** ~~like it says it is~~ **in its mission statement, students expect the mission statement to be fulfilled** ~~in some way~~**.**

We then revise, adding concrete details and arrive at the following:

> **Students expect that Tusculum will fulfill its mission statement which names the school a service institute.**

By cleaning up overly wordy phrases, you will keep your readers focused on your argument, undistracted by confusing or awkward language.

• • • •

If you follow these three rules, you will go a long way toward cleaning up your prose, making it lighter and more attractive—and easier to carry.

> As revising is sometimes the most important step, I take this step seriously, because it can make or break you.
> ~Mason Carnett

One final note: This section on editing highlights three important stylistic problems that student writing often contains. Additionally, young writers often struggle with specific grammatical and punctuation problems, but these are so various and the different kinds of errors so numerous that I cannot include them all in this book. If your instructor tells you that you need to work on a specific kind of grammatical error, I would direct you to the very excellent resources of the Purdue Online Writing Lab located at https://owl.english.purdue.edu.

II. ENGLISH 110: THE JOURNEY BEGINS

English 110: Sample Schedule
Residential College

The following is a sample schedule that your instructor may or may not choose to follow. In either case, it will give you an idea of the basic frame for the class.

Week One: Exploring Topics for Analysis and Argument	
Possible Activities	Reading essays and stories
	Responding to your reading with your own ideas
	Learning about audience, appeals, and basic argument techniques (you may review the first part of this book on the writing process)
	Analyzing visual arguments like advertisements and fliers
	Creating visual arguments

This week's activities will likely culminate in your having chosen a text to analyze for the *rhetorical analysis paper* and a topic of interest (perhaps related to the rhetorical analysis) for your later argument paper.

Week Two: Drafting the Rhetorical Analysis	
Possible Activities	Examining your text's intended claims and evidence
	Learning more about audience and examining your text's intended audience
	Learning more about ethos, pathos, and logos and locating examples of these in your chosen text
	Examining your text's language use, including rhetorical tropes and schemes
	Drafting your rhetorical analysis

This process will probably end with your completion and submission of the rhetorical analysis paper.

Week Three: Drafting the Argument Paper	
Possible Activities	Creating questions to guide your inquiry into your chosen subject
	Answering those questions from your own experiences, ideas, reading, and observations, as well as asking friends and classmate's opinions
	Learning about and conducting primary research such as interviews, surveys, or observations
	Learning about and outlining a convincing claims structure with the evidence you have gathered
	Drafting your argument paper

This process will probably end with your completion and submission of the argument paper.

Week Four: Revising Both Major Papers	
Possible Activities	Peer review
	Post-draft outlines
	Read-alouds
	Instructor conferences
	Copy-editing

At the end of this week, you will submit your portfolio to your instructor..

We hope that you will both enjoy and learn from this process, and that your ability to make and analyze an argument will develop, preparing you for English 111 and other courses here at the college.

English 110: Sample Schedule
Gateway Program

The following is a sample schedule that your instructor may or may not choose to follow, but will give you a basic idea of the class framework.

Week One: Exploring Topics for Analysis and Argument	
Possible Activities	Reading essays and stories
	Responding to your reading
	Learning about or reviewing basic argument techniques (you may be asked to review the first part of this book)

Week Two: Introduction to Rhetorical Analysis	
Possible Activities	Learning about audience and the rhetorical triangle
	Learning about audience appeals such as ethos, pathos, and logos
	Learning about rhetorical schemes and tropes
	Choosing a text for analysis

Week Three: Drafting and Revising the Rhetorical Analysis.	
Possible Activities	Drafting of the rhetorical analysis
	Self analysis and revision
	Peer review, post draft outlines, read-alouds
	Instructor conferences

Week Four: Introduction to Argument	
Possible Activities	Reading and examining argument essays and using them to generate topics
	Discussing argument styles and evidence types

	Creating questions to guide your inquiry into your chosen subject and answering those questions from your own experiences, ideas, reading, and observations, as well as those of friends and classmates
	Learning about and conducting primary research such as interviews, surveys, or observations
Week Five: Drafting and Revising the Argument Paper	
Possible Activities	Learning about and outlining a convincing claims structure with the evidence you have gathered
	Drafting your argument paper
	Peer review, post draft outlines, read-alouds
	Instructor conferences
At the end of this week, you will submit your portfolio to your instructor.	

We hope that you will both enjoy and learn from this process, and that your ability to make and analyze an argument will develop, preparing you for English 111 and other courses here at the college.

Chapter 4: Rhetorical Analysis
Learning the Ways

Welcome to English 110! For many of you, this is the first writing course you have taken at the college and thus the beginning of your journey as a college writer. We encourage you to read through the first section in this handbook and familiarize yourself with the steps in the writing process. You will be using those steps throughout this course as you compose two different genres of common college-level writing: an analysis paper and an argument paper. You will work through the processes of prewriting, drafting, revising, and editing with your instructor and classmates for each of these papers, both of which are detailed in this and the following chapter. And while your instructor may teach the writing of these two papers in either order, this hand-handbook will begin with the analysis paper. The analysis paper will give you an opportunity

to study the way an experienced writer makes an argument and analyze the moves that she or he makes to convince readers. Just as you would on any journey that promises potential peril, you should look to those more experienced for guidance. On my own trek through the Amazon, I carefully followed my guide, Silver, walking where he told me to walk, paying attention to those things he pointed out, avoiding those pitfalls he warned me against. You, too, can look to experienced guides who have successfully negotiated the complex and sometimes dangerous paths of persuasive writing, learning their moves, observing their maneuvers and stratagems, and learning from them how to construct successful arguments.

In examining the motives and methods of these published writers of argument, you are doing what we call *rhetorical analysis*. Aristotle defined *rhetoric* as "the available means of persuasion." In other words, rhetoric encompasses all of the tools a writer uses—claims, evidence, language, appeals, etc.—to persuade a reader. In a *rhetorical analysis*, then, a writer examines the tools another author has used to make an argument and adjudges their success or failure.

Choosing & Deconstructing a Text

It is important to note that, while arguably every text makes claims and arguments, a rhetorical analysis is typically performed on texts designed specifically to persuade. That means that you will not be analyzing literary texts or other works that, though they may be obliquely persuasive, are not designed explicitly for that purpose. A literary analysis differs in both aims and process from a rhetorical analysis, so in choosing your text, be sure you've chosen one specifically designed to persuade through the use of claims, subclaims, and evidence.

Once you have chosen the text you would like to analyze, you need to begin to break it down, or *deconstruct* the argument. Imagine a complex cloth woven of many different threads—your task it to take apart the cloth and examine the threads individually. Some of the threads, or parts of an argument, that you might examine include,

- The author's claims and subclaims
- The author's use of evidence

- The author's ability to appeal to readers
- The author's use of language and rhetorical tropes

In each case, you will carefully examine every part of the argument and then analyze what the author has done, for what purpose, and to what level of success. Please note that in a rhetorical analysis, you are not *responding* to the argument topic itself, nor are you contributing your own ideas on the topic. Instead, you are analyzing the structure of another's argument and judging its persuasive power.

ANALYZING CLAIMS & SUBCLAIMS

To analyze an author's claims and subclaims, it's a good idea to first outline the argument so that you have a solid handle on exactly what the author was trying to persuade readers of. Once you have a good grasp of the primary arguments of the piece, you can then begin to analyze the success of these arguments. With the outline in front of you, ask yourself the following questions:

> My most important piece of advice in writing the rhetorical analysis paper is finding the author's claims because if you do that then you know exactly what the author is going after.
> ~Austin Bishop

- Is the argument thorough? Has the writer addressed possible counterarguments? Are there obvious arguments or counterarguments that the writer has left out? Is there something else you feel the writer should have addressed but did not?
- Is the argument accurate? Has the writer made claims that you feel are questionable or poorly supported?
- Is the argument up-to-date and timely? If the article or essay is an older one, is there information that is no longer relevant? Has new knowledge clarified any part of the argument, making it obsolete?
- Is the order of claims and subclaims convincing and easy to follow?

All analysis papers should contain a summary of the claims and sub-claims made in the text being studied and a consequent analysis of the success of those claims. The following example is taken from an analysis of Marjorie Garber's book, *Vested Interests: Cross Dressing and Cultural Anxiety* by Neil Bartlett. Bartlett here examines Garber's claims, both those he sees as successfully made, and those he finds lacking:

> Marjorie Garber's thesis in *Vested Interests* is challenging and simple: Cross-dressing isn't an aberrant, eccentric or minority art form; it is a mainstream cultural activity which makes evident the deepest ways in which our ideas of who we are and who we aren't are structured. [. . .]
>
> A chief virtue of Garber's book is its gorgeously wide frame of reference, which strays across periods, cultures and media with real authority. The expected material—Shakespeare's transvestite heroines—is dispensed with early, and then it's down to the real crazies: Nancy Reagan, Rambova, Elvis, Liberace.
>
> This breadth of reference becomes also a problem. If cross-dressing is everywhere, if all instances of such acts are equal parts of one massive, central cultural conundrum, then differences get dissolved. In particular, we lose sight of the issue of who loses and who gains in the battle of dressing and cross-dressing. [. . .]
>
> When Garber insists that playing with dress is part of a large and endlessly reflective cultural system, she is of course right. But she doesn't really engage with the fact that this cultural system is also a war, with winners and losers.

So while Bartlett finds Garber's claims to cover a "gorgeously wide frame of reference," both historically and culturally, he also critiques what he finds as an absence: the lack of acknowledgement that cross-dressing most often constitutes a violation of cultural expectations that frequently draws reprisals.

Once you've had a chance to outline and examine each of the claims the author made, you may decide that there are gaps, or places where more or better claims were needed. Or perhaps you will feel that the author made his or her point successfully, supporting it with an adequate number of claims with no obvious absences. Either way, make sure you provide a summary of claims made and an analysis of their success.

Evaluating Evidence

Similarly, after dissecting an argument, you may decide that, while the claims and subclaims were accurate and thorough, the evidence used to support them was not. Or perhaps you decide that the evidence used to support them was notably sufficient and well-done. Whether you would like to praise or critique, analyzing an author's use of evidence is another important part of a rhetorical analysis. To analyze the use of evidence, you might ask yourself the following questions:

- Is each claim supported with sufficient evidence to be convincing?
- Is the evidence timely and up-to-date?
- Is the evidence convincing? Is it accurate and truthfully represented?

The following example is taken from an analysis of Arnold Ludwig's book, *King of the Mountain: The Nature of Political Leadership*, by Larry Arnhart. Arnhart finds that Ludwig includes an impressive amount of evidence to support the first half of his central claim: that political leadership in all major contemporary societies has been dominated by men. Arnhart writes,

> Arnold Ludwig's book shows that the political history of the 20th century confirms the claim of Aristotle and Darwin that male dominance of politics is rooted in human biological nature. Ludwig argues that the male desire to be the supreme political ruler expresses the same biological propensities that support the dominance of alpha males among monkeys and apes. He supports his argument with a meticulous analysis of the 1,941 chief executive rulers of the independent countries in the 20th century. He illustrates his points with lively anecdotes from the lives of the 377 rulers for whom he had extensive biographical information. (64)

However, despite this impressive body of evidence, the second half of Ludwig's central claim—that such political dominance is biologically dictated—is found by Arnhart to be insufficiently supported with evidence:

> If Ludwig is right about males having a stronger propensity to dominance than females, then he should be able to show the underlying neurophysiological mechanisms that support this difference. But he offers little more than some casual references to higher levels of testosterone among males. (64)

In this example, then, the author of the analysis finds the argument being studied to have made sufficient claims but to lack impressive enough evidence to support those claims.

CATEGORIZING AUDIENCE

The success or failure of a claims structure, including its evidence, relies in large measure on how well it was constructed to appeal to a specific audience. The shape a text takes—its flavor, tone, and quality—is dependent on three elements that are located outside the text itself but which influence its construction: the topic, the writer, and the audience. These three elements constitute the three points on what is commonly known as the Rhetorical Triangle:

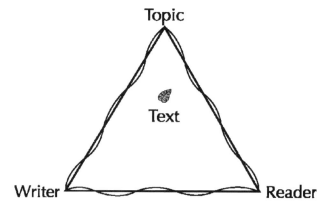

Figure 4.1: The Rhetorical Triangle

If any point on the triangle changes, the shape of the text itself changes. It seems fairly obvious that a text written by Mary and a text written by

Guillermo, even if they are about the same topic and written to the same audience, will be very different texts. After all, Mary and Guillermo are unique individuals with different points of view.

Likewise, it seems self-evident that Mary, writing a paper on the Supreme Court's decision to overthrow the Defense of Marriage Act will produce a considerably different text from the one she will later write about the effects of second-hand smoke. Clearly, changing the topic of a paper changes the shape of the text itself.

What seems less obvious to many young writers, however, is how differently two texts should appear when both are written by the same writer and on the same topic but to different audiences. For example, let's say that Guillermo wishes to write about the controversy surrounding Genetically Modified Foods (GMOs), a topic about which he is very passionate. The first text, written to an audience of GMO opponents who follow his blog, *Poisoning Our Food Supplies*, will look considerably different from the other text, written for his Tusculum biology class. He will choose different language, adopt different tones, and select different evidence to communicate to these very different audiences.

Thus we can see that changing any point on the rhetorical triangle changes the shape of the text itself. Consequently, a writer's awareness of the way in which the rhetorical triangle works helps him or her to develop the topic in such a way as to appeal to the target audience. Authors with a keen awareness of audience customize their writing—the kinds of claims they make, the evidence they use, and the language they employ—to suit their intended readers.

An important part of writing a rhetorical analysis, then, is to evaluate how well an author has appealed to his intended audience, beginning first with an identification of that audience. Look at the following excerpt from an analysis of Phyllis Zagano's book, *An Argument for the Restoration of the Female Diaconate in the Catholic Church*, by Margaret Eletta Guider. Guider here identifies the intended audience of Zagano's book and then comments on the strengths of her audience appeal:

> You need to make sure that you understand what the author's main idea and audience are. Understanding these two key pieces will strengthen your paper like none other.
> ~Rushi Chauhan

> Well researched and well written, the book anticipates the interests, the questions and the needs of thoughtful individuals and committed communities of faith who are willing to wrestle with the dynamics and ambiguities of history, authority, possibility and grace. Though Zagano's context for inquiry is the United States, she is keenly aware of the broad implications of her study for the church as it seeks to respond to the people of God in a global context. To this end, Zagano's grounding in the Roman Catholic tradition enables her to serve as an interpreter for the local church as well as an interlocutor for the world church. I predict that far beyond the borders of the church in North America, this book will have a reading, a relevance and a repercussion that may exceed the author's expectations.

Guider also expresses some concerns with the possible reception of certain members of Zagano's audience:

> Though Zagano's conclusions may leave some readers with a new or renewed sense of hope, it is reasonable to assume that others may find her tenacity in resurfacing the neuralgic question of women's ordination a serious affront to the teaching authority of the church.

However, Guider doesn't see this as a weakness of Zagano's argument but rather of the contemporary situation of many readers within the Catholic Church. In other words, she has described who she thinks Zagano's readers will be and which of those readers will be receptive—and which resistant—to her argument. Likewise, you should include an analysis of likely readers of the argument you are analyzing, what you think their reception of the text will be, and why you believe this.

Appealing to Readers

In addition to analyzing *who* the audience for a piece is and how well you think an author reached that audience, you will also need to examine specific types of evidence and their success or failure in reaching an audience. You already know that you need to analyze the sufficiency and quality of the evidence used to support an argument. In addition, however, you will need to examine *how* that evidence might be used to appeal in specific ways to the target audience. Aristotle defined three specific *types* of evidence that an author might use to persuade readers: Appeals to Pathos, Appeals to Ethos, and Appeals to Logos.

Appeals to Pathos

The first way evidence might appeal to an audience is by reaching their emotions. Emotional appeals, or *appeals to pathos*, seek to convince readers to support an argument by drawing on their emotions. Take the following example from President Barak Obama's first inaugural address:

> As we consider the road that unfolds before us, we remember with humble gratitude those brave Americans who, at this very hour, patrol far off deserts and distant mountains. They have something to tell us, just as the fallen heroes who lie in Arlington whisper through the ages. We honor them, not only because they are the guardians of our liberty, but because they embody the spirit of service, a willingness to find meaning in something greater than themselves.
>
> And yet, at this moment, a moment that will define a generation, it is precisely this spirit that must inhabit us ALL.

Here, President Obama seeks to enlist the support of Americans by appealing to their sense of patriotism and their pride in the brave soldiers—both current and past—who have supported our freedom with their service and their lives.

When trying to spot appeals to pathos in a text, you should keep an eye out for any evidence that seeks to rouse listeners'/readers' emotions in any way. Some common ways that argumentative texts appeal to pathos are included in Table 4.1.

Common Ways to Appeal to Pathos

Kinds of Evidence	Emotional Effect
Descriptions	Detailed descriptions help the reader visualize what the speaker is speaking or writing about—a powerful way to help readers or listeners see the issue from the writer's perspective.
Narrative	Stories often appeal to our emotions, whether of pity, sorrow, humor, patriotism, anger, pride, etc.
References to Identity	Anything that might make listeners feel that they are a part of a group usually does so through appeals to emotions. For example, drawing on listeners identities as Americans, as Good Family Men and Women, as Mothers, as Tennesseans, as Conservatives, as Christians, etc. allows the speaker to identify her- or himself as a part of a group and thus evoke emotions of solidarity and unity.
References to Tradition	Whether it's religious, familial, national, or ceremonial, people generally respect, even reverence, tradition, and evoking tradition thus allows a speaker to appeal to his or her audience's emotional connection to that tradition.

Table 4.1: Appeals to Pathos

Appeals to pathos can be very powerful. In fact, in the *Encyclopedia of Rhetoric*, L.D. Greene claims that "Of the three appeals of *logos, ethos*, and *pathos*, it is the [last] that impels an audience to act." How often have you known, logically, that you should do something but haven't done it because it was too hard, too inconvenient, too boring, etc.? By contrast, how many times have you done something you know you *shouldn't* because your emotions were involved? Obviously, emotional appeals can be quite powerful. And in the hands of a skilled and ethical rhetorician, they can move an audience to positive action. In the same way, in the hands of an unethical user, they can serve to *manipulate* audiences into taking action. In the next section in this chapter, we will discuss some of the fallacies of argument that result from the unethical or simply sloppy use of appeals. Fallacies resulting from a poor use of emotional appeals include *bandwagon appeals*, *stereotyping*, and *appeals to false emotion*.

Appeals to Ethos

Appeals to ethos seek to garner the support of readers by convincing them that the author is a person of knowledge, good will, and integrity. In other words, appeals to ethos tell a reader, "You can trust me; I know what I'm talking about and I wouldn't lead you astray." Look, for example, at the following excerpt from Franklin D. Roosevelt's first inaugural address in 1933:

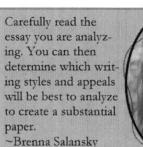

> Carefully read the essay you are analyzing. You can then determine which writing styles and appeals will be best to analyze to create a substantial paper.
> ~Brenna Salansky

> And I am certain that on this day my fellow Americans expect that on my induction into the Presidency, I will address them with a candor and a decision which the present situation of our people impels. This is preeminently the time to speak the truth, the whole truth, frankly and boldly. Nor need we shrink from honestly facing conditions in our country today.

In 1933, the country was firmly in the grip of the great depression. Roosevelt had been optimistically voted in as president in the hopes that he would have fresh new perspectives to offer in solving the crisis. In this first inaugural address, then, he attempts to establish a trust and a rapport with the American people by framing himself as a person of honesty and courage. In this way, he seeks to convince his audience to trust his arguments about what must be done.

There are many different ways to make ethical appeals, but the most common are summarized in table 4.2. In all cases, however, writers use ethical appeals in order to establish trust in their character which can then be extended to a trust in their arguments.

Common Ways to Appeal to Ethos

Kinds of Evidence	Effect
Use of Established Reputation	Often an author or speaker who enjoys celebrity status (in the arts, in politics, even in academics) will rely on that reputation to convince audiences to follow along with an argument.
Declamations of Knowledge or Experience	Often, authors will tell stories the sole purpose of which is to show readers the author's knowledge of and experience with the topic. This convinces readers that they can trust what the author is saying since her or his claims stem from experience and not merely from second-hand research.
Appeals to Authority	Not only might an author seek to convince readers by demonstrating his or her own credibility, but they might do so by showing the support of authorities whose knowledge, experience, and reputations are well-established. Any time a writer cites another authority, they are borrowing that person's ethos in the service of the argument being made.
Assurances of Good Will	Sometimes authors will convince audiences to lend their trust by showing that their motives for making the argument are noble.
Claims to Character	In addition to motive, authors will sometimes seek to convince readers to trust them by demonstrating good character. They may claim to be honest, to care about their families, to love their country, to care about the environment, etc. Any evidence that makes the author look like a good or caring person is an appeal to ethos.

Table 4.2: Appeals to Ethos

And just as in the case of emotional appeals, appeals to ethos can be used either ethically or unethically. When used unethically, appeals to ethos might devolve into the fallacies of *ad hominem attacks, appeals to false authority,* and *appeals to dogma.* These will be further described in the next section.

Appeals to Logos

The final kind of audience appeal described by Aristotle is the appeal to logos, or logical appeal. While the previous two kinds are important, an academic argument, to be truly convincing, should rely primarily on this type of appeal. Appeals to logos include many different kinds of evidence, including inductive and deductive reasoning, statistical and scientific support, analogies, and cause-effect reasoning. These are each described in Table 4.3.

The following is an example of an appeal to logos from Kathy Freston's article "Vegetarian is the New Prius." The article is supported by paragraph after paragraph of statistics showing the dramatic environmental impact of raising farm animals—all appeals to logos. Near the end of her argument, she assures readers that making the change to vegetarianism won't be as hard as they might think:

> Doing so has never been easier. Recent years have seen an explosion of environmentally-friendly vegetarian foods. Even chains like Ruby Tuesday, Johnny Rockets, and Burger King offer delicious veggie burgers and supermarket refrigerators are lined with heart-healthy creamy soymilk and tasty veggie deli slices. Vegetarian foods have become staples at environmental gatherings, and garnered celebrity advocates like Bill Maher, Alec Baldwin, Paul McCartney, and of course Leonardo DiCaprio. Just as the Prius showed us that we each have in our hands the power to make a difference against a problem that endangers the future of humanity, going vegetarian gives us a new way to dramatically reduce our dangerous emissions that is even more effective, easier to do, more accessible to everyone and certainly goes better with french fries.

In order to convince readers that not only *should* they adopt an environmentally-friendly, vegetarian lifestyle, but that doing so is fairly *easy*, Freston here uses a series of examples to demonstrate this ease. Vegetarians, she says, can now easily find tasty food both at popular restaurants and in the grocery stores, and she offers specific examples to back up her claim. Moreover, new vegetarian converts can look to experienced practitioners, and for this, too, she offers examples. Using inductive reasoning, then, Freston convinces readers that going veg is a piece of cake.

Common Ways to Appeal to Logos

Kinds of Evidence	Effect
Inductive Reasoning	Inductive reasoning is reasoning by example. In this type of evidence, then, an author will make a claim and then support that claim with a series of examples demonstrating its generalizability.
Deductive Reasoning	Deductive reasoning involves tracing a chain of logic, often in the form of "if, then" statements. Beginning with factual statements upon which all parties can agree, deductive chains then guide readers through a series of increasingly complex claims, each based on the establishment of the claim that precedes it. One famous example is the deductive chain made by Socrates which starts with the factual claim, "All men are mortal," followed by the next claim, "Socrates is a man," and concludes with the final claim, based now on the acceptance of the previous two: "Socrates is mortal."
Statistical and Scientific Support	People are especially convinced by statistical and scientific evidence, and when used well, it can, indeed, shore up an argument to impressive heights. But be cautious: some authors manipulate statistics to meet their ends. A critical reader approaches these appeals with caution, acknowledging, however, that when done well, they are particularly powerful.
Analogies	Analogies help readers to see a topic more clearly by comparing it to a topic with which readers are already familiar. Done well, analogies can help to clarify and contextualize issues for readers.
Cause-Effect Reasoning	Tracing the connections between events, their causes, and their effects, can be a powerful way to move readers to action or belief.

Table 4.3: Appeals to Logos

Unfortunately, it is especially easy for logical appeals to be constructed poorly and consequently to lead to fallacies of argument. Fallacies that result from the poor or unethical use of logical appeals include *straw man, false analogy, red herring, circular reasoning,* and *slippery slope,* all of which are described in greater detail in the section that follows.

Avoiding Fallacies

When an author uses a particular rhetorical device (e.g. appeals to ethos, pathos, or logos) and pushes the device beyond the bounds of either ethics or reasonableness, the argument then devolves into *rhetorical fallacy,* or *fallacy of argument.* There are dozens of different kinds of rhetorical fallacies, but some of the most common are detailed below.

Appeals to Pathos Gone Awry

Bandwagon Appeals

Remember that appeals to identity and tradition, when used ethically and for reasonable purposes, are excellent and powerful examples of appeals to pathos. By reminding people of their loyalties, their identities, and their heritage, writers can urge audiences to take positive action in the interest of those communities. However, sometimes authors encourage readers to adopt an attitude, buy a product, or take an action based *only* on the nebulous claim that, because others do it, buy it, or believe it, so too should the reader.

The following is a famous example of this type of rhetorical fallacy. In his book, *How I Found Freedom in an Unfree World,* Harry Browne provides a road map to what he believes is true freedom: getting rid of the expectations of others and the constraints we might feel to make them happy. He writes,

> Everyone is selfish; everyone is doing what he believes will make himself happier. The recognition of that can take most of the sting out of accusations that you're being 'selfish.' Why should you feel guilty for seeking your own happiness when that's what everyone else is doing, too?

It's OK to act selfishly, Browne seems to say, *if that is what everyone else is doing.* But the fact that others might do an action is not reason enough for a critical and ethical thinker.

Stereotyping

Another way that appeals to identity might be used unethically is in the rhetorical fallacy of *stereotyping*. While drawing on a shared identity can be a powerful way to engage emotion, writers need to be careful about lumping all members of a group together, assuming that they will all think, look, or act the same.

The following example is from "Why Men And Women Get Married" by Jenna Goudreau in *Forbes Magazine*. Here, Goudreau relies on the tenuous claim (supported by Gray, whose famous book *Men are from Mars* is full of such stereotyping), that all (or at least *most*) women feel a certain way about marriage, while men feel the opposite:

> For all the young women who've chewed their nails to the skin anticipating a proposal, it may be a relief to know that, yes, men still want to get married. But there's a critical difference between the sexes. In broad terms, when a woman falls in love, just like the Trinity character in *The Matrix*, she knows he's The One. But a man's readiness can be seen as a life stage. To call on *The Matrix* again, a time when he's ready to take the red pill.
>
> "He first needs to feel like he knows what he's doing in the world and where he's going," says John Gray, relationship counselor and author of the *Men Are from Mars, Women Are from Venus* books. "Women are more concerned about who they're going with."

Stereotyping is an extreme form of categorization. We all categorize things. Doing so is an important way for us to understand and make sense of the world. But when categorization goes too far—when it leads us to assume that all members of a group can be easily understood and defined—then it crosses into the realm of stereotyping, a classic rhetorical fallacy.

False Appeals to Emotion

Appeals to emotion, as we discussed in the previous section, are not inherently bad or fallacious. Appealing to emotion can be a powerful way for a writer to motivate her or his readers to action. However, such appeals become logical fallacies when A) they are not supported by other kinds of evidence, B) they are used for unethical ends, or C) they are used to urge a belief rather than an action.

Gary N. Curtis, author of *The Fallacy Files*, explains that "appeals to emotion are always fallacious when intended to influence our beliefs, but they are sometimes reasonable when they aim to motivate us to act." Our desiring something to be true, he explains, is not a valid argument for the acceptance of its truth. On the other hand, desire *is* a valid reason to pursue a goal or action, providing the goal or action is an ethical one.

Religious arguments often use appeals to emotion to encourage belief. Take, for example, the following from Christian writer Paul Little's *Know Why You Believe*:

> There are many reasons to believe that God is very much alive and active in the universe.
>
> Think about humanity's overall longing for something beyond what we see. It's this longing that causes people to turn to religion for answers. . . . This inner longing was described by Blaise Pascal, the great 17th-century mathematician, as "the God-shaped vacuum" in every human being.

Here, Little makes the argument that because people *long* to believe in God, God must be real. And while this reasoning may work as a bolster to individual belief, it is not an example of valid evidence in an argument. (Incidentally, just because something cannot be proven to be true, it does not follow that it is therefore false.).

■　■　■　■

Appeals to Ethos Gone Awry

Ad Hominem Attacks

Ad hominem means "against the person," and ad hominem attacks are attacks against a person's character. While it's perfectly acceptable to question the credibility of an authority and their expertise on specific issues (were I to have the presumption to write on nuclear physics, for example, critics would—quite fairly—question my authority to do so), ad hominem attacks attempt to discredit an opponent by attacking them in areas tangential or unrelated to the argument at hand or by smearing their character or calling them names. The following example, taken from *Conservative News and Views*, does both:

> Citing the Clinton sex scandal, RoseAnn Salanitri claims that Bill Clinton is a liar like unto the "father of all liars." Moreover, she claims, it is only "those who have been enchanted by the Liar in Chief [who] will accepts Clinton's remarks" and his endorsement of Barack Obama for a second term.

Salanitri not only attacks Clinton on a personal level (comparing him to Satan), but she also attempts to divert attention from the real issue—Clinton's endorsement of Obama—by referencing an unrelated personal matter—Clinton's infidelity. Ad hominem attacks are essentially distraction techniques, attempts to divert readers' attention from the real subject of the argument.

Straw Man

An important part of many kinds of argument is the addressing of alternate viewpoints. However, when a writer misrepresents her or his opponents' arguments, then the writer has fallen into the **straw man** fallacy. Taken from the straw men that used to be set up as target practice for sports like archery and even football, it means to set up a false opponent in order to more easily knock her or him down. The following example comes from a speech given by Senator Rand Paul at The Conservative Political Action Conference. His argument is that President Obama, who had cancelled White House tours for school children due to financial restrictions, should rethink the programs to be cut:

> So what I ask the president, if he wants to let the school children back in the White House, what about the $3 million that we spend studying monkeys on meth? Does it really take $3 million to discover that monkeys, like humans, act crazy on meth? (March 14, 2013).

In this example, Senator Paul is misrepresenting his opponent's position by oversimplifying, even misrepresenting, the research being funded. While it is true that the National Institute on Drug Abuse receives funding for a research project on the effects of methamphetamines on rhesus monkeys, the purpose of such research has both complex and reasonable purposes. As Marilyn E. Carroll, leader of the team of researchers describes it, "the main objective of this research is to develop nonhuman primate models (rhesus monkeys) of critical aspects of addiction that will yield useful information for the prevention and treatment of drug abuse." The research team is testing the effects of different treatment models which will eventually help them to treat humans addicted to this dangerous and difficult-to-overcome drug. Paul's oversimplification of the research is set up simply as a straw man, making his opponents' position look ridiculous so that he can then knock it down. He pays no attention and gives no respect to the complexity of his opponents' argument. This is a common rhetorical fallacy and one that you will need to be very careful not to duplicate in your own writing.

Appeals to False Authority

Using the voice of authorities to back up claims is an important part of making an argument. Writers draw upon the reputations of experts in order to lend ethos to their arguments. This is a necessary and well-respected part of argument. However, when a writer uses a single expert to support a point, or even worse, draws on "experts" that are either of questionable credibility or whose expertise is not widely recognized, they are initiating the fallacy of **appeals to false authority**.

In the following example, Clavius, a sixteenth-century mathematician and astronomer, argued that because Ptolemy's astronomical theories paralleled that of ancient philosophers, his theories must be superior to Copernicus's:

> One may doubt whether it would be preferable to follow Ptolemy or Copernicus. For both are in agreement with the observed phenomena. But Copernicus's principles contain a great many assertions which are absurd....For according to the philosophers, a simple body like the Earth can only have a simple motion....Therefore, it seems to me that Ptolemy's geocentric doctrine must be preferred to Copernicus's doctrine. (cited in Engel 144).

Here, Clavius abandons the need to debate the theories through logic and evidence and instead relies on questionable authorities (the philosophers) to make his argument. (And incidentally, as it turns out, Clavius was wrong: Copernicus was the man to back).

As this example demonstrates, however, there are some authorities in any given culture that hold such weight that often writers will fail to recognize the insufficiency of such authorities as the only evidence offered. Moreover, drawing on authorities that have meaning in one culture but not another will fail to convince readers that do not share the writer's reverence for those authorities. For example, arguments that claim that something is true simply because the Bible said it, or because the President, or Shakespeare, or Grandmother said it, are all examples of appeals to false authority.

■ ■ ■ ■

Appeals to Logos Gone Awry

Circular Reasoning

We earlier discussed the importance of deductive reasoning in creating arguments. In a deductive argument, writers build a chain of logic, stating premises, which lead to other premises, which lead to other premises, leading finally to a logical conclusion. The **circular reasoning** fallacy occurs when writers use as one of the premises for their argument the very conclusion they are trying to prove, or else use as a premise a claim that actually needs to be proven, that is not accepted as fact (they use a conclusion *as* a premise). Take the following example from Sam Harris's famous anti-Christian polemic as an example:

> Atheism is not a philosophy; it is not even a view of the world; it is simply an admission of the obvious. In fact, "atheism" is a term that should not even exist. No one needs to identify himself as a "non-astrologer" or a "non-alchemist." We do not have words for people who doubt that Elvis is still alive or that aliens have traversed the galaxy only to molest ranchers and cattle. Atheism is nothing more than the noises reasonable people make in the presence of unjustified religious beliefs.

In order to understand Harris's fallacious reasoning, let's outline his claims and conclusion.

> Central Claim: Atheism *is* reality.
>
> Premise One: No one who *isn't* a thing (an astrologer, an alchemist, etc.) needs to identify himself as such.
>
> Premise Two: Being a religious believer is to be a specific thing.
>
> Premise Three: Being an atheist *isn't* being a specific thing: it's just reality.
>
> Therefore, Atheism is reality, because atheism is what is real.

This is a classic example of circular reasoning because the real issue—is atheism the obvious and logical choice?—is here stated as one of the premises of the argument (premise number three). Many readers can accept as valid premises the first two of Harris's argument. However, the third premise is really a conclusion disguised as a premise—that atheism is simply the realistic choice. Using as evidence to support a claim the very claim itself shows a lack of the kind of logic and reason that Harris is so loudly demanding throughout his book, a flaw you need to assiduously avoid in your own argument construction.

Red Herring

The **red herring** fallacy gets its name from the practice of distracting hounds from the scent of their pray with a smelly fish—a red herring. And in argumentation, a red herring distracts readers from the real issue at hand by introducing information that is irrelevant or tangential to the central argument, as in the example below.

In February of 2012, Treyvon Martin, a young black man in Sanford, Florida was shot by George Zimmerman, a white member of a self-appointed neighborhood watch group. In the wake of the shooting, the media debated extensively the culpability of Zimmerman, who claimed that he was acting in self-defense. In the weeks and months following the shooting, the media hotly debated Zimmerman's claim, examining the circumstances of the shooting, the 911 call placed by Zimmerman, the testimonies of Zimmerman and other witnesses. Into these arguments appeared a number of red herrings as well, as in the following example from the UK newspaper *The Daily Mail*:

> Trayvon Martin was suspended from school three times in the months before he was shot dead by a neighborhood watchman, it emerged today. . . .
>
> The new claims, revealed in a leaked report, paint a different picture of a teenager who frequently found himself in trouble with authorities. . . .
>
> Earlier, he had been suspended for skipping school and showing up late to class. And most recently, in February, he was suspended again when officials found a 'marijuana pipe' and an empty baggie with traces of the drug.

In a blog article for the *The New York Times*, Rober Mackey wrote that "a wave of vitriol was aimed at the young victim . . .last weekend." And indeed, after President Obama voiced support of the young man's family, the attacks on Martin's character multiplied. But in addition to being offensive in nature, these attacks on Martin's character are also red herrings. Even if Martin were a poor student, often suspended, and even if he were a user of marijuana, how are any of those claims (which later proved to be highly suspect anyway), evidence of Zimmerman's guilt or innocence? In fact, attacking the character of the victim is a common red herring practiced by supporters of the accused who have little in the way of solid argument or evidence in order to distract from this lack.

Slippery Slope

An important part of making a logical argument is considering the repercussions of the claim. If we accept a proposal to provide students with their textbooks, for example, (an argument that my students like to make), we would then need to examine the impact of accepting this proposal—which might include a raising of tuition to cover the attendant expenses. Carefully examining the possible impact of a proposed claim is a crucial part of making a responsible argument. However, when a writer attempts to dissuade readers from accepting a claim by predicting dire and unreasonable repercussions, then they have fallen prey to the ***slippery slope*** fallacy. Professor Hadley Arkes, in his arguments against gay marriage, makes just such a mistake:

> If it [marriage] could mean just anything the positive law proclaimed it to mean, then the positive law could define just about anything as a marriage. Why shouldn't it be possible to permit a mature woman, past child bearing, to marry her grown son? In fact, why would it not be possible to permit a man, much taken with himself, to marry himself?. . .Although I am not predicting that, if gay marriage were allowed, we would be engulfed by incest and polygamy, . . .what is being posed here is a question of principle: what is the ground on which the law would turn back these challenges?

Although Arkes claims that he is "not predicting" that gay marriage will lead to the scandalous and ridiculous things he has named above, he certainly is strongly implying such a prediction. And this is a classic example of how slippery slope fallacies work.

False Analogy

Earlier, I wrote that using analogies was one way to help readers to understand complex ideas by likening those complexities to things the reader is already familiar with. As such, *analogy* is one method of appealing to logos. However, when a writer likens two things to one another in an unfair way—either by pushing the analogy too far or by comparing things very obviously unlike—they have fallen prey to the fallacy of ***false analogy***. Look at the following example from Professor Susan Wooley, interviewed by *New York Times* columnist Molly O'Neill about the dangers of America's obsession with dieting:

> We know that overweight people have a higher mortality rate than thin people. We also know that black people have a higher mortality rate than white people. Do we subject black people to torturous treatments to bleach their skin? Of course not. We have enough sense to know skin bleaching will not eliminate sickle-cell anemia. So why do we have blind faith that weight loss will cure the diseases associated with obesity?

Here, Wooley likens overweight people to black people and skin bleaching to weight loss. The problem with this analogy is that Wooley has taken it too far. Of course skin bleaching will have no effect on sickle-cell anemia, but there is much evidence that, in fact, dieting may help overweight people to avoid many of the health drawbacks of obesity. In this way, then, the two things are not at all comparable and consequently constitute a false analogy.

Either/Or Fallacy

Sometimes writers or speakers will attempt to win an argument by positing that there are only two approaches to the issue—theirs and their opponent's. Moreover, the opponent's position is usually oversimplified or made to look dangerous, unappealing, or stupid. Of course, in reality, there are almost always more than two ways to approach a problem or issue, so the use of the ***either/or*** fallacy presents an over-simplification of the problem in order to manipulate audiences into aligning with the writer/speaker.

In the wake of the terrorist attacks of 9/11, many such fallacies were bandied about, from both sides of the aisle. For example, in an address to congress on September 20, 2001, President George W. Bush warned both other countries and those in our own country who were urging a more cautious approach that, "Either you are with us, or you are with the terrorists."

Bush was not alone in trying to manipulate audiences in this way. Hillary Clinton made similar claims on September 13, 2001, when she warned, "Every nation has to either be with us, or against us."

These examples provide excellent illustration of the dangers of either/or fallacies. In the emotionally-charged aftermath of the terrorist attacks, and aided by rhetoric like that above, people of dissenting opinions—who didn't believe we should charge immediately into Afghanistan, or who in any way attempted to understand why the terrorists had done what they had done—were villainized and abused. After all, if they weren't "with us," they must have been "against us," right? This is the danger of reducing the complexity of an argument to only two narrow options.

Faulty Causality

As a writer of arguments, you will inevitably make causal claims. Looking for the reasons that something happened, and examining the effects of actions and incidences is one very important kind of argument. However, such claims need to be backed up with both common sense and solid evidence. Simply because one thing follows another does not mean that the one *caused* the other. Children are prime users of this particular fallacy. Jealous that my niece was getting to talk to me on the phone the other day, for example, my nephew jumped up from his seat to grab the phone from her and in the process, spilled his juice. "Look what you made me do!" he screamed.

My nephew had fallen prey to the fallacy of **faulty causality**—incorrectly identifying the cause of a problem or issue. We see faulty causality practiced by adults who should know better, too. Take, for example, the following from a report issued by a White House Task Force under President Ronald Reagan. The task force was charged with examining the state of "family values" in the United States, and sparked one of the decade's most virulent and partisan arguments. Republicans argued that the liberal media combined with too-easily accessible welfare programs were leading to a breakdown in traditional family values (The television show *Murphy Brown* became the famous representative of this breakdown for conservative media), while Democrats argued that the report was nothing but "an embarrassment" of conservative Christian "tantrum" throwing. Faulty arguments were made on both sides, but the one below, from the official White House report, is a striking example of faulty causality:

> There is increasing evidence that the easy availability of welfare has greatly increased the incidence of child poverty. For example, the highest increases in the rate of child poverty in recent years have occurred in those states which pay the highest welfare benefit.

The only evidence cited by the report was the correlation between the poverty rates in some states with the percentage of welfare monies spent in those states. The problem with such reasoning, as many of the opponents of the report pointed out, is the assumption that the availability of welfare *caused* the increase in child poverty (the implied argument being that because parents could access welfare, they then chose to have more children). However, the report failed to establish that the one actually *caused* the other, and in fact, ignored several reputable studies showing absolutely no correlation between the availability of welfare and the choice to have more children. The report ignored many other, more probably causes of the rising rates of child poverty: inflation, job loss, the mass-movement of manufacturing to overseas plants that took place during the Reagan era. All of these are more likely causes of child poverty than the availability of welfare, and all of these would also lead to greater need for welfare monies, thus accounting for the correlative rise in the percentage of welfare dollars sent to the most impoverished states.

This example illustrates the danger in mixing up *correlation* with *cause*. Just because two things are happening at the same time does not mean that one is causing the other. There could be a third phenomenon happening that is causing both, or there could, in fact, be no connection at all, the correlation being merely coincidental.

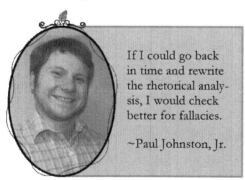

If I could go back in time and rewrite the rhetorical analysis, I would check better for fallacies.

~Paul Johnston, Jr.

■   ■   ■   ■

As we have seen, there are a number of ways for writers to fall victim to faulty reasoning.

Being a critical reader means watching for such sloppy thinking and purposeful slights-of-hand. And an important part of the rhetorical analysis paper is calling out authors who attempt to use these fallacies in their arguments.

Recognizing Figures of Speech

Remember that a rhetorical analysis examines not only *what* authors say, but equally importantly, *how* they say it. You have already learned to examine the claims made and the validity of the evidence used to support those claims, spotting faulty evidence along the way. Now it is time to turn your attention to the author's use of language itself.

The term **figures of speech** refers to the use of language in surprising ways. There are two distinct kinds of figures of speech: tropes and scheme. Tropes play with the meaning of language; schemes play with the sounds of language. We'll look at only the most common of each of these (though there are dozens of different types, and if you are interested in this kind of study, we encourage you to research them more extensively).

Rhetorical Tropes

Otherwise known as *figurative language,* rhetorical tropes, in the words of Terrence Hawkes, are defined as "language which doesn't mean what it says." Figurative language tropes, then, say one thing, but actually mean another. Some common tropes are defined below.

Metaphor

A metaphor is the comparison between two seemingly unlike things that yet share an important characteristic. Metaphor is often used to help readers understand new concepts or to make ideas more colorful and attention-grabbing.

I love this metaphor from comedian and song-writer Bo Burnham:

> Love is a homeless guy searching for treasure in the middle of the rain and finding a bag of gold coins and slowly finding out they're all filled with chocolate and even though he's heart broken, he can't complain because he was hungry in the first place.

In this example (from his song "Love Is"), Burnham compares love to a search for treasure, a search in which the seeker doesn't find what he was initially looking for but discovers, after exploration, that it was actually what he needed but just didn't know he needed. By comparing two unlike things, Burnham helps us see love in a colorful and memorable new light.

You'd think metaphors would be easy to spot—after all, when we employ metaphor, we are saying something with a meaning different from the literal. They should stand out, right? But as George Lakoff and Mark Johnson point out, metaphors are ubiquitous in human language—they are everywhere. We even *think* in terms of metaphor. And sometimes, they are so inherent a part of our thinking and speaking, that we don't even recognize them *as* metaphors. Think of these common phrases, so often used that it's hard to separate the literal from the metaphorical:

- The journey of life.
- The light of understanding.
- The fruits of knowledge.
- The heart of the matter.

And on and on. We use metaphor almost unconsciously to express difficult ideas and to give life to abstract concepts. And so metaphors are often hidden from our conscious awareness. In digging them out for a rhetorical analysis, however, you will become more attuned to the metaphors we use in everyday life. Just don't expect this process to be easy!

Simile

Like metaphors, similes allow writers to decorate their texts, to evoke images in the minds of their readers, and to simplify difficult concepts by likening them to more readily-comprehended concepts. However, unlike metaphors, which declare that one thing *is* another, similes compare two unlike things using the words "like" or "as," as in the following example from Stephen Crane's *Red Badge of Courage*:

> In the eastern sky there was a yellow patch like a rug laid for the feet of the coming sun.

Because you can look for the key words "like" and "as," finding similes is sometimes easier than finding metaphors. But you'll soon discover that they, too, are an everyday part of our common speech and thought.

Personification

Another kind of language that "doesn't mean what it says," personification is the assigning of human attributes to inanimate objects. The following is an example from Toni Morrison's *Tar Baby:*

> Only the champion daisy trees were serene. After all, they were part of a rain forest already two thousand years old and scheduled for eternity, so they ignored the men and continued to rock the diamondbacks that slept in their arms. It took the river to persuade them that indeed the world was altered.

Words that alert you to the personification in this passage include "serene," "ignored," and "persuade," all adjectives or verbs typically assigned to humans but here applied to the trees and river.

Hyperbole

Finally, hyperbole is the term we give to the purposeful exaggeration of the size or scope of a thing. When you say to your roommate, "I'm so tired I'm going to die!" or "I have a million pages to read before tomorrow," you are employing hyperbole. So, too, was Gabriel Garcia Marquez in the following example:

> At that time Bogota was a remote, lugubrious city where an insomniac rain had been falling since the beginning of the 16th century.

Of course, the rain had not literally been falling for 300+ years; but Marquez's hyperbole highlights the idea that Bogota is a city where rain is frequent. Note that there is also some personification going on here as Marquez describes the rain as "insomniac," an adjective typically applied to humans.

■ ■ ■ ■

Rhetorical Schemes

Like rhetorical tropes, rhetorical schemes act as decoration for a text, creating sound, texture, and, consequently, appeal. However, schemes do so by playing with the *sound*, rather than the meaning, of language. Some common rhetorical schemes are defined below.

Alliteration

Alliteration is the repetition of a letter or sound at the beginning of successive words. Alliteration draws readers' attention to a sentence or group of sentences and creates interest. The following example is from British Prime Minister David Cameron in an article entitled "There Are 5 Million People on Benefits in Britain: How Do We Stop Them Turning into Karen Matthews?" in the UK's *Daily Mail*:

> The details are damning. A fragmented family held together by drink, drugs and deception. An estate where decency fights a losing battle against degradation and despair.

The repetition of the letter "d" at the beginning of words in these sentences draws attention to their importance. "Damning" is already an impactful word, but it is emphasized when combined with the other evocative words that follow: "drink," "drugs, "deception," "degradation," and "despair," all of which are at odds with the single positive "d" in the group, "decency." This contrast, highlighted by the sounds of the word, emphasizes "decency's" inevitable overpowering.

Anaphora

Anaphora is the repetition of an entire word or phrase at the beginning of successive clauses. Like alliteration, anaphora draws our attention to important words and sentences and emphasizes them, makes them memorable. Take the following example from Scott Russell Sanders's essay, "Under the Influence:"

> How far a man could slide was gauged by observing our backroad neighbors--the out-of-work miners who had dragged their families to our corner of Ohio from the desolate hollows of Appalachia, the tightfisted farmers, the surly mechanics, the balked and broken men. . . . **We saw** the bruised children of these fathers clump onto our school bus, **we saw** the abandoned chil-

dren huddle in the pews at church, **we saw** the stunned and battered mothers begging for help at our doors.

The repetition of the words "we saw" at the beginning of successive clauses draws attention to the fact that, though people saw and knew of the abuses happening in their community, they did not act. "We saw" is a passive phrase, and thus makes more terrible the crime and the despair.

Epiphora

Related to anaphora, epiphora is the repetition of a word or phrase at the *end* of successive clauses. The following example comes from an interview on CBS's *The Early Show* with Aaron Broussard, the President of Jefferson Parish, Lousianna. Following the disasters of Hurricane Katrina, a frustrated Broussard told *Early Show* anchor Harry Smith that he was fed up with FEMA's administrative leaders:

> Take whatever idiot they have at the top of whatever agency and give me a better **idiot**. Give me a caring **idiot**. Give me a sensitive **idiot**. Just don't give me the same **idiot**. (cited in Dakss)

Broussard's repetition of the word "idiot" at the close of successive clauses has clear purpose; it aptly demonstrates his frustration and lack of respect for those who were in charge of cleaning up the disaster.

Antithesis

Antithesis is another fun one. It means the placement of sentences or phrases in juxtaposition with those to which they are opposed to create a balanced meaning. Think of Patrick Henry's "Give me liberty or give me death."

The following example is from Pulitzer-prize winning columnist Anna Quindlen about Hillary Clinton:

> Hillary has soldiered on, **damned if she does, damned if she doesn't**, like most powerful women, expected to be **tough as nails and warm as toast** at the same time.

Juxtaposing phrases or sentences of opposite meaning draws attention to the gulf between them. In this case, readers' attention is drawn to the impossible situation Clinton finds herself in, unable to satisfy the opposing expectations of a society resistant to women's power.

■   ■   ■   ■

You've now thoroughly dissected the text you are analyzing:

- You've outlined the claims and evidence and analyzed their validity and effectiveness;
- You've decided who the audience is and analyzed the ways in which the author appeals to that audience through ethos, pathos, and logos;
- You've carefully scouted the text for rhetorical fallacies;
- And you've analyzed the author's use of language and how that might appeal to a reader.

All of these things—claims, evidence, appeals, and language—are important parts of an argument. The central question of a rhetorical analysis, then, is how well did your author use them? In the use of language, of appeals, of claim, and of evidence, did your author successfully and ethically convince their target audience to think, believe, or do something? Analyzing this success is the very heart of rhetorical analysis.

■   ■   ■   ■

In the following student paper, you can see how one student analyzed a text for rhetorical effectiveness. While Mamie focuses her analysis on the three appeals, ethos, pathos, and logos, a rhetorical analysis might alternately focus on any of the tools described above. In a short five to seven page paper, however, you should focus only on the most powerful tools used by the author to convince readers. Trying to list every appeal, trope, and scheme used by the author will make your paper cluttered and chaotic. In her paper, then, Mamie felt that Carter's audience appeals were most powerful and focused both her thesis and her analysis on those.

Student Example of a Rhetorical Analysis

Mamie Hassell

Dr. Morton, Professor

English 110

10 Dec. 2013

Rhetorical Analysis of Stephen L. Carter's
"The Insufficiency of Honesty"

> Mamie begins with narrative. She has a fairly short, but very effective, personal anecdote about her own experience with honesty. With regular spacing, the narrative would take up about 2/3 of a page, no more, which is an appropriate length for a paper of 5 to 7 pages.

When I was a child, my mother always read Laura Ingles Wilder to me. She said, "The real things haven't changed. It is still best to be honest and truthful, to make the most of what we have, to be happy with simple pleasures, and to have courage when things go wrong." Throughout my childhood, I attempted to live by these virtues. As I got older, living by these principles became much harder. Relationships came along that made me believe I was not good enough, so I improved my story a little bit. Eventually, I got caught up living a life that I did not want. Freeing myself from this life was the most redemptive feeling. Honesty is defined as being liberated from all deceit. Throughout our lives, several of us attempt to achieve honesty. The question is, is honesty enough? Many of us forget to abide by our moral codes. In contrast to simple honesty, integrity is living by a firm adherence to a strong moral code. Finding people of integrity is becoming more and more rare, especially with the current mindset of people in the Western hemisphere. They get caught up with life and often forget what they stand for.

In the article, "The Insufficiency of Honesty," Stephen L. Carter confronts those who flee from their responsibilities and use honesty as their excuse. Carter claims that the Western way of thinking is quite corrupt. <u>Using appeals to ethos, pathos, and logos he creates a compelling argument: that being honest is not always adequate, and sometimes people may be honest, despite acting without integrity.</u>

Carter addresses his audience to inform them of these beliefs. It seems the audience would be generally uninformed regarding the idea that honesty does not always equal integrity. Due to the word choice and use of generalizations, it is implied that Carter is addressing an academic audience. Though aiming towards this audience, he does not exclude nonacademic readers, though it may be more challenging for them to grasp all concepts clearly.

The most effective appeal to pathos used by Carter utilizes a narrative. "A man who has been married for fifty years confesses to his wife on his death-

---

Side annotations:

Here, she examines the primary claims of the article (though this section could be longer). The final sentence of this paragraph is Mamie's thesis: she evaluates Carter's argument (claiming that it is "compelling") and names the major tools she will examine.

In this paragraph, she names and discusses Carter's target audience.

Here, she begins her examination of pathos with a good topic sentence.

bed that he was unfaithful thirty-five years earlier. The dishonesty was killing his spirit, he says. Now he has cleared his conscience and is able to die in peace" (320). Carter uses this narrative because everyone can relate to the theme; it pulls on one's heartstrings. Most people would agree that this action, though honest, was not done with integrity. This appeal clearly allows the reader to grasp the concept Carter is arguing. Though the man told the truth, he did not have anything to lose for his mistake since he was dying, so he acted without integrity. He simply desired to clear his own guilty conscience; he did not consider the traumatizing effect it would have on his wife. Carter utilizes this narrative to make the reader almost question his or her own acts. This gives the reader that desired connection that helps the author win an argument.

> In this and succeeding paragraphs, Mamie describes a specific example of the appeal she is examining (in this case, pathos), considers that example's effect on readers, and explores the impact of that example on Carter's overall argument.

In addition to emotional appeals, Carter also used many appeals to ethos to convince the readers of his established reputation and good character. His opening sentence establishes him as an educated person of high reputation. He writes, "A couple of years ago I began a university commencement address by…" (319). By establishing himself as someone of high reputation and intelligence, the audience will be convinced that his credibility is automatically higher, therefore improving his appeal. Carter then continues on to use appeals of good character and integrity by using the "Momma's Boy" technique. He says, "As my mother used to say, you don't have to tell people everything you know"(320). This establishes him as a "good ole' boy" which allows the reader to perceive he has good character and strong family ties. Carter does this to advertise himself to the audience. By creating this feel, readers are convinced of his character.

Carter's final appeals to ethos utilize the same techniques. He says, "As it happens, I believe- both as a Christian and as a secular citizen who struggles toward moral understanding- that we can find true and sound answers to our moral questions"(322). He uses Christianity to signify a strong sense of goodwill, integrity, and character. This appeal may backfire on a nonreligious audience; yet if this happened, the argument would not be completely forsaken.

Using this line, "but I do not pretend to have found very many of them [answers], nor is an exposition of them my purpose here" (322), Carter comes off with a sense of humility. This strongly implies to readers his good character and extreme moral values.

Carter uses these multiple appeals to ethos to convince the reader that he has intelligence, established reputation, goodwill, integrity, and excellent character, yet he still has

> While Mamie gave us only a single example of an appeal to pathos (which is sometimes sufficient), she has now given *four* excellent examples of appeals to ethos. The number of examples given, as well as the depth of analysis and thought shown here, makes this, in my opinion, the strongest part of her paper.

humility. Thus readers are more inclined to accept his premises.

> While appeals to pathos and ethos are important to Carter's argument, appeals to logos are really central. He uses examples to show that his claims can be generalized. This technique is called inductive reasoning. Carter uses another narrative to convince the reader of his claim, that honesty does not equal integrity. He begins, "Having been taught all his life that women are not as smart as men, a manager gives the women on his staff less challenging assignments then he gives men" (321). Carter states that because of the man's ignorance, his company and his employees are evaluated unfairly. Although he honestly believes that men are smarter than women, he betrays true integrity for accepting that stereotype. Carter uses this example to increase his claim's stamina.

A really nice transition sentence begins this paragraph, giving the analysis a sense of unity and coherence.

Another example of inductive reasoning can be detected in the following narrative. "Or the problem differentiating honesty from integrity may be more complex, as when a man who was raised from birth in a society that preaches racism states his belief in one race's inferiority as a fact, without ever really considering that perhaps this deeply held view is wrong. Certainly the racist is being honest- he is telling us what he actually thinks- but his honesty does not add up to integrity" (319-320). He

Many students struggle to understand appeals to logos. Here, Mamie does a nice job describing how inductive reasoning functions as a form of logos.

includes this narrative to give the readers' another example of how the concept, "honesty does not equal integrity," applies to different situations. Using multiple examples of how something applies to his claim, Carter provides the reader with the ability to strongly understand the concept through generalizations.

> Mamie's conclusion gives readers her final assessment of Carter's essay. She judges it "quite compelling," with "strong appeals." She also circles back to her introductory narrative, a nice concluding strategy.

Largely, Carter's article is quite compelling. He strongly appeals to the readers' sense of judgment, logic, and emotion using various rhetorical techniques. He persuades readers that honesty is not always enough, and that they should strive for integrity. As my mother always taught me, "it is best to be honest and truthful," yet after reading "The Insufficiency of Honesty," I believe now that it is not enough to simply be honest and truthful, and that we should strive for integrity to live moral and virtuous lives.

CHAPTER 5: THE ARGUMENT PAPER
Taking the Lead

Now that you have observed and analyzed the steps taken by a professional writer/trekker, it is time to strike off on your own. In making your own argument, you will be leading readers through the complexity of an issue of your choice, helping them to navigate the difficult choices and confusing paths. You will cut down the weeds of false information for them and help them to see the path to a reasonable conclusion.

As did the professional writer whose work you just studied, you too will need to carefully consider, 1) the claims you are making and the order in which you should make them, 2) who your audience is and what kinds of evidence will appeal to them, and 3) what kind of tone and style will not only best suit you as a writer but will also appeal to your audience and appropriately frame your topic.

Unlike the professional writers that you have just studied, however, you will not be drawing on the ethos of outside experts. The kinds of arguments you make in English 110 come largely from your own ideas and experiences, though you may draw on the ideas of those around you as well. With that difference in mind, we encourage you to otherwise follow the examples of the professional guides you have just read as you begin your own journey through the jungles of argument.

Starting with Curiosity

"No one begins any writing project without posing a question," writes Professor Desirae Matherly. Indeed, she claims, every worth-while writing project begins with curiosity. It is this curiosity that drives us to write, to try to find the answers to the problems or issues we have observed.

Thus we might also claim that every piece of writing begins with observation. For example, if your professor has assigned course readings and you are developing your argument topic from those readings, you might observe your own feelings and reactions to the topics of your reading. If your instructor wants you to develop your topic from real life situations, you will want to observe the world around you with greater attentiveness to find what resonates with you, what makes you question.

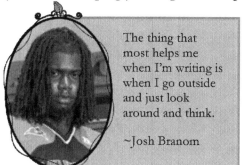

The thing that most helps me when I'm writing is when I go outside and just look around and think.

~Josh Branom

In either case, as Bruce Ballenger writes in *The Curious Reseracher*, "it's the writer's curiosity—not the teacher's—that is at the heart of the college research paper" (7). You will absolutely write a better paper if you begin with something that intrigues you, that you want to know more about.

In my own class, I ask students to begin by taking photographs around campus. *What is happening on campus that catches your eye?* I ask them. Their own curiosity then guides them as they begin observing life on campus with greater attention. What problems do they notice? What amazing things are people doing that deserve attention? What buildings/people/practices/traditions have intriguing or mysterious histories worthy of exploration? From these photographs, they develop paper topics that capture that essence of curiosity.

Similar questions might be posed about whatever the topic of your course. Within the theme your instructor has chosen, ask yourself, "What are common problems that need solved? What are under-celebrated achievements that deserve attention? What are interesting or intriguing events that people ought to know about?" Choosing a guiding question will eventually lead you to your central argument or claim—the answer to your question—but that comes later, after much thought and exploration.

Evolving Subclaims from Questions

Now that you have a guiding question that you would like to answer in your argument paper, you can begin to think about other, smaller questions that arise from that central question. For example, in the sample argument paper at the end of this chapter, the student, Yesenia Flores, began with the guiding question, "Why does Tusculum have such a low graduation rate for Latino students?" In preparation for writing an answer to this question, she brainstormed other questions that she thought might arise as a natural part of exploring this central question. Her list included questions such as,

- Is it true that Latino students are graduating in low numbers? How do we know?
- Are there cultural factors affecting the graduation rate of Latino students?
- Are there language issues affecting the graduation rate?
- Are there other issues I haven't thought of yet that are affecting the graduation rate?
- What can Tusculum do to better help these students?
- What can friends and family do?

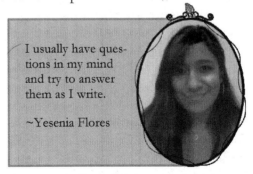

> I usually have questions in my mind and try to answer them as I write.
>
> ~Yesenia Flores

With these questions in mind, Yesenia was ready to begin searching for answers. She began by reflecting on her own experiences. As a first-generation college student from a Latino family, she had a lot of experience with the challenges of attending college. In addition, she talked to others—both students and authority figures at the school—

who were able to offer additional insights. Later in this chapter you will learn more about different methods of generating evidence to answer your guiding questions. For now, I simply want to emphasize the importance of beginning your paper with an open and inquiring mind.

Considering Audience

When forming your guiding questions, you will also want to consider who your audience is and what they will need and want to know about your topic. Are they well-informed? Likely to be interested? Are they specialists or novices to the topic? Are they in your camp or hostile to your stance? The answers to these questions will help you determine what information to include in your paper and how to frame it.

For example, if you have a well-informed audience, you will need to spend less time on background information than if you have an audience new to your topic. Likewise, if you have readers who are likely to be interested in your topic, you can plunge right in with your argument, whereas if you have readers who are reading from a sense of duty rather than interest, you will want to spend some time in the beginning wooing them and winning their interest.

Your language choices, too, will be affected by your intended audience. If you are writing an email to a friend, for example, your language is probably informal and full of slang, and you probably don't pay a great deal of attention to the conventions of style and grammar. Academic audiences, by contrast, generally expect formal language and the use of Standard English grammar conventions. But even within the designation of the "academic audience," there are differences. Different academic disciplines, for example, have different expectations for pronoun usage and the kinds of evidence that are acceptable. And an academic audience composed of professors or other specialists differs from an academic audience composed primarily of students. For that matter, an audience of freshmen probably has different needs than an audience of seniors. So deciding precisely who your intended audience is can help you make a host of stylistic and organizational decisions.

When I ask students who the intended audience for their papers is, they very often look at me dumbfoundedly: "Well, you, of course," they respond. Discussion closed. And yet, while it is true that I am an important part of their audience (whether we like it or not, I will be the one to eventually assign a grade to their writing), I'm not the only potential reader. In fact, in some cases, I want my students to envision a wider audience, or even a more specific audience. Perhaps it's just their classmates, but perhaps they envision something beyond even that. Maybe they want to write a piece for the *Pioneer Frontier*, or a letter to the Dean of Students. These real-world audiences are worth considering as you formulate your topic, though you should discuss with your professor if writing to these kinds of real-life audiences would be acceptable for your particular assignment.

In either case—whether your teacher and classmates form your intended audience, or you are writing to a theoretical real-world audience, it will help you decide on your writing approach if you first picture your potential readers, their interests, experiences, backgrounds. What kinds of questions would *they* have about this topic? What kinds of evidence would be most convincing to them? As an exercise to help them do this, I ask my students to write a little narrative about three potential readers. Making up a background and a personality for these three imaginary readers allows students to give concrete images to their imaginary readers and more realistically imagine what these readers might want to know about their topic.

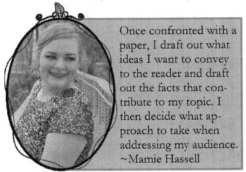

Once confronted with a paper, I draft out what ideas I want to convey to the reader and draft out the facts that contribute to my topic. I then decide what approach to take when addressing my audience.
~Marnie Hassell

I would like to insert a note of caution here: in imagining your readers and trying to make your writing appeal to them, be careful not to subordinate your own interests or ideas to those of imagined readers. While a consideration of your audience is certainly important, those considerations must be combined with your own voice or the writing will fail to appeal to anyone, including yourself. The worst thing you can do is ask, "What would my teacher like to hear?" and then give him or her exactly that. With Frank Cioffi, I assert that the thing writing teachers most want "is to *learn something new*" (24). Startling ideas, new insights, unusual bits of knowledge—these are exciting to those of us who have made learning and teaching our life-long pursuit, and these are exactly the things that will never happen in your writing if you subordinate your own unique point of view to what you think your readers want to hear.

Choosing Your Evidence

Now that you have carefully formulated a series of guiding questions garnered both from your own interests and those of your potential readers, you are ready to begin answering those questions by considering the evidence of your own experiences as well as the experiences and ideas of those around you. This search will lead you to answers, your answers will become claims, and your claims will in turn be supported by the evidence you have gathered.

Found versus Generated Evidence

In chapter two of this book, I detailed several different kinds of evidence that writers use to support their claims including personal experience, expert opinions, statistics, examples, and analogies. All of these kinds of evidence can be gathered in one of two ways: found or generated.

If you are to "find" evidence, we must assume that there is evidence lying around, waiting for discovery. And of course there is—generally in a library or online. To find evidence, you must search for it, and this requires research skills that you will be taught in English 111.

However, there is another way of gathering evidence, evidence that does not yet exist, and *won't* exist until *you* generate it. You will do this kind of research through primary research collection.

Let's look a little more closely at these two very different methods of evidence collection. Let's imagine that you have chosen to write a paper about the Appalachian story-telling tradition. In order to support your claims, you want to include expert opinions. You have two ways to gather such opinions: you can find them in books, articles, and websites. . . or you can go to the Jonesborough Story Telling Festival and talk to the experts yourself.

Similarly, you might search for statistics—or you might generate them. For example, if you want to show that Appalachia's story-telling tradition is valued by the people of Appalachia, you might read a book, looking for the number of people who attend the Storytelling Festival each year. Or you might choose, instead, to do a survey of Tusculum College students and find out how many of them have attended the festival, generating your own statistics in support of your claims.

In English 111, we will give you detailed instructions on how to find secondary evidence (that found in books, articles, and internet sources), how to judge their credibility and worth, and how to use and cite them correctly. In English 110, then, we do not want you to use *found* evidence. But we do want you to use *generated* evidence. Depending on your professor, you may be asked to rely primarily on personal experience as the main method of evidence generation, or you may be encouraged to use a combination of the following types.

Generated Evidence: Personal Experience

At some point in your paper-writing past, you have probably been told to avoid the word "I" in academic writing. Most of my students are surprised when I tell them that not only is using "I" perfectly acceptable in my discipline and many disciplines at the College, but that using the first-person pronoun is actually *required* for this assignment.

So why are students so often discouraged from using personal experience and the first-person "I"? Two reasons: first, it's a very old rule much touted in the middle part of the twentieth century when instructors of writing (a fairly young discipline at that time), sought to gain equal footing with their then-more esteemed colleagues in the sciences by adopting similarly objective-sounding language. And second, there are still several disciplines for whom first-person is not considered appropriate. Some fields in the social sciences like psychology and sociology, and the hard sciences (biology, chemistry, physics) discourage the use of both personal experience and the first-person pronoun when writing for their disciplines. Objective research is expected in these fields, and the researcher is expected to remove, as much as possible, his own preconceptions and prejudices from the research process. In other fields, however, such as literature, creative writing, art, history, communications, and political science, we encourage writers to own and acknowledge their worldviews and the influences that have led them to make arguments. For this reason, we encourage both the use of personal experience and the use of the first-person "I." Because of the different beliefs across the disciplines regarding the use of first person, whenever you are given writing assignments, it would be safest for you to ask professors for their preferences.

Regardless whether personal experiences are encouraged or discouraged, they are rarely sufficient for building an entire argument. You will almost certainly have to support your own experiences with other forms of evidence. The following sections will give you some additional ways to do this.

Generated Evidence: Interviews

Remember those questions that you came up with that helped you begin to formulate the outline of your paper? These questions might also serve (with refinement) to direct your evidence gathering. One of the ways you might do this is by asking those questions of others who have experience or expertise in your subject.

Interviews are best done in person so that you have an opportunity to observe the body language of the person you are talking to and modify your questions accordingly. If, for example, you ask a question and then observe that your interviewee begins to fidget, looks down at her hands, or otherwise looks uncomfortable, you might modify or even withdraw the question. If, however, your interviewee finishes a response but looks as if he would like to say more on the topic, you might encourage him to continue. For this reasons, in-person interviews are the most effective. However, since this is not always possible, there will be times when you need to conduct your interviews over the phone or even online via email. These are both acceptable forms of interviewing, though NOT simply because they are easier than setting up an in-person interview.

Regardless of the medium of the interview, there are some steps you should take in preparation to the make the experience comfortable for your interviewee and efficacious for your own research.

First, make certain to set up the interview in advance and give your subject time to prepare. I know the block system can make timely preparation difficult, but give your participants at least a little bit of time to prepare to speak with you—never "drop in" unannounced.

Second, you must prepare your questions carefully in advance. If possible, it may even a good idea to send your questions in advance, though you may opt instead for the authenticity of spontaneous answers. In either case, however, be careful. This act of preparation also creates what Sunstein and Chiseri-Strater call an "ironic contradiction": "While it's critical to prepare for an interview with a list of planned questions to guide your talk" they explain, "it is equally important to follow your informant's lead" (220). So you must create questions ahead of time and prepare carefully for the interview, but you must also be prepared to alter, elaborate on, create anew, or even abandon questions when you are in the interview so that you get the most important information and allow your informants to share what *they* feel is most important.

Furthermore, in preparing questions, you should keep in mind that there are two different kinds: open and closed. Closed questions ask for information—facts about the informant or about the background of the topic. Yes/no questions also fall into this category and should be especially limited. Closed questions are necessary parts of an interview, but they should not dominate the interview. Instead, the majority of the interview should

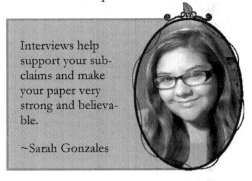

Interviews help support your sub-claims and make your paper very strong and believable.

~Sarah Gonzales

be spent on *open questions*, questions that investigate the ideas, opinions, and experiences of the interviewee. Open questions often take the form of the examples below:

Please tell me about the first time you encountered X.
What other experiences do you have with X?
What do you think is causing X?
Would kinds of solutions do you envision for problem X?
Can you tell me some specific stories where X was a factor?

These sorts of questions allow your interviewees to share their experiences and ideas in whatever depth they choose. But should they hesitate, you should reformat the question, ask it in a different way, or ask a related question. The goal is to elicit substantive, not merely factual information. As Sunstein and Chiseri-Strater explain, in an interview, you should aim to "make your informant your teacher" (240). Allow participants to share their expertise and let their experience guide the interview.

Generated Evidence: Surveys

While interviews give you detailed, substantive evidence to support (or refute) your claims—what we call *qualitative data*—surveys give you evidence that is *quantitative* and *generalizable*. "Quantitative data" is data that can be calculated numerically. As we discussed in the previous chapter, statistics are especially effective appeals to logos, and readers often find this form of evidence particularly convincing. Conducting surveys allows you to generate your own statistics about your immediate community.

Statistics generated in this way are also "generalizable," meaning that the information gathered can be said to apply to a majority of people in that group. While the information gathered from interviews is *specific* and *detailed* (both important qualities in in-depth evidence gathering), it cannot be claimed that the information gathered in that way represents others' views. Information gathered in surveys, by contrast, represents the views of a large number of people and thus can be more easily generalized.

While a well-designed survey can be invaluable in creating and supporting claims about how a group works or thinks, surveying is also the method most fraught with the risk for error. In designing questions for surveys, you must make certain of the following:

1. **Questions must be easy to understand**. Have others read over your questions and make certain there is no possibility for misinterpretation. If it later turns out that respondents have misunderstood the questions, then your results are invalidated. And unlike interviewing, surveying does not offer the opportunity for your to reframe or alter confusing questions during the process of administering the instrument, so you must make certain going in that the questions are absolutely clear.

2. **Questions must not be leading**. A student once gave me a survey to fill out on the adequacy of handicap facilities on campus. The survey opened with the question, "Don't you agree that the handicapped students on this campus deserve

more parking?" She clearly had an answer in mind when she asked this question; her agenda was clear. Well-designed survey questions, however, should be free of bias. Respondents should not be able to guess your personal beliefs about the topic from the questions.

3. **Questions should be limited in number**. According to Lunsford and Ruszkiewicz, in their book *Everything's an Argument*, respondents resent being asked to answer more than about twenty questions, so it is important that you decide exactly what information you are seeking and limit your questions to that number.

4. **Questions should be easy to tabulate**. Do not ask the same kinds of open questions you might ask when interviewing. Surveys should consist almost entirely of closed questions. Yes/no questions are easy to tabulate as are questions that ask respondents to rank their responses on a numeric scale. For example,
    How useful did you find the textbook for this class? Please circle the number that most closely represents your feelings:
    5 (extremely helpful)
    4 (somewhat helpful)
    3 (minimally helpful)
    2 (not helpful)
    1 (useless—I hated it)

In addition to asking the right kinds of questions, you should plan carefully for the correct distribution of your survey. Surveys should be distributed to an adequate number of people to represent the population you are discussing. If you survey too few participants, then your data will not be truly representative. On the block system, surveying large numbers of people is rarely practical. However, you should be aware of the error rates associated with the number of participants a survey includes and do your best to survey the largest number of people possible.

A survey sample of 100 people is subject to an error rate of approximately 10%. In other words, with this sample size, there is a 10% chance that your statistics failed to generalize the true average of the population you are studying. If you cut that sample in half, surveying only 50 people, you raise the error rate to approximately 15%. A sample size of only 20 participants creates an error rate of 22%. That means that your statistics are only 78% reliable! ("Sample Size"). Discuss with your professor what error rate is acceptable before planning your survey.

Generated Evidence: Observations

In the case of both interviews and surveys, researchers run the risk of respondents altering their responses to fit what they think the researcher wants to hear or what they think they ought to say. One way around this pitfall, then, is to conduct *observations* instead. Formal observations, like interviews and surveys, require the researcher to plan in advance. While informal observations of people's behavior may be useful for anecdotal (story) evidence, they do not have the same reliability as formally-structured observations. When setting up a formal observation, the researcher should,

1. **Write down the questions you would like answered by your observations before you begin**. This will help direct your research and keep you on task. For example, if you are interested in how students utilize the library, you might write down questions such as "How many students use the computers in the center of the library?" "How many students use the study area in the back of the library behind the periodical shelves?" "How many students check out books from the library stacks?" etc. You can then observe for a planned period of time, counting the numbers of students who do these particular things. If you simply show up at the library with the vague notion that you want to observe how students use the library, you won't gather the right kind of data to make your case.

2. **Plan where, when, and for how long you will conduct the observation**. For example, if you want to know how great a need there is for increased handicap facilities on campus, you might plan to sit in front of Virginia Hall for a two-hour period and watch how many people with physical disabilities are forced to either struggle with the door or wait for someone to open it for them (since we do not have a motorized door opener). That's the "where" and "how long." But you should also note that not all times of day will be equally fruitful. Observing from 11:00 to 1:00, for example, would allow you to see students exit-

ing the building after morning classes and entering for afternoon classes—a much more relevant time period than 6:00 to 8:00 in the evening.

3. **Write down your observations as they are happening**. Have a notebook or a laptop with you and write down both what you see and how you interpret it right away. Don't rely on your memory to record your results.

4. **Finally, be both unobtrusive and respectful**. Don't make people uncomfortable. This is both unprofessional and ruins your results, since people who feel they are being watched tend to alter their behavior.

Formal observations require careful planning and careful attention, but when done well, the results are both generalizable and authentic.

Generated Evidence: Experiments

The most common way of generating evidence in the sciences is through the use of experiments. In these fields, such research is meticulously controlled and gathered. And while this method is less used in other disciplines, there are still interesting ways to set up an experiment that might enable you to support your claims in other kinds of arguments.

For example, suppose you want to explore how well Tusculum College students follow directions. In this case, you might gather some willing participants and guide them through a series of direction-following exercises, then record how well they did. Or perhaps you are interested in seeing how effective the Moodle tutorials are. You might ask your willing participants to follow one of the tutorials to perform a task in Moodle, then record how well they did.

Such experiments allow you to set up circumstances in which you can specifically test your hypotheses. For this reason, they can be a useful alternative to observations because you know that your research will yield results (in observations, by contrast, you are at the mercy of chance). For this same reason, however, others might argue that you have set up artificial parameters that do not mirror real-life and thus your evidence is of questionable value. Would a person trying to follow directions during an experiment try harder to be precise, for example, knowing that they were being observed? Possibly. And for this reason, Lunsford and Ruszkiewicz caution that "such experiments should be taken with a grain of salt" (503). On the other hand, useful data can be gathered from experiments. You have both the opportunity to observe your participants in a controlled field and question them afterward, combining some of the best of the methods listed above.

■   ■   ■   ■

Your 110 professor will certainly have preferences about which types of generated evidence it is acceptable for you to use in this paper, so before proceeding with any evidence gathering, make sure you have discussed the assignment parameters with him or her.

Organizing the Essay

You began your writing process by exploring possible topics; you then chose a topic you were curious about and about which you wanted to learn more; you made a list of questions that you and your potential readers would want answered about that topic; you gathered information that would allow you answer those questions from primary research methods. It is now time to organize all of this information into a formal argument essay.

There are three primary argument styles that describe the structure of most written arguments. Your personal preferences, along with those of your professor, as well as the subject matter, will determine which style you adopt. Each of the three is explained in brief in the following pages, but because different professors prefer different styles, be prepared for *your* professor to give additional details on the style or styles he or she prefers.

The Classical Style

Developed by Greek and Roman rhetoricians over two thousand years ago, the Classical Style was primarily an oral argument style. As such, it has a very clear, easy-to-follow structure so that listeners could follow the speaker's movements through the separate parts of the argument. We sometimes call this style the Aristotelian Style because it is primarily from Aristotle's writings that we know how the argument was structured.

The Classical (or Aristotelian) Style works especially well on controversial topics or on topics where the speaker/writer is attempting to win readers over to her or his position from other, already defined positions. In my experience, the Classical Style is the one most often taught in high schools and universities, and many of your professors will expect to see elements of this style in your papers, though I encourage you to play with the elements and make them your own. None of the styles I am describing should be slavishly followed: always make room for your own voice and personality in your writing.

The Classical Style is made up of six basic parts:

1. The first is the *Exordium*. Literally *to begin* or *to urge forward*, the exordium was designed to capture listener's attention and introduce them to the topic. In chapter two of this book I detailed several methods for winning the interest of readers in an introductory paragraph, and I encourage you to revisit that chapter for ideas.

2. The second part of the argument is the *Narratio*, or *narrative*. In this part, writers describe the history of the topic, detailing who is involved, what the parameters of the discussion are, and what the present state of the topic is. This section is largely background information. The length of this section will depend on your audience and their current knowledge of the topic.

3. The *Divisio* is the third part of the Classical Style. Here, writers present their position on the topic and *divide* the argument into the separate claims that they will present in the remainder of the speech or writing. This is usually presented in the form of your central claim.

4. The fourth part, which occupies a majority of the argument, is the *Confirmatio*. Literally *the confirmation*, writers here provide evidence for their position. This will occupy the majority of body paragraphs. In the pages that follow, I will further discuss the kinds of claims and evidence appropriate to the *confirmatio*,

though I encourage you to revisit chapter two for a more detailed discussion of different kinds of evidence.

5. The *Refutatio*, the fifth element of the Classical Style, can actually come before the *confirmatio* depending on the preferences of the writer, or might even be mixed in with elements of the *confirmatio*. In the *refutatio*, or *refutation*, writers acknowledges counter arguments and then refute them, showing why their position is superior to that of opponents.

6. The argument thus completed, the final part is the *Peroratio*, or *end* (per) *of speech* (oratio). Here, speakers or writers summarize the main points made and call on audiences to act. The summary of main points is particularly important in oral discourse because speakers need to remind listeners of what has gone before and help them to keep the shape of the argument in their minds. However, please note that for a *written* paper of fewer than ten or so pages, a summary conclusion is generally discouraged. Even when using the classical style, then, I encourage you to adapt one of the alternate concluding methods detailed in chapter two of this book.

■   ■   ■   ■

The Toulmin Style

In his 1958 book *The Uses of Argument*, Stephen Toulmin outlines a method for argument that has hugely impacted modern composition and rhetoric practices. In fact, many of the terms that I have used in this book, including *claims* and *subclaims* are borrowed from the style developed by Toulmin.

The Toulmin Style shares a lot of features of the Classical Style. Similar to the Classical Style, for example, the Toulmin Style requires writers to make clear claims and back them with evidence (though the Toulmin Style encourages appeals to logos above other kinds of appeals).

Perhaps what makes the Toulmin Style most persuasive, however, is its emphasis on the delineation of *warrants*, or the assumptions that lie behind the claims we make and the evidence we accept. A Toulmin argument, then, is made up of three important parts: the claims, the data, and the warrants.

1. Claims: As we've earlier discussed, a claim is an assertion that is both debatable and in need of evidence to support it. For information about how to make and structure claims, please see chapter two.

2. Data: In Toulmin terms, data is the evidence we use to support our claims. In chapter two, we discussed several kinds of evidence: personal experience, expert opinions, statistics, examples, and analogies. And in chapter four, we explained how writers might structure that evidence in order to appeal to either ethos, pathos, or logos. While all kinds of evidence are appropriate in the construction of a Toulmin argument, those kinds of evidence that appeal to logos are especially emphasized.

3. Finally, a Toulmin argument makes explicit the *warrants* or assumptions that underlie the claims we make and the evidence we accept. Warrants are statements of the big, universal beliefs we hold about the world and about right and wrong. We might say that warrants are the declarations of our worldviews, the written statements of our assumptions about how the world works.

Sometimes, these assumptions lie in our minds uninterrogated, dwelling in our subconscious but not brought to the surface, not articulated. But even if we haven't thought about them or put them in words, these worldviews underlie all of the claims that we make. They also lie behind the kinds of evidence we accept as truthful or convincing. Because people often do not acknowledge their subconscious assumptions, they may get frustrated with others who do not agree with them, unable to see *why* what is so clear to them is not clear to others. In most such cases, this is because the two parties are operating under different worldviews. Let's look at an example to help clarify what we mean by both worldviews and warrants.

Example:

Jenny has just moved into an apartment with three other girls. The apartment, however, has only three parking spaces, so one of the roommates is going to have to park on the street. Since parking on the street is sometimes scarce, this means that the unlucky roommate may have to walk quite a distance from car to apartment.

Jenny works at a convenience store and her shift begins at 5 am. She feels that, for this reason, she should get one of the parking spaces, especially as one of the roommates, Delinda, is a student and doesn't have to be to class until 12:30 pm. Delinda contends that the parking space is *hers*. She, after all, has been living in the apartment and paying rent longer than any of the other girls.

So who is right? Should Jenny have the parking space or should Delinda? If you believe that Jenny should get the parking space, then you probably share a worldview with Jenny:

Jenny's Claim:	Jenny should get the parking spot
	because
Jenny's Evidence:	she has to be to work earlier and it is harder for her to walk far in the cold, early morning.
Worldview underlying this claim:	When awarding limited goods or privileges, special consideration should be given to those who bear the greatest hardships.

If you chose Delinda, however, you are probably operating under a worldview that looks something like this:

Delinda's Claim:	Delinda should get the parking spot
	because
Delinda's Evidence:	she has lived in the apartment the longest.
Worldview underlying this claim:	First-come should be first-served. Time is the measurement of worthiness under this worldview.

The Toulmin method requires writers to make explicit these worldviews so that readers can judge the case with greater clarity. Moreover, when people involved in a debate are honest about the assumptions that underlie their claims and the claims of their opponents, it allows them to more easily see where their opponents are coming from and reach equitable solutions. In this case, perhaps Jenny would agree to reimburse Delinda for the use of the parking space, thus acknowledging the years of rent money that Delinda has put into the apartment, while Delinda can put up with a little bit of hardship in acknowledgment of Jenny's greater difficulty.

Think about the kinds of worldviews that underlie the following claims:

- Marriage equality should be granted by the federal government to same-sex couples since the current Defense of Marriage Act is simply unfair.
- Tusculum should allow students to live off campus since other schools allow their students to do so.
- All children should be encouraged to play a sport since sports teach socialization and sportsmanship skills.

If you agree with any of these statements, it is because your worldview corresponds to the assumption underlying that argument. Defining and laying out that assumption is an important—and ethically honest—move, and one strongly encouraged in the Toulmin Style.

Finally, the Toulmin method also encourages writers to consider and address counterarguments, just as the Classical method does. Again, however, writers are expected to consider the worldviews underlying their opponents' claims and to state these as a warrant. Writers may then refute those warrants and their subsequent claims.

● ● ● ●

The Rogerian Style

At a conference I recently attended about the teaching of college-level composition, one speaker claimed that we have been teaching argument as the primary mode of writing for decades, and, he claimed, "we have apparently taught it too well." All of the political bickering and backstabbing, and the unwillingness, even inability, of our country's leaders to see the validity in their opponents' ideas is the result of argument run amok. No one is really *listening* to anyone else, he claimed; instead, everyone is making impressively laid-out and well-supported arguments (as we, their composition teachers have taught them to do) that advance their party's agendas without any hint of compromise. Maybe, he said, the days of teaching argument should be over (Pagnucci).

It was a similar frustration that led a group of writing teachers in the 1970s to look to the work of psychologist Carl Rogers, whose theories about group therapy had had profound success in bridging gaps between patients. Might we also, these teachers wondered, use Rogers's ideas to bridge the gaps between parties in an argument? In their book *Rhetoric: Discovery and Change*, Richard Young, Alton Becker, and Kenneth Pike lay out a methodology that seeks to apply Rogers's nondirective therapy to the writing of argument. Rogerian argument, as they termed it, should thus have four parts:

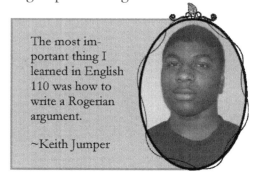

> The most important thing I learned in English 110 was how to write a Rogerian argument.
>
> ~Keith Jumper

1. *The Introduction.* Here, the writer lays out the problem in great enough detail to demonstrate her full understanding of the subtleties of the problem. One key part of the introduction must be a demonstration that the opponent's position is understood.

2. *The Context.* In this part of the text, the writer lays out the contexts in which his opponents' position may be valid. This requires writers to play what Peter Elbow calls "the believing game," to place himself in the position of his opponents and argue for them.

3. *The Position.* Here, the writer lays out her position and describes the circumstances in which her solution would be most valid.

4. *Conclusion.* This is the section in which the writer demonstrates how his opponents could benefit from adopting elements of the writer's position.

Rogerian arguments are difficult. They require us to set aside our feelings of outrage, of urgency, of uncompromising conviction and try to see our opponents' points fairly, without prejudice. Imagine having an argument with someone you love and respect—you would likely try to see their point of view and validate it, even as you respectfully disagree. That's what is called for in a Rogerian-style argument. And I tend to think that a number of the problems in our current political system cited by the speaker at my conference could be dealt with if our leaders replaced some of their vitriolic argument styles with more Rogerian methods.

■ ■ ■ ■

Which of the three argument styles you pursue depends on your personal preferences, your professor's requirements, and the demands of your topic. In all likelihood, you will mix elements of each to form your own argument style. These methods simply give you a place to begin, a way to start organizing and conceptualizing your claims. In the end, the best arguments represent the voice and personality of their authors rather than a rigid adherence to a specific style.

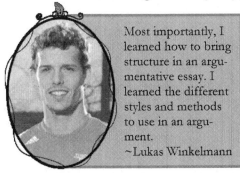

> Most importantly, I learned how to bring structure in an argumentative essay. I learned the different styles and methods to use in an argument.
> ~Lukas Winkelmann

DEVELOPING STYLE & VOICE

At this point, I want to remind you that the third point on the rhetorical triangle—one of the points that determines the success of the writing—is the writer. **You.** You have already considered your topic, carefully choosing your claims and sorting through and selecting convincing evidence. You have also already considered your audience, what kinds of claims and evidence will convince them, and what kind of tone you should adopt to appeal to them. We want to remind you, then, that your voice, your personality and style are also an important part of the success of this project.

I can tell my father's voice when he calls me on the phone. Similarly, I can identify my favorite writers by the tone of their writing. I can *hear* their voices, in the kinds of words they choose, the length of their sentences, the construction of their writing, the formality or informality of their prose, and many other things. When I was a student, my favorite comment I ever received on a paper complimented my personal style. "Your writing fairly sparkles," my professor wrote. What a compliment! So what is your writing personality? Short sentences? Long sentences? Sarcasm? Wit? Seriousness? Playfulness with vocabulary?

This injunction to include your personal voice and style doesn't mean that you should write exactly as you speak. Just as you have various voices that you use in speech—you talk to your boss differently than you talk to your bff—you should adopt an appropriate tone, even while preserving your individual voice in writing. In academic texts, this means you will need to adopt a slightly more formal tone—seldom use slang or curse words, employ some longer, complex sentences, employ a more advanced vocabulary. But learning to mix those requirements with the voice that represents your personality is what takes writing from tepid to great. Unfortunately, we can't give you any shortcuts or easy lessons on developing voice. You'll just need to practice. Read over your prose often and ask yourself, "Does this *sound* like me?"

■ ■ ■ ■

Student Example of an Argument Paper

As you read the following paper, you will notice that it is organized in three distinct, though clearly related, sections: the first, in answer to the question "Is it true that Latino students are graduating in low numbers? How do we know?" establishes that there is indeed a problem; section two explores several reasons why this might be true, answering the question, "What factors are causing this problem?" And section three, in answer to the question, "What can we do?" proposes ways that the school could help more of these students to successfully complete their degrees. From this example, then, you can see the way that inquiry guides the research and organization of a solid argument. You can also see the way that different kinds of evidence—in this case, personal experience, personal observations, and interviews—help support and strengthen claims.

Yesenia Flores

Dr. Sheila Morton

English 110

25 Nov., 2013

Latin Students' Graduation Rates at Tusculum College

> Yesenia begins with a quotation from a famous person, a good introductory strategy.

"Our language is the reflection of ourselves. A language is an exact reflection of the character and growth of its speakers," said Cesar Chavez, American farm worker, labor leader, and civil rights activist. For most people residing in the United States of America that prominent language is English. The next rising language in the States is Spanish. Similar to the rising Spanish language, its speakers, too, are rising in number. Just in the Greene County area, ten years ago, I saw there were very few Hispanics in the area. If you wanted to see Latinos, you had to go to The Catholic Church Of Notre Dame or even recently closed store and restaurant LA Chichiua. However, when I enrolled in Tusculum College, I thought there would be more Hispanics since America's population is becoming more diverse. However, when I found out the number of Latino students, and especially the graduation rate for the Latino population, I was shocked. I decided to interview Mrs. Stokes, Director of the Trio Programs and The Living-Learning Community for Latinos on campus for more information on the graduation rate of Hispanics in Tusculum College. Mrs. Stokes stated, "In spring 2012, the Hispanic graduation rate was zero." With this knowledge, I started to become worried since I am a Hispanic student attending Tusculum, and all the while, Tusculum College's Hispanic graduation rate is nonexistent. To clarify, I am a Tusculum Hispanic student, yet there are no Hispanic graduates from Tusculum. What happens to Tusculum's minority undergraduates that did not graduate from Tusculum College, specifically the Latino population? To put it this way, what is the cause for Tusculum College to have such a low graduation rate for the Hispanic students? Is Tusculum College not culturally appealing to them? Is the environment not right? Is there not enough financial aid? What are the reasons for these Hispanic students who attend Tusculum College yet do not to obtain their degree here? And what can the school do to help them?

From the information I gathered for the low Hispanic graduation rate, three topics always came into the discussion: citizenship, financial aid, and family. First, let us discuss how citizenship can have a strong impact on a Hispanics' education. Citizenship for Hispanics has always been a pressing topic, not just for local states

Here, Yesenia gives some background on her topic to show readers that there really is a problem needing to be solved.

Yesenia's central claim is actually framed as a guiding question or set of questions.

Her first sub-claim is found in the second sentence of this paragraph: citizen status is one potential cause of the problem.

but also for the federal government. Consequently, in the past years the Hispanic news channel Univision that my family and I watch has kept Latinos informed regarding changes that could affect us as well as other Hispanics in America. One of the news items that Univision anchored was how President Obama proposed a solution to Congress in 2009 called "The Dream Act." However, the bill was vetoed by the senate the following year. That has not necessarily stopped Hispanic students without legal documents from attending a higher education, but it has made it more expensive. Some examples are my close friends Jose and Anabel Franco. When we were applying for colleges, Anabel and Jose did not have legal documents from the United States. However, they could still attend college by enrolling as international students. On the other hand, if they decided to do that then they wouldn't be eligible for financial aid, and the cost of schools like Tusculum College in 2013-2014 for tuition, including room and board, adds up to $30,750.

> As evidence to support this subclaim, Yesenia cites things she's seen on television as well as the experiences of others she knows.

That brings me to my next topic, financial aid. Is there enough financial aid going around for the high rising population of Latinos? There are indeed Hispanic scholarships that help pay financial costs like the CANFIT Program Scholarships that I was interested

> After a transition sentence, Yesenia frames her second subclaim as a question, a technique she is fond of.

in applying for. The problem with these particular kinds of scholarships is that the scholarships are targeted to very specific groups of Hispanics students (such as females, or students from specific states). Right now I am attending Tusculum because of my good grades in High school, because of being a minority female, and because my parents having a low-income. However, the money that is given to me by the Hope Scholarship and other scholarships isn't enough. I still had to take out students loans and alone this year I have to pay the state back around 5,800 in U.S dollars. As a Hispanics female I need all the financial aid that is given since I have no experience in the workforce and I have to pay for school myself.

> Personal experience provides the primary evidence for this paragraph.

Another thing to consider is the fact that Hispanic families tend to be large. In my family alone there are eight of us not including my aunts, uncles, grandparents, etc. There are many reasons why Latinos have big families (which includes both nuclear families and even extended families), but it remains true Hispanics are very family oriented. However, the large amount of family members of these Hispanic students could be another reason for their success or failure in college. In my interview with current senior David Nunez he stated," I was the first in my family to attend college." He continued by saying, "In my first years,

> This subclaim, more traditionally formed as a statement, claims that the large size of Hispanic families may be another reason for the low graduation rates.

I felt I wasn't being helped much [by my family]." As stated above most Hispanic families are large, and as a result they tend to spend more money on food, clothing, entertainment, etc. Consequently most of these Hispanic families are at or around the poverty line, so the head of the household would have to work very hard to make up for it. I have experienced this myself. Both my parents had to work long hours, so to save on money, my aunts would take care of my brothers and I. When my brothers were old enough to work, they left home, while I in turn had to look after my younger family members. Since then my extended family has moved, but if today I had to do what I did five years ago I would probably not be attending college.

> Evidence for this claim includes both personal experience and the results of an interview she conducted with a fellow Latino student.

My next possible reason why the Hispanic graduation rate is nonexistent in Tusculum College is perhaps the cultural gender roles among Latinos. Latino men vary depending on what country they reside in, from their height and stature to the color of their skin. However, one thing remains true: wherever you may find a Latino man, he will bring an aura of "machismo." In his YouTube documentary *Machismo: A Cultural Barrier to Learning*, Arizona State University student Nick Newman states, "One result of the machismo is that young males may not want to ask the

> An interesting subclaim begins this paragraph and leaves the reader saying, "tell me more."

questions necessary to be successful in school…. many Mexican-American boys regard education as a feminine pursuit." My own father thought my thirst for knowledge was ridiculous when I was a little girl. He thought it would serve me better in the world if I stayed in the kitchen to learn from my mother the household responsibilities. It wasn't until later on when I was enrolled in school that he realized that, unlike his sons who are big and strong, I had a sort of intelligence that could allow me to become a politician, army general, heck even a president.

The Hispanic women, like the Latino men, also have to overcome obstacles to successfully accomplish a higher education. I have met many brilliant Latin women who could accomplish great things on their own. The problem with these Hispanic women is that they often have a negative mentality. One of my good friends Karen is one of these brilliant Latina women whom I am talking about. She is very creative and resourceful, and I truly believe she could make her own clothes boutique or become a make-up artist. However she kept looking for reassurance first from her own father, and then over time, from her daughter's father. Most Latinas have this mentality that they cannot overcome problems on

> Yesenia's use of a documentary film is technically secondary research and thus not encouraged in English 110. But movies and documentaries are less formal secondary sources, so your instructor may allow their inclusion. You should always ask before using them.

> Again, personal experience and the experience of others that she knows provide the evidence for this claim. Notice that Yesenia never makes claims without providing a variety of supporting evidence. This is what makes her paper so strong.

their own; they must look to the men who are head of the household, the ones who possesses the most "machismo." The breaking of these gender roles and the limitations included is what I truly believe will make a difference in the graduation rate of Hispanics, both male and female, at Tusculum College.

> Another subclaim, arguing that Latin culture's approach to time makes higher education difficult is backed up with personal evidence and even a quote from a Tusculum syllabus.

Even so, the Latino students may not be accustomed to Tusculum's fast-paced "block system" that clashes with their own Latin culture. In Tusculum's webpage it states," Over the course of a year you will take eight different classes, each one for three and one-half weeks (18 class days) at a time." Every Tusculum course's syllabus includes the rule, "three absences will fail you automatically; three tardies are equal to one absence." Now Hispanics tend to be easy-going people who enjoy living for now and believe helping others is a first priority, which makes them infamously known for being on "Latin Time." I myself cannot even count the times I have been on "Latin Time" because of my family that has made me late to an important event. How could I explain "Latin Time" to professors when they themselves know virtually nothing of Latin Culture? For all they know, I could be making this up.

Another quality that has been taught at an early age to these Latinos but that makes college work in the States difficult is the Spanish language. In America, the language that is expected to be spoken is English. English is a difficult language to learn if you weren't taught to speak it at an early age. Personally it took me around 5 or 6 years to learn the English language and that was because I was more exposed to the language as a child by going to daycares and entering grade school earlier. But for a person that hasn't been exposed to the language as much as I have, for more recent immigrants, for example, that would make it all the more difficult to learn, and for most Hispanic students, that is the case. There are days when even *I* don't understand what a professor's English instructions mean. If English as a second language is a problem for many Hispanic students, are they getting the right amount of help inside and out of the classroom? All of these things, then, are likely contributing to the low graduation rate at Tusculum.

However, one solution that might help the Latino graduation rate is mentoring. David Nunez, a current student at Tusculum, stated, "I had SSS (Student Support Services) guiding me." I also am a member of the SSS group. In SSS they give you a mentor to help you

> Notice the sheer number of claims Yesenia makes about "causes"—this is her sixth! Obviously, a lot of critical thinking went into the design of this paper.

> Yesenia now moves on to her final set of subclaims, these dealing with potential solutions.

Flores 9

out in any way for freshmen or newly transferred students. My mentor is current student Sarah Jackson. Although, I don't see her often since I am a commuter, she is very useful in helping me understand what is expected in certain classes. Not only her, but the SSS staff as well are a big help to me. Karen Cox, David Smith, and Sarah Gardner are very thoughtful and dedicated people who accomplished this wonderful student organization that truly does help students in any way it can from a simple ride to Walmart to a recommendation for a Graduate school. If more Latino students were given such mentoring, I think our numbers would increase.

> Evidence is once again comprised of personal experience and evidence garnered from an interview.

A similar support group for Latinos on campus is the newly formed Latino Club, Latin Link. It is not just open to Hispanic students in Tusculum but to anyone who is interested in learning about Hispanic culture. One of the events they hosted was the Ernie G. comedy show. Not only was the show amusing, but Ernie made many people aware of some Hispanic attributes in our culture. In a sense it made me proud to be Hispanic. Even though I was born an American citizen, there are culture differences that set American Latinos and other non-Hispanic Americans apart, things like "Latin Time." I do try to help those persons who weren't aware of the reasons why Hispanics do certain things to

> Her next subclaim speculates that the new Latin Link club may offer a part of the solution.

understand. Sadly, I cannot inform everyone, but with the newly established Latin Link I am sure more people will be educated on the subject of Hispanics and our culture.

The last solution I will talk about is the Latino Living-Learning Community. In a way, they are striving to provide a sort of guidance to these Hispanic students attending Tusculum. The director of the Latino Living-Learning Community, Mrs. Jeanne Stokes felt this was a way they could ensure the graduation rate of Latinos at Tusculum College. In my interview with Mrs. Stokes, she claimed, "One reason we instituted The Living-Learning Community" was because we were "thinking they would have a group of students of like kind and that they would have classes together, and if they have language issues they could help one another. That was one of our thoughts and just to also provide a support system in addition to their [other] support systems." She also said that, "Mrs. Gietema [Professor Deborah Gietema—from the math department] and I are available to the students whenever they need assistance in addition to the other support system that are here on campus. So we hope by targeting that population that we might be able to support them with all the support they need to be successful and

---

Yesenia saves her most powerful claim about possible solutions for last—a common and intelligent move because it leaves readers with the strongest point uppermost in the minds.

Again, Yesenia's evidence is composed both of personal experience and interview responses. Here, she includes an interview with an authority figure on campus. The variety of interviews (with both students and faculty), strengthens her argument by providing multiple points of view.

likely to stay." I know for sure as a member of this community that they helped make my transition to Tusculum a lot easier. The Living-Learning Community has provided me not only with a support group, but also with students who have gone through classes that I may be struggling with. With my Living-Learning peers, there isn't the cultural or language barrier that would normally get in my way, and I feel this is what will help the most to increase Tusculum's Hispanic graduation rate.

> She ends with a "full circle" concluding strategy (see chapter 2), which works nicely to give readers a sense of tidiness and completion.

Working together in this way, I believe that Tusculum will soon see many more Latino students graduating. As Cesar Chavez said "We cannot seek achievement for ourselves and forget about progress and prosperity for our community... Our ambitions must be broad enough to include the aspirations and needs of others, for their sakes and for our own."

Works Cited

Machismo: A Cultural Barrier to Learning. Dir. Newman, Nick. *YouTube.* 16 Aug. 2011. Web. 8 Dec. 2013.

Nunez, David. Personal Interview. 1 Dec. 2013.

Stokes, Jeanne. Personal Interview. 2 Dec. 2013

II. ENGLISH 111: THE JOURNEY CONTINUES

English 111: Sample Schedule
Residential College

The following is a sample schedule that your instructor may or may not choose to follow. In either case, it will give you an idea of the basic frame for the class.

	Week One: Discovering Your Topic
Possible Activities	Reading essays, stories, or even a novel & responding in writing with your own experiences and ideas
	Talking to people about possible topics and interests
	Prewriting activities such as brainstorming, freewriting, sketching, and mapping
	Doing preliminary research to help you choose and narrow a topic
	Creating and exploring questions to guide your research
	Writing exploratory essays about your chosen topic
This week's activities will likely culminate in your writing and submitting a research proposal.	

	Week Two: Researching Your Topic
Possible Activities	Surfing the web to gain background information on your topic
	Visiting the library to find articles and books
	Interviewing those who know about your topic or conducting surveys, observations, or experiments
	Analyzing sources and selecting the ones that will best help you answer your research questions
	Reading and annotating your sources
This process will probably end with your completion and submission of the annotated bibliography.	

Week Three: Drafting Your Research Paper	
Possible Activities	Choosing specific passages from your sources to summarize, paraphrase, and quote
	Placing those sources into conversation with one another and showing where they differ
	Learning to use all of those sources to support the most important part of the paper—your ideas and discoveries
	Learning to organize all of those voices into a coherent essay that readers can understand and learn from
	Drafting your paper

This process will probably end with your completion and submission of the research paper.

Week Four: Revising Your Paper	
Possible Activities	Peer Review
	Post-draft Outlines
	Read-Alouds
	Instructor Conferences
	Copy-Editing

At the end of this week, you will submit your portfolio to your instructor.

We hope that you will both enjoy and learn from this process, and that you will feel better prepared for the kinds of research assignments you will inevitably encounter in future classes and even out in the workplace.

English 111: Sample Schedule
Gateway Program

The following is a sample schedule that your instructor may follow. Regardless, it will give you an idea of the basic frame for the class.

Week One: Discovering your Topic	
Possible Activities	Reading essays, stories, or even a novel and responding in writing with your own experiences and ideas
	Talking to people about possible topics and interests
	Prewriting activities such as brainstorming, freewriting, sketching, and mapping
This week will likely end with the submission of a central research question and a collection of personal experiences or narratives in support of that question.	

Week Two: Preliminary Research	
Possible Activities	Choosing a topic
	Doing preliminary research in encyclopedias and on the web to gain background information about your topic
	Writing exploratory essays about your topic
	Creating and exploring questions to guide your research
This week will likely end in your drafting a research proposal on your chosen topic.	

Week Three: Finding and Analyzing Sources	
Possible Activities	Visiting the library to find articles and books
	Conducting interviews, surveys, observations, or experiments

	Analyzing sources and selecting the ones that will best help you answer your research questions
By the end of this week, you will likely have written and submitted the annotated bibliography.	
Week Four: Drafting Your Paper	
Possible Activities	Choosing specific passages from your sources to summarize, paraphrase, and quote
	Placing those sources into conversation with one another and showing where they differ
	Learning to use all of those sources to support the most important part of the paper—your ideas
	Learning to organize all of those voices into a coherent essay
This week will likely culminate in submitting the first draft of your research paper.	
Week Five: Revising Your Paper	
Possible Activities	Peer Review
	Post-draft outlines
	Read-alouds
	Instructor Conferences
	Peer Editing
At the end of this week, you will submit your final portfolio	

We hope that you will both enjoy and learn from this process, and that you will feel better prepared for the kinds of research assignments you will inevitably encounter in future classes and even out in the workplace.

CHAPTER 6: THE RESEARCH PROPOSAL
Choosing your Conversation

So you've passed English 110 and are readying yourself to begin a new adventure. In English 111, you will build upon the skills you developed in English 110, but in addition to constructing tight, well-organized arguments, you will also bring these arguments into conversation with those already constructed by other scholars and writers. In other words, you will now add *secondary research* to your argument process.

In 1973, philosopher and composition theorist Kenneth Burke developed a powerful metaphor to describe the academic research process. He likened the beginning of the process to entering a party. When you first enter, he said, you notice that there are lots of people standing around talking, some of them quite heatedly. You join one of these groups and for a while, you listen to what they are saying. When you feel that you are adequately filled in on the topic and what has been said about it, you then begin offering your own ideas. People respond to you. You respond to them, and the conversation continues to expand.

To extend our previous metaphor, you might imagine that finally, after much trekking through the jungle, learning its paths and its secret treasures, you now arrive at a village. The people that live there are eager to share their knowledge with you, but you must listen and observe carefully--after all this is a brand new culture and you don't yet know the customs

and moirés. As soon as you feel confident that you understand them, you begin sharing your own culture, ideas, and experiences in a fruitful exchange. They add to your knowledge, you add to theirs, and both sides are richer for the conversation.

That is what academic research at its best does. It introduces you to the conversations that are ongoing in the academic world, conversations that have been happening between scholars for thousands of years and that become increasingly complex as our knowledge widens and expands. You need to listen in on this conversation for a while before you can pitch in, but once you have caught the tenor of the arguments being made, you can then contribute your own insights and experiences, widening the conversation even further. It's an exciting adventure you are about to embark upon.

Navigating the Research Process

If you were to travel to a foreign land and meet a new group of people of a culture foreign to your own, what would you be most interested in finding out? Would you like to know about their family constructions? Courtship rituals? Marriage rites? Gender roles? Or would you be interested in their arts and architecture? Their ways of constructing and passing on knowledge? Or perhaps you would be interested in their beliefs, religious, political, and ideological. There are so many questions to pursue, so many possible conversations to engage in. The first step in the research process, then, is to find out which of these conversations most interests you at this time. Your professor may help to steer you toward certain kinds of research topics depending on the themes of the class, but the determination of the final topic will be largely up to you.

Determining a good research topic is crucial since you will be working intensely with this topic for the next several weeks. Choosing too hurriedly can lead to disaster: not only in terms of a poor grade, but also in weeks of boredom and frustration. To help my students avoid rushing into a topic, I constructed the graphic in Figure 6.1.

> Choose a topic that interests you, and you care about. If you are passionate about it, it will be easier to convince your reader that it is a worthy cause that deserves attention.
> ~Brenna Salansky

Following this plan will help you to avoid choosing poorly and suffering throughout the research process as a result.

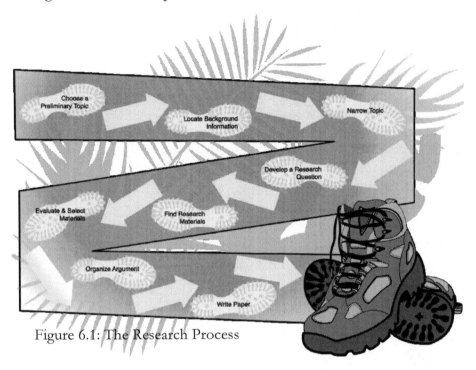

Figure 6.1: The Research Process

Each step in this process is discussed in further detail in this and the following chapters. We'll begin with step one—choosing a preliminary topic.

Finding Your Topic

Choosing a Preliminary Topic

One way to begin finding a suitable research topic is to work from your readings. By this point, your professor has likely assigned you to read and respond to a series of essays or articles, a novel, a few stories, or a set of poems. Whatever your assigned reading materials, it would be helpful for you to keep a running list of topics that are inspired by your readings.

Other professors may ask you to begin, not by reading and responding to other's writing but by examining your own life and experiences. You might be asked to write a series of reflections that explore possible research topics that stem from your own story or from the stories of those around you.

In either case, doing a daily brainstorm of topics will help you to have plenty of choices when the time comes for you to actually begin writing. If you find yourself stuck for ideas, please revisit chapter two of this textbook for ideas on topic generation. Make sure you keep a working list of possible topics as you do, so that when the time comes, you have plenty to choose from and can choose a topic that both interests you and will be researchable.

■ ■ ■ ■

Using Background Research to Narrow Your Topic

After carefully considering your options and choosing a topic that interests you, you must then narrow that topic to something both *researchable* and *grounded*. "Researchable" means that the topic should be broad enough that you can write eight to ten pages about it, but narrow enough that you can treat the topic fully within those page constraints.

"Grounded" means that the topic is one that responds to and is well-founded upon current research and contemporary academic conversations. You want to make sure that your topic is neither too dated nor too obvious. Questions that have long since been answered don't make for very interesting research, so you need to show an awareness of current debates or questions in the field you are interested in.

To achieve these two goals, you will need to do some preliminary research. This means looking up your topic in a few *generalized* and *specialized* encyclopedias. A "generalized encyclopedia" has information on a wide range of topics, and while the entries are not usually incredibly detailed, a generalized encyclopedia offers a great breadth of information on a large number of topics. By contrast, a "specialized encyclopedia" is focused around a single, specific area of study such as "music" or "literature," or even more specifically, around such narrowed areas as "jazz" or "nineteenth-century British literature." Some examples of generalized encyclopedias accessible from Tusculum's library include *Encyclopedia Britannica*, *The Columbia Encyclopedia*, and even *Wikipedia*. Examples of specialized encyclopedias include *The Encyclopedia of Social and Cultural Anthropology, The Encyclopedia of American Folk Art,* and *The Encyclopedia of the History of American Management.*

Our library has two databases that will allow you to search a number of both generalized and specialized encyclopedias: Credo Reference and Gale Virtual Reference. Using either of these databases will allow you to look up your topic in dozens of reference works at once.

Let's look at an example. If your English 111 course were structured around the broad theme of "families" or "family dynamics," you would probably have read a number of articles about different kinds of families. You would probably also have done some reflection and writing about your own family. Perhaps along the way, you became interested in the topic of adoption and now feel that you would like to write your paper on this topic However, *adoption* is a pretty broad topic—you could arguably write an entire book (or two or three) about the complexities of adoption. Consequently, you need to narrow your focus. So you go the library webpage and search CREDO Reference, typing "adoption" into the search bar. Your search yields over 1,500 results, all from different encyclopedias, dictionaries, and other reference materials. This is, obviously, too many for you to read, but that isn't the point of this exercise. Instead, you would simply select a few promising-looking entries and skim through them.

One entry that you may choose to focus on in this case is from *The Hutchinson Unabridged Encyclopedia.* If you click on that entry, you will get a screen that looks like that in Figure 6.2. You would then skim the article, looking for key words, subheadings, and related links. Focusing on these will help you develop narrower and more specific topics related to adoption. For example, after skimming the article pictured, you might come up with a list of subtopics that looks something like this:

> Adoption without parental consent
> A child's right to know his/her history and original name
> Adoption of children from poor countries
> Black market adoption
> Adoption via Internet agencies

You now have several much more narrow topics that might interest you and be more appropriate for a paper of eight to ten pages. And that from only a single three-paragraph encyclopedia article! Imagine the list of topics you might create after scanning several more such articles.

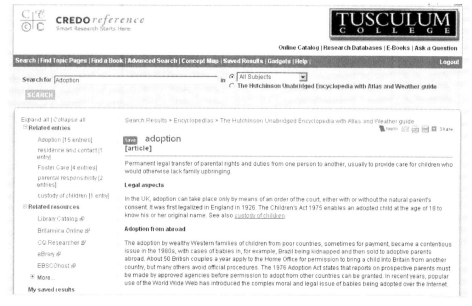

Figure 6.2: Credo Reference

• • • •

Using Wikipedia

You have probably been told by teachers and professors—more than once, I would guess—that Wikipedia cannot be used in any type of academic research paper. And those teachers and professors were right—Wikipedia should never be cited in any kind of finished academic project. The reasons for this have probably also been explained to you, or you have guessed them—Wikipedia is an open-source collaborative project that anyone, regardless of their situation, education, or credibility, can contribute to. For that reason, the potential for misinformation is persistent, making Wikipedia a non-credible research source.

So why am I even talking about it? Well, because I *love* Wikipedia. I think it's brilliant. I wish I had invented it. I want to start a fan club for the person who did. And just because I recognize the potential weaknesses of the global collaborative writing project that is Wikipedia, I also recognize its genius and the situations in which using it *is* appropriate. Such as right now, at this stage in your writing process. When you are gathering background information on a topic and using that background information to narrow your topic, Wikipedia is as useful (sometimes more so because of its ease of use and accessibility) as any other encyclopedia. Moreover, despite the potential for misinformation, several studies have shown Wikipedia to average the same number of factual errors as other major encyclopedias. As Professor Reid Priedhorsky explains, "there is an intense, ongoing review of articles by a community of deeply committed editors," editors who watch avidly for misinformation and correct it within hours, sometimes minutes, of its creation (cited in Crovitz and Smoot 259). So as you skim encyclopedia articles looking for narrow, researchable topics, please feel free (unless your instructor has given you specific instructions to the contrary) to use Wikipedia. Also be aware, however, that this is for the purposes of *background research only*.

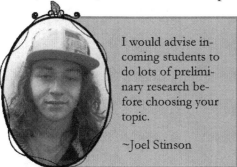

I would advise incoming students to do lots of preliminary research before choosing your topic.

~Joel Stinson

Neither Wikipedia nor (generally) any other encyclopedia constitutes acceptable source material for citation in an academic paper.

Final note: for an example of the way that one group of students in an English 111 class narrowed their broad topic to more researchable topics, please consult the section on "Prewriting: Mapping" in chapter one of this handbook.

Formulating a Research Question

To further help you refine your topic and begin planning your research strategy, you need to frame your research topic as a question. Any good research topic can be explored using different avenues; the research question helps you to choose one of those avenues and direct your research in more meaningful ways. Moreover, formulating a good research question is the key to formulating a good central claim since your central claim will be the *answer* to your research question, an answer arrived at after thoughtful and careful research.

A research question might be one of several types. For example,

Existence Questions

Existence questions ask such things as, "What is happening?" "What has happened in the past?" "What will happen in the future?" "What is the state of the topic?" and "Is there a problem in the current state of the topic that needs addressed?"

For example, if we return to our previous considerations of the topic of "adoption," we might formulate an existence question that looks something like this:

> "With the Internet now a common way for consumers to procure nearly any goods or services they desire, what is the future of adoption? Will children, too, be simply another 'consumer good' to be purchased online?"

Cause or Effect Questions

These are really two different, though related, types of research questions. A Causal Question might ask such things as "What brought this about?" "Why are we doing this?" and "What is the purpose or motive for this?"

Effect Questions, by contrast, focus on the *effects* of an action or phenomenon by asking things such as "What will this lead to?" "How might this be changed?" and "What are the long-term repercussions of this?"

For example, you might ask about adoption,

> "What are the emotional effects on both children and parents involved in the adoption process?"

Or you might ask,

> "Why are more and more children from abroad being adopted by American parents? What are the primary causes of this trend?"

The first is an effect question, the second a causal question. Please note that even if you ask a causal question, you will probably also address, though to a lesser extent, some of the effects, and vice versa. But the bulk of your paper should focus on either one or the other, cause or effect.

Comparison Questions

Comparison questions, obviously, ask you to compare two things, either to show their similarities or to emphasize their differences. These questions address such things as "What other ideas, concepts, texts etc. is this like?" "What are the fundamental differences between two ideas?" and most importantly, "What can we learn from such comparisons?"

For example,

> "What are adoption proceedings in Europe like compared to those in the US and how can understanding these differences help us to strengthen the adoption process so that it is safer and more fulfilling for both parents and children?"

Values Questions

Values questions allow you to explore the merits of a topic based on its value, personally or socially. These questions often take the following forms: "What is good?" "What is bad?" "Is this ethical?" "Will it benefit society?" "Will it help people?" and "Will it help me and/or my readers?"

> I liked the topic that I chose so it made the paper enjoyable. . .make sure you choose a topic that you enjoy or writing the paper will be miserable.
> ~Ashleigh Taylor

For example,

> "Should children of adoptive parents be told their original names and histories as young children? Is it ethical to withhold such information from them, or will the detrimental effects of telling them at too young an age outweigh such ethical considerations?"

■ ■ ■ ■

Choosing the right research question is essential. This question will guide your research and help you formulate your claims. Choosing well from the beginning will make the entire process much, much easier, so give this step some careful thought and consideration.

Drafting the Proposal

Once you have a working research question, you are nearly ready to begin the research process. However, your instructor would first like to check over your progress to this point and make sure that you are headed in a productive direction. For that reason, he or she will ask you to write a *Research Proposal*.

It's important that you understand how to write a research proposal as this kind of document is very commonly asked for in academia. Every time I undertake a piece of research, whether it be for presentation at an academic conference or for potential publication, I first have to submit a research proposal and receive the "go-ahead" from whatever governing body is in charge of that academic venue. For example, when I decided I wanted to write this textbook for Tusculum College composition students, I had to submit a research proposal to my colleagues in the English Department. At the commencement of every chapter, I submit a smaller version of that original proposal, seeking their approval for the text I intend to include in that chapter. As experts, they review my intended research plan, offer suggestions for modification, and finally give me the go-ahead. The research proposal, then, is an acknowledgement by you, as a scholar, that what you are writing is indeed a part of an ongoing academic conversation. In this case, you are holding a portion of that conversation with your professor, and it behooves you to begin that conversation before you commence the in-depth portion of your research.

The form and structure of research proposals varies from discipline to discipline, and even in English 111, different instructors will want you to shape your proposal differently. Your individual instructor will give you specific criteria for the proposal. However, in general, a research proposal will usually require the following:

A Contextualization of your Topic

You will likely be asked to discuss where your interest in this topic stems from and what the current state of the topic is from your preliminary background research. This is the part of the proposal wherein you justify the importance of your research topic.

A Research Plan

In some disciplines, you will spell out the methods of data collection you plan to employ and the methods by which you plan to analyze that data. In other disciplines, such as English and the other humanities fields, you will discuss where you intend to seek information and the timeline you intend for the gathering of your research.

Your Research Question

You will almost certainly be required to include your research question in the proposal, so make sure you have spent adequate time developing a rich and productive research question. Sometimes, you will also be required to venture a preliminary answer to the question (in some disciplines, this is called your hypothesis).

Two Sample Student Research Proposals

The following are examples of research proposals submitted by English 111 students. Because the expectations differ considerably from instructtor to instructor, I've included examples from two separate courses. Despite the differences, however, the essential elements described above can be found in both.

Running Head: AMERICAN GANG CONSPIRACY 1

The American Gang Conspiracy: Influence of Gangs

Throughout the History of America

Jonathan Nash

Tusculum College

> Jonathan's class used APA format. Your English 111 class may use either MLA or APA. We'll talk about these differences in future chapters. Appendices A, B, and C provide formatting directions for both styles.

Author Note

This paper was prepared for Dr. Sheila Morton's English 111

class at Tusculum College

AMERICAN GANG CONSPIRACY   2

Research Paper Proposal:

The American Gang Conspiracy: Influence of Gangs Through-

out the History of America

Why I Am Interested in This Topic

Being born and raised in Brooklyn, New York and living most of my life in metropolitan areas, I have observed that gangs play a noticeable role in the culture of city life. From the countless crimes committed daily, to secret societies that seemingly run the streets, gangs have molded many cities over the past decades into how they currently run. Evolved from the earliest gangs dating back to the 1800's, such as the Chinese Triad's and the Italian Mafia, modern gangs have taken more of a mainstream role in pursuing their interests.

Throughout my life, I have witnessed the effects of a gang driven community first hand. I spent most of my teenage years living in a largely populated city in South Florida, just outside of Miami. The city was home to over 275,000 residents, housing seven high schools with over 6,000 students in each one. Attending North Fort Myers High School, I quickly had to adapt to the struggle that students faced attending schools in a large city. Despite the campus' scenery looking postcard ready, the

> The contextualization of the topic usually occupies the largest part of the proposal. Here, Jonathan describes his interest in this topic for both personal and intellectual reasons. He shows that he's done some preliminary research as well by citing historical gangs.

school faced its downfall internally. With many students being active participants in major gangs, all students and faculty, especially freshmen, were forced to walk the halls with caution. The presence of gang activity hindered the learning opportunity for many students. I can recall one evening in class when everyone heard a dispute coming from outside. As the instructor begin to get up to check on what was occurring, a gun was fired, missing its target and blowing out the glass window in the neighboring classroom. Sadly, this was not an uncommon occurrence.

> Adding to his personal experiences with the topic (which are detailed and extensive—one of the reasons this is a good proposal), Jonathan has looked around at some preliminary sources such as the political cartoon cited here.

Witnessing youth participation in gangs has not only affected schools, but the community outside school as well. I personally know many people who were pressured into joining a gang just for the opportunity to feel safe. This cooperation in gang activity at such a young age is how the culture of the city is set. As depicted in the "Join or Die" political cartoon illustrated by Benjamin Franklin, people living in the city are generally given two options: a life of violence and crime, or a life of fear and paranoia.

The topic of gang affiliation interests me for personal reasons. My parents, living over forty years of their life in New York City, have told me many gloom tales of living in a city dominated by gang related crime. One that is imbedded in my memory is how my uncle, my father's brother, was mugged and beaten to death walking home from work one night. This incident happened roughly one week before I was born.

I have also chosen this topic in reaction to Myers' novel *Monster*. Gang life can directly be related to the decisions the young adults of Steve Harmon's neighborhood made and the various gangs that internally run a prison. It disgusts me to read about groups of people, such as Evans, Cruz, and King, pressuring another into committing a crime, for I know that this truly does occur in the lives of youth in cities. Also, despite the fact that gang influence in the jail Harmon was held in was never stated, individuals who are in gangs can better assimilate to prison life with other members of their gang present to protect them.

Gang presence has affected my family throughout the many places we have lived. Gangs have shaped the community of large cities into their control by offering their own fellowship, and instilling fear in those who do not accept. I am interested in further learning of the foundations of gangs, their

> Jonathan also relates his topic choice to the class readings—another way to contextualize his topic.

influences in public life, and how they continue their underground culture that is seemingly indestructible.

My Proposed Research Topic and Research Question

The topic of gang influence on the culture of city life can be approached from various angles. One can begin by researching the history of the formation of gangs throughout the world, following that up with major migrations and movements of gangs in and to America's cities. One can also research the effect of gang related activity of different time periods of American history and how it has evolved to modern standards.

My planned research question is "How does the influence of gangs positively and negatively affect the culture of life in major cities?" Without research, I believe that throughout history, gangs have been a major influence in city politics, communities, prison life, crime, and youth. I assume that gangs cause more negative effects on society by going against and under the law in order to run their operations.

However, I also want to explore the surprising idea that gangs may sometimes have a positive impact. While it goes against the law to change what they see fit, it can also be

Having contextualized his topic, Jonathan then moves onto his research plan, describing the kinds of information he will be seeking.

He also gives his proposed research question and explores possible answers to the question, answers which will be found through research.

viewed as an act of rebellion from the people. Americans perceive some rebellious acts throughout history as heroic, from overthrowing oppressed governments to labor unions fighting for better working conditions. Despite the negative connotation that gangs have been deemed with, groups of people in cooperation to fight for what they believe in does not have to be viewed as criminal.

    Personal experiences that tie me to this topic are stated in the previous section, detailing the circumstances I have dealt with due to gang activity. Upon further thought, gangs, through history, have played the role of government of the people more closely than politics has offered.

Heather Honeycutt

Dr. Clay Matthews

English 111-30

25 Oct. 2011

Burning the Filter

At one time or another, you have probably considered the annoyances of tobacco, like second-hand smoke and health concerns, but have you ever considered the vital importance of it? I am not talking about cigarettes, snuff, or any of the other products made from tobacco, but rather the tobacco itself. Have you ever considered how the loss of this crop could affect our economy and the people of the community?

My intentions are to produce a research paper about the tobacco farmers of Greene County, Tennessee. Historically, tobacco was the top cash crop for the county and it remains one of the top five cash crops today. Now, due to increased government taxes, imports from other countries, reduction of exports, and lowered public demand due to health concerns revolving around the use of tobacco, the number of tobacco farms and the size of those that remain have decreased. The dominance of the tobacco crop in the county keeps shrinking.

Heather's class used MLA formatting.

Notice that Heather begins with a strong intro strategy

In this paragraph, she begins the contextualization of her topic. Note that she has done some solid preliminary research to ground her topic.

Honeycutt 2

As the price of tobacco has decreased, the income made from growing and selling tobacco has also diminished, which has forced many farmers into seeking a second source of income to survive. Some have completely given up on farming tobacco and have chosen to farm other lucrative crops or have chosen full-time jobs outside of agriculture. The goal of this paper is to show how the many drawbacks and hardships that tobacco farmers face have affected their lives and the lives of their families. I want to discover the history of the farmers I study and compare their lives when they started farming versus their lives as tobacco farmers today.

> Here, Heather includes her primary research question: What are the drawbacks and hardships of tobacco farming today and how does it compare to previous times?

Tobacco farming is a very hands-on work, which requires many able-bodied people. I aspire to learn the process of tobacco farming. I want to know all the steps required to plant, grow, harvest, bale, and sell the crop. I also seek to find the relationships between the workers. Is a special bond needed to work such a labor-intensive job? Are there bonds created while doing this work? I plan to find out what types of workers the farmers have on staff. Are the workers friends, family members, community members, or migrant workers?

> Here she continues with some of the other questions that are driving her research.

The topic of tobacco farming intrigues me simply because it is so unfamiliar to me. I am not so distanced from the subject that I am unsure of where to begin, but I feel that I am very much an outsider to the tobacco farming community. As a child, I was exposed to a small portion of the labor required to prepare tobacco after it is harvested, but because I was uninterested at the time, I never thought to ask questions about the task being performed or its significance. I presently find myself taking an interest in tobacco because, until recently, I have never considered it to be an important part of my local community. I never realized that tobacco significantly affected the economy. As a citizen who is opposed to tobacco usage, I want to see how the crop is helpful to our society.

> She describes her personal experience and her initial reaction, but also shows that she is keeping an open mind, letting the research inform her opinions.

My topic is localized in Greene County; therefore, all field working sites will be somewhat convenient to access. There are also many field working possibilities for personal interviews and observations. I believe that tobacco farmers as a subculture is well-suited to field work due to the fact that they have been overlooked for quite some time. As tobacco farming continually shrinks, so are the voices of those who built those farms. Someone needs to bring their hardships and opinions to the light of the public.

> In these and the following paragraphs, Heather describes her research plan. Her class is focused on "fieldworking" a kind of research that emphasizes primary research gathering (the kind of "generated evidence" described in chapter 5).

I plan to search out various tobacco farms in the Greene County area and request permission to visit these farms and speak with several people involved with their upkeep. I plan to interview the owners of the tobacco farms and ask a number of questions concerning their history with tobacco, the current issues they face, how they feel about the government regulations, as well as other questions. I would also like to examine the family life of the tobacco farmer. Through these interviews, I hope to gain a better understanding of how numerous issues have affected the life of the tobacco farmer. Also, I intend to find a former tobacco farmer who has given up tobacco farming in search of another source of income. I want to find out their reasons for the switch as well as how farming once affected their lives.

> Finally, she describes how she intends to combine her primary research with secondary research, finding books or articles that will help her understand the economics of tobacco farming. This is an excellent example of a research plan.

To understand how tobacco farming influences the city of Greeneville and the community as a whole, I am going to seek a reference that can help me compare past economic health with the current state of economic well-being. Before I can fully understand my subculture, I must gain some general knowledge about it. First, I must find a source to help me understand more about the process and steps of tobacco farming. I plan to find a written source to help me with this task; however, I would also find it helpful to be able to immerse myself in the subculture by completing hands-on work in the field. I anticipate finding other materials that can aid in learn ing what regulations and taxes the government has placed on the growth and sell of tobacco.

Through studying the tobacco farmers of Greene County, I hope to gain a better understanding and appreciation of the things I never before found important. I now realize that this crop is a huge part of our economy. Tobacco products are bought daily throughout the country. Without this crop, our economy would suffer a major upset. Although I know tobacco products are unhealthy, it is beneficial to the American way of life. There lies the irony.

CHAPTER 7: ANNOTATED BIBLIOGRAPHY
Listening to Others

If academic research is like a complex, ongoing conversation, then the first thing you will need to do, once you've decided which conversation to join, is to listen carefully to the other participants, gauge the tenor of the conversation, and understand the debates that are current and ongoing. As you read about your topic from the various perspectives of different scholars, you will find that you agree more with some and less with others. In fact, you might find that you actually *disagree* with some of the conversation's participants, that their world view is too different from your own, or that their claims are unconvincing to you. Not until you have developed this kind of familiarity with the views and stances of the participants in the academic debate are you ready to begin contributing your own ideas. The Annotated Bibliography allows you a place to explore these various views, to organize them and set them in conversation with one another before you begin responding to them in the final research paper.

In essence, an **annotated bibliography** is a compilation of sources, listed according to the conventions of one of the major formatting styles (e.g. APA, MLA, Chicago, CBE, or Turabian), and containing a summary and analysis of each source. Your instructor will decide which formatting style you should use as different disciplines prefer one or the other. The two most common, APA and MLA, are described in Appendices A, B, and C. Since an annotated bibliography is a common assignment in

many upper-division courses, you should always check with your instructor regarding which style is appropriate.

There are several reasons to write an annotated bibliography, and in your scholarship at the college, you will probably be asked to do so for any or all of these reasons. Dr. Mike Bodary, professor of English at Tusculum, describes some of the primary reasons to write an annotated bibliography:

- If you are doing a research project with multiple sources (let's say 15 articles spread through 10 journals), then an annotated bibliography helps you to keep track of what useful articles are where, what the information is about, and how each author/artist might be relevant to your research topic.

- If you regularly do research in one specific area, an annotated bibliography can be accessed multiple times for multiple papers—making life easier for you!

- If you are trying to summarize important works in an area of common research (e.g., a comprehensive overview of black holes in astrophysics) that would be highly useful to academics or graduate students, you might create an annotated bibliography large enough to be sold as a book. (These books are very useful to academics and researchers because they summarize a large body of research quickly, allowing people to better find information relevant to their own research or interests.)

- If you are a student in a class where you have to do a research paper, you might have a really mean professor who makes you do a stupid annotated bibliography. (Bodary 2).

The last most likely describes your current reasoning, though you may find the bibliography useful enough to appreciate reasons one and two as well. At any rate, the first place to begin is by finding credible sources.

Selecting Sources

Selecting credible, reliable, convincing, and interesting sources is the first step to writing a good research paper. Deciding which sources fit the bill, however, depends very much on the type of writing project you are undertaking and the discipline in which you are writing. Some disciplines and some projects demand primary research, while others need only secondary research. Very academic projects require lots of peer-reviewed sources, while others are content with popular sources. In English 111, we will try to introduce you to all of these kinds of sources and help you understand how to choose appropriate sources for a variety of writing situations. In the paragraphs that follow, we list some of the types of information you will want to pay attention to when choosing your sources. For some professors, the annotated bibliography may include a reflection on some or all of these categories. For others, you will use these categories to help you *choose* your sources, but you will not be required to reflect on those choices in the bibliography itself.

Finding enough sources was the hardest part, so use all of your time wisely.

~Taylor Lewis

Primary and Secondary Sources

If you as an author want to have credibility of your own, you need to make certain to include a variety of sources and source types. However, you need to be sure as you do so that you understand which of those sources are more authoritative and carry the most weight. In chapter five, you learned about different kinds of primary evidence and how to conduct your own primary research. Your instructor may ask you to carry out one or more of these kinds of primary research and include them in your bibliography. Primary research gives you an opportunity to really contribute to the academic conversation, to add something that wasn't there before to the ongoing scholarly discussion. But whether or not your instructor wants you to *conduct* primary research, they will likely want you to find print sources of both primary and secondary research conducted by others. Sometimes, determining whether or not a source is a primary or a secondary source is difficult. A primary source can be described as one in which the researcher is not removed by either time or other researchers from the source of study, whereas a secondary source is one in which the researcher and object under study are removed by at least one level. To help make this clearer, I offer Table 7.1, adapted from that created by librarian Susan Thomas of the City University of New York:

	Humanities	Sciences & Social Sciences
Primary Sources	First-hand accounts of events, recorded at the time the events happened (such as diaries, autobiographies, letters, newspaper articles, photographs, speeches, interviews, surveys, observations, and government records)	First-hand reports of primary research by the researchers themselves (such as the reports of clinical trials, scientific experiments, psychological experiments, case studies, surveys, observations, and interviews)
	Creative works (such as novels, plays, poems, sculptures, paintings, and films)	
Secondary Sources	Those in which a second party analyzes or interprets the primary sources (such as biographies, histories, reviews, and journal articles that analyze or interpret creative works or historical events)	Those in which a second party analyzes or interprets the results of primary research (such as books or journal articles that summarize and analyze the findings of clinical studies and scientific or psychological experiments)

Table 7.1: Primary and Secondary Sources

Your professor will likely have a list of minimum requirements for the number of primary and the number of secondary sources they would like to see on your bibliography. Having a good mix of source types on your bibliography will show that you are well rehearsed in the academic conversation as it presently stands.

Publication Source

In addition to analyzing a work's value as a primary or secondary source, you must also consider the venue in which the source was published. There is a kind of hierarchy of credibility in relation to print and digital sources. As a general rule, peer reviewed books and journal articles are more credible than magazine or newspaper articles, which are in turn more credible than online sources. The following is a list of the most common forums for publication and a brief explanation of their place in the hierarchy.

Peer-reviewed books and journal articles

"Peer review" refers to the process a publication undergoes before it appears in print. It means that the book or journal article was reviewed for content, quality, and overall contribution to the field of study by scholars who are actively involved in that field. This is (usually) the most credible kind of source because it has already been evaluated by people who know the subject well. That doesn't mean that you don't still need to evaluate its relative merits as well, only that you can start with an assumption that it is likely on the "credible" side of the street. Most of the books and journal articles that you will find in the library are from peer-reviewed sources.

Magazine and newspaper articles

While magazines and newspapers do have editors who review their writers' work, these editors are not usually scholars or specialists in the field being written about, and thus their reviews are not as critically reliable. For this reason, magazines and newspapers are not considered peer-reviewed sources. Moreover, magazine and newspaper articles do not often *create* knowledge in a scholarly field, they merely report, or summarize, the work of scholars who are doing so. This is the primary difference between a journal and a magazine: journals provide a place for scholars in a field of study to share their ideas, their research, and to debate topics important to that field. Journals, then, are the place where new knowledge is creat-

> Find good sources you know you can work with...If you don't find good sources right away, keep searching!
>
> ~Tiana Erickson

ed. Magazines merely report on those discoveries and debates *post facto*, and this is why they are lower in the hierarchy.

Web sources

This category is particularly complex as there are vastly different kinds of sources on the web and these will require extra attention from you, the researcher, to fully assess their credibility. Just as you would with any source, you should assess web sources by examining the publisher (or sponsoring organization), author, intended audience, date of publication, critical reception, and relevance of the source (all of which criteria are detailed in the following pages). In addition, however, you should also pay attention to URL endings. The following are the most common URLs and what they mean.

- **.gov** These are government sites, belonging either to the federal, state, or occasionally county governments. This URL ending is highly restricted, which means that only federally approved sites can use this domain ending. For that reason, you can usually count on **.gov** sites being fairly credible and the information being reliable.

- **.edu** These are education sites, belonging to officially accredited, post-secondary educational institutions. Again, this URL ending is highly restricted, so only eligible colleges and universities can obtain one. Therefore, websites with this URL are usually pretty credible. One caveat to this, however: some colleges allow students to create websites that utilize the college's **.edu** domain for learning purposes. You don't want to site a student project as an authoritative source, so make sure you know who the author of the page is before you accept the source as credible.

- **.org** This domain ending was originally intended to signify non-profit organizations and was once highly restricted for that purpose. Today, however, nearly anyone can get a website with a .org ending. The majority of **.org** sites are still nonprofits (including many charities, political parties, religious organizations, and various interest groups), and for this reason, many professors will encourage you to use **.org** sites. It is vital, however, that you first research the sponsoring organization and make certain that they are a legitimate nonprofit before you begin citing any information given on the site. It is also particularly important with **.org** sites that you research and understand the agenda of the organization—just because a group is a registered non-profit does not mean that their agenda is an admirable one. Even the white supremacist group, Aryan Nation, has a **.org**, but that doesn't mean that you should consider them a legitimate source.

- **.com** This domain ending signifies that you have opened a "commercial" site, and this, of course, is the most common domain name on the web. However, **.com** sites are no longer restricted to commercial entities, which means that anyone, no matter their age, intelligence, experience, education, or agenda can get a **.com** site. This makes these sites a little bit dangerous because it is sometimes difficult to discover the true author or organization sponsoring the site. A 10-year old with mad computer skills can design a beautiful and convincing web site, but that doesn't mean that the information is reliable or credible. For this reason, some professors will prefer that you not use **.com** sites at all, while others will ask you to restrict your search to only certain kinds of **.com** sites (such as well-known news sources).

- **.net, .biz, .int** These domain endings all had original purposes as well. **.net** sites were intended for businesses associated with networking, such as internet service providers. **.biz** was for general businesses. And **.int** was designed for international organizations. However, in the last few years, all three of these domain endings have become open to the public and you should approach these sites with the same kind of wariness with which you approach .com sites.

Understanding what kind of web site you are using is important, and paying attention to URL endings can help you to do so. But as with any other source, print or digital, you will also need to analyze your web sources using the other methods listed here.

■ ■ ■ ■

Publisher

In addition to publication *source*, you should pay attention to the actual publisher. Books and journals published by academic presses, for example, have been through a rigorous selection process and are consequently usually both reliable and credible. Oxford University Press, Cambridge University Press, University of Chicago Press, Harvard University Press: these are among the top publishers of academic books and articles. In general, if your book or article is published by a university press, you can be assured that it has gone through a rigorous process of selection and review.

University presses are not the only credible publishers, however. There are a number of important independent and commercial presses. In fact, according to the Association of American Publishers, approximately 60% of scholarly works are currently published by commercial publishers. There is no way for me to list all of these presses here. It behooves you, then, to look up non-University presses and make sure that they enjoy a solid reputation and that they publish primarily academic, rather than popular sources.

When looking at non-academic sources (like magazines and journals), make sure that you know the reputation and agenda of the publisher as well. For example, periodicals with deep political biases may not be as credible as news sources with a greater sense of objectivity. You can always look up the reputation of a publisher online, and especially for publishers that you are not familiar with, this is a good idea.

■   ■   ■   ■

Author

Once you have ascertained the credibility of the publication itself, you need to examine the author's own credibility. Begin by asking questions: Who is the author? What is his interest in the topic? What kind of training or experience (professional and educational) has this person had in the field you are researching? Does she teach at a university? If so, which one and for how long? Has he published anything else in the field? Have you seen her name cited by other works? Has he won any awards? Has your professor mentioned this author?

Answers to these questions can often be found in the biographic blurb of the source you are consulting, especially if your source is a book. Journal articles, too, sometimes have biographical information about the author. If your source has no biography attached to it, you should do a web search for your author (though be careful not to mix the author up with others of the same name).

■ ■ ■ ■

Intended Audience

Asking yourself who the intended audience for a publication is will help you to assess the scholarly depth of the source. There's nothing wrong with a book intended for elementary children, for example, but understanding that this is the intended audience will help you to assess whether or not this is an appropriate source for use in a college-level research paper. In general, you want to select sources whose audiences are at least at the level of *your* readers, i.e. college students and higher. The more specialized the intended audience for a piece, the more difficult, but also more authoritative, the source is likely to be.

■ ■ ■ ■

Date of Publication

For some disciplines and some topics, the date a source was published profoundly affects the source's worth. For example, if you are researching the best approaches to treating leukemia, you certainly don't want to draw on sources from the early 20th century. If you are researching literary interpretations of *Othello*, however, the date a source was published is far less important. As a general rule, when researching topics in the sciences and social sciences, you don't want any sources older than a decade. This rule is less important for research in the humanities, although you will still want the majority of your sources to be recent, showing that you are up to date on the current state of the academic conversation in the field.

■ ■ ■ ■

Critical Reception

Understanding how your source was received by other scholars in the field gives you another hint as to the source's value in the disciplinary conversation. If your source is a book, look to see if there are any book reviews. These will let you know how other scholars viewed the worth, accuracy, or reliability of the book.

Google Scholar provides you another way to discover how the book or journal article was received by showing you how many other scholarly works cited that source. To find this information, simply open Google in your web browser and click on the tab at the top labeled "Scholar." In the search box, enter the name of the article or book you are citing. The entry will then look something like that in Figure 7.1:

Figure 7.1: Citation Information from Google Scholar

> **Home in Harlem, New York: Lessons from the Harlem Renaissance Writers**
> SH Bremer - Publications of the Modern Language Association of ..., 1990 - JSTOR
> ... And **Harlem, New York**, their capital city within a city, was the center. Whether or not they happened to be living there at any particular time, the **Harlem Renaissance writers** regarded **Harlem** as their pri- mary, symbolic **home**. ...
> Cited by 14 - Related articles - All 2 versions

This information will tell you how many other scholarly works (at least those contained within Google's extensive databases) have cited the article or book you are analyzing. This information then gives you an idea of how well-respected that source is in the scholarly community. The more citations a work has, generally the more respected, and thus credible, it is.

■ ■ ■ ■

Relevance

Finally, you need to analyze the source's worth to you, the researcher. Does the source offer new information, a different viewpoint, or a unique perspective? How does it interact with other sources in your bibliography? How do the author's ideas compare to your own ideas? How useful will this source be to your research? Don't make up your mind about a topic before you have finished your research. Instead, make sure that you are finding sources from multiple perspectives and that you carefully consider all of these before deciding on your own argument. A source that merely parrots what other sources have said is not particularly helpful (this is why purely informational sources such as encyclopedias are generally used for background information and not as sources for the building of an argument). Finding sources with different points of view will allow you to see the topic in all of its complexity and make some intelligent decisions about where *you* stand.

■ ■ ■ ■

Some professors will want you to discuss some or all of these criteria for evaluation in your annotated bibliography. Others will only want you to use the criteria to select your sources but will not require you to reflect on those methods in the bibliography itself. You should make sure you understand the requirements for your particular course before you begin.

Writing Summaries

Regardless of whether or not your professor wants your annotated bibliography to include reflections on the categories of source credibility listed above, you will always be required to write a summary of each of your sources.

A summary is an overview of the main ideas of an argument in an abbreviated form. In an annotated bibliography, a good summary should usually be anywhere from six to twenty sentences long (a solid paragraph in length). For shorter articles or websites, you might need only six or eight sentences. For longer works, such as books, your summary will necessarily be longer. Regardless of length, however, a good summary should always do the following:

- It should contextualize the argument by showing the larger conversation of which the source is a part
- It should *always* present the primary argument of the source,
- And it should detail main supporting arguments

Many times, students will start their summaries with something like this:

> In his article "Home in Harlem, New York: Lessons from the Harlem Renaissance Writers" Sidney H. Bremer gives several ways that the Harlem Renaissance writers illustrated what an "urban home" can look like.

As an overview of the main argument of the article, this sentence is lacking in several ways. First, while it tells *what* the author does in the article, it fails to explain the central argument made. Secondly, it fails to contextualize the argument in any way for readers. A far better overview of the main argument might look like this:

Context — In his article "Home in Harlem, New York: Lessons from the Harlem Renaissance Writers" Sidney H. Bremer critiques the outdated definition of "home" that American cultural has traditionally valorized: the country cottage with white picket fence and mother and father (both white) fulfilling traditional family gender roles. This is not the "home" that most of us grew up in, and yet this cultural image, Bremer contends, continues to exert its force on our imaginations, making many of us feel alienated from the urban landscapes that really are our "homes." **Central Claim** — *However, he explains, the writers of the Harlem Renaissance offer an alternative image: their writing helped to define a "home" built in an urban landscape that fosters community, loyalty, and a supportive cultural.*

The second example is much better than the first because it introduces the academic conversation that the article is a part of (some parties in the conversation perpetuate a traditional definition of home, and it is with these parties that Bremer is dialoguing). It also states the main argument—not only that Bremer "gives several ways" that Harlem Renaissance writers defined an urban home, but the actual ways that they did so: fostering community, loyalty, and a unique culture.

Having already completed summaries over my sources helped a lot when writing my paper.

~Kylee Nolan

After you have contextualized the argument and stated the primary point, you then need to give an overview of supporting arguments. For example, using the above article as our case, we might finish out the summary thus:

> Bremer explains that Harlem-as-home was created by these writers in their celebration of Harlem's "textures, persons, and arts" (p. 49). It was described by them as being essentially "organic" unlike the mechanized views of city life more traditionally promulgated. These writers depicted Harlem as life-giving, nurturing, and sexually exciting, a place where the senses were heightened and the intellect stimulated. Moreover, Bremer argues, though

the poverty and ghettoization of Harlem's residents cannot be overlooked, they nevertheless formed a community where people interacted in the streets and felt themselves to be an extension of family. The view of Harlem as presented by these Renaissance writers emphasized the vitality, artistry, organicism, and community of Harlem's neighborhoods. And while this vision may often times be idealized and unrealistic, still, Harlem Renaissance literature offers us an alternate dream of "home" to contrast with the country cottage vision. A true *Urban* Home.

After reading this summary, we could probably guess what the major sections of the article are about, even without having read the article. In fact, from this summary alone, we could outline all of the major points of the article:

Central Claim:

Harlem Renaissance writers helped to define the image of an "urban home" different than the traditional country home represented in much of literature.

Subclaims:

- This urban home was defined as textured and artistic
- It was represented as organic, not mechanical
- It was also presented as life-giving and magical
- Its community was quite close, people viewing one another as extended family
- These representations often ignore the poverty and oppression—it's an idealized view of home.
- Nevertheless, it offers us an alternative vision of what "home," an *urban* home, can mean.

To sum up, then, a good summary gives readers 1) A contextualization of the argument, 2) the author's primary point, and 3) a clear, though abbreviated, explanation of supporting points such that the reader has a clear overview of the article's organization.

As you begin writing your own summaries, it will help you to follow these steps:

1. Decide who the author is conversing with. What are the alternate points of view that the author is addressing? This will help you to contextualize the argument.
2. Locate the central claim and put it in your own words.
3. Outline the article, and then put that outline in paragraph form.

And voila! You have a thorough summary.

For some disciplines, and thus for some professors, a thorough summary is all that is required in an annotated bibliography. For others, you will also be required to analyze the source for quality, reliability, and credibility using the criteria discussed previously. You should ask your professor what information he or she requires and pay careful attention to the assignment sheet.

• • • •

The following pages give examples from annotated bibliographies taken from different English 111 classes. Though the requirements differ slightly, each contains a thorough and detailed summary and demonstrates careful attention to both source selection and citation.

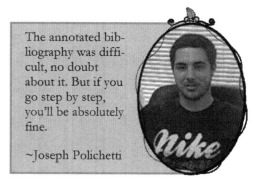

The annotated bibliography was difficult, no doubt about it. But if you go step by step, you'll be absolutely fine.

~Joseph Polichetti

This first example is from one of my own English 111 students, Grace Arthur. Grace was writing her paper in recognition of the many good things done by Doctors Without Borders as well as the many challenges that organization faces. Her course requirements included APA formatting, as well as a thorough analysis of sources using many of the criteria listed above. This particular entry is a bit lengthy, but a good example of a thorough analysis.

> Hopkins, M., Grimwood N. & Holton-Roth D. (Director & Producers). (2012, May 16). *Living in emergency*. [Documentary]. Red Floor Pictures. Retrieved from http://www.youtube.com/watch?v= gcb8tAaGjWw

Entries formatted according to APA guidelines.

> In this documentary video, Hopkins claims to show the world what MSF [Médecins Sans Frontières] does in the field along with the triumphs and struggles that the staff faces every day. It begins by showing many scenes from Liberia and goes on to explain that they are the only medical group allowed in to help. There are more than one million people in the city, and the Mamba Point Hospital that MSF set up is the only free emergency hospital there. The audience is introduced to many different doctors that are working in the area, in the Congo, and in other small villages. While the majority of the staff consists of veterans, many are on their first mission. Each of the workers face challenge ranging from tough decisions to undesirable working conditions. The staff learns to work together as a team, but this does not mean that tensions do not arise. Many of the workers get frustrated at each other and the fact that they cannot save everybody. They soon learn how demanding a job out in the field can be. They all face their fears of a new experience or the trials that come when reentering the field. This documentary remarkably shows both the accomplishments and struggles that come when one is working in the field for MSF - and it is not what most people would like to assume it is.

Grace begins her summary section with the director/author's main claim. She then goes on to detail the other major sections of the film and the claims made in each.

> An English-American filmmaker, Hopkins' *Living in Emergency* documentary is his most famous work. He attended grade school in the United Kingdom and then attended Georgetown University. He worked as an assistant to Scott Rudin in New York and worked on several small

Here, Grace reflects on the experience and credibility of the filmmaker.

> She also examines the critical reception of the film, including other works that citit and its popularity on YouTube.

films there. Following his job there, he started his non-fiction story telling independent production company. With this company he created multiple films that are similar to this documentary. This film has two different versions – English and French – and is cited by websites such as New Cultural Frontiers and American University Washington, DC. I think that Hopkins plays an important role in the field with this film. Because he runs an inde pendent production company that focuses on non-fiction story telling, this film is a perfect fit for his work. He is able to convey raw emotions and stories and help the audience really understand and feel as though they are in his place during this time. On YouTube, the English version of this documentary has over 27,000 views in less than a year. He is reaching people with his work through his independent company.

> In this final section, Grace looks at how this source is in conversation with her other sources and with her own developing point of view.

Hopkins' documentary is one that shows what life is really like when working in the field for MSF and I think that it makes a respectable claim that is very relatable to many of the other sources for this paper. He works to show the world all of the struggles that come from working in the field with Doctors Without Borders alongside the valuable things that they do. In doing this, he is able to show a viewpoint that is different from many of the other authors. The website for Doctors Without Borders shows almost all positive actions done by the organization. It is their main website, so they do want to promote that because they need sponsors and followers. However, Hopkins shows raw footage and interviews that allow you to feel as though you are in the camp with the doctors and staff. These two sources do connect, but it is not in the exact same way. His claim does connect in a similar way to Redfield's peer-review because they both show some of the aspects that

> you do not always see up front from the organization for publicity reasons. The documentary does not differ from my world-view, but it did open my eyes to many new aspects of the organization. I had an idea, but I did not know how tiring, stressful and intense situations could be out in the field. I agree fully with what Hopkins did when filming and releasing this documentary because I think that many other people in the world cannot fully wrap their minds around the situation until they see it either. In my paper, I plan to use this source as a way to show how hard it can be for these workers, but how they still continue to work for MSF because they believe in the goal of the organization.

Of course, not all of your annotations need to be this lengthy, but Grace's is a good example of the kind of thoroughness that some entries may require.

The next two examples are from student Anisha Bell, who took Dr. Clay Matthews's English 111 course. Her class requirements were a little bit different from Grace's. Anisha's bibliography is in MLA format. And while Anisha was expected to *choose* her sources by carefully evaluating credibility, such evaluations were largely a separate assignment, only a short analysis of credibility and relevance was required in the actual bibliography itself. The bulk of the entry, then, is summary with a couple of sentences of analysis. Which style of annotation your professor prefers will be explained to you in your class.

Anisha's research paper was a fieldworking project examining the subculture of cross-dressers in Johnson City. Because she was doing fieldwork, her bibliography includes many more primary research sources (see the second example given below).

MLA Format

Ekins, Richard. *Male Femaling: A Grounded Theory Approach to Cross-dressing and Sex-changing.* New York: Taylor & Francis Routledge, 1997. Web.

Anisha's summary begins with the book's central purpose and then details the way the book is divided into subclaims about the stages of transgendering.

In this book, Richard Ekins takes a closer look into the complex psychology behind individuals who choose to undergo sex changes as well as those who decide to practice cross-dressing. Ekins examines how both the public and private arenas of the lifestyle intermingle with one another via mainstream media and personal motivators. For example, Ekins describes five distinct stages in which a person considering transgendering must push through; the first stage simply plants the idea of transgendering within the mind of a person, while each subsequent stage continues to foster the idea until finally it is enacted upon. An extensive amount of research consisting of numerous informants garnered over the course of seventeen years is utilized to neither condemn nor advocate the validity of an individual's gender practices, but rather record the way in which the informants work to manage their lives while in the process of transgendering. This book is relevant to my overall project because it provides a substantial reasoning as to why people choose to participate in cross-dressing.

Here she begins the brief analysis of her source, commenting that it shows "extensive research," and that its purpose is objective, "to record" rather than judge.

Anisha ends with a brief explanation of how this source will benefit her project.

Though shorter, this is also a good example of an annotation, with its clear, succinct summary and analysis.

Love, Vanity. Personal interview. 5 Nov. 2011.

Saturday night I visited New Beginnings, a gay club in Johnson City. Along with taking extensive field-notes, I also got the chance to interview Vanity Love, one of the drag queens in attendance. She gave me some insight into her life and explained why she chose to start dressing in drag. Ever since the age of six, Vanity Love was attracted to the frills of girlhood. "I always wanted to play with my sisters and their toys, the football my dad gave me stayed at the back of my closet for I don't even know how long". Love revealed that she had been dressing in drag for over ten years and had no urge to ever go back to the way things were before drag. "Vanity is the person I've always wanted to be. No way I'm going back to being that guy with no life." This interview validates the majority of my research. Vanity Love is much like the drag queens I have read about in that she is dissatisfied with her life as a male and therefore, must dress in drag to feel complete. This interview is relevant because it delivers a real-life account and validation of my research.

> Here Anisha again does a good job summarizing the main claims of her source and explaining how that source will be relevant to her own project. Primary research adds depth and interest to a paper.

CHAPTER 8: THE RESEARCH PAPER
Joining the Conversation

You have now trekked through the jungle, navigating the pitfalls of the writing process, of topic selection, and of research. You have chosen your conversation, listened as others have expressed their knowledge and ideas. You've chosen your allies and your opponents, gathered your own thoughts, and are ready to join the debate. All of that preparation will help you as you embark on the final writing project of your career as a composition student—the final research paper. It's here that you will combine the things you have learned about prewriting, reading, analyzing, studying, note-taking, and drafting. Please review the first section of this book to remind yourself of some of the crucial lessons on drafting and revising, and remember all that you learned in English 110 about formulating a convincing argument.

Organizing the Essay

In English 110, we talked about organizing your argument essay around the kinds of questions you and your readers might have about your topic. The same holds true for the 111 research paper. If you conducted any primary research for the annotated bibliography, what kinds of questions did you ask in your interviews or surveys? As you conducted your secondary research, what questions did you have in your own mind as you searched and read? These question will provide the basis for your research-paper subclaims.

As illustration, we offer the following excerpt from a recent English 111 research paper. Grace Arthur, in her paper "Traveling for a Cause: Doctors Working Together to Improve the World," argues that "many people do not fully understand why these non-profit surgical organizations [such as Doctors without Borders, Operation Smile, and Mabuhay Deseret] exist and

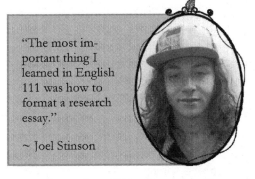

"The most important thing I learned in English 111 was how to format a research essay."

~ Joel Stinson

why others donate to them." However, she writes, "I believe that these organizations are uniting medical personnel and other workers together to positively benefit the world." This belief became Grace's central claim. As she researched her topic, she had many questions in her mind, questions that, when answered, became her subclaims.

For example, Grace's paper answered the following questions in the following order:

- What volunteer medical organizations exist that enable volunteers to help the poor and needy?
- What are these organizations doing to benefit the world?
- What are the dangers and drawbacks of volunteering?
- Considering these dangers, why do the volunteers participate?
- How are they raising awareness among the public?

- What can we, the general public, do to help in these noble goals?

Some of these questions required only a single subclaim paragraph to answer them; some required several. But by beginning with organizing questions, Grace was able to keep information about the same sorts of topics (for example, what the benefits of volunteering might be), together in her paper, and the logical progression of information gave her paper coherence and focus.

Initially, it may even help you to write your guiding questions as subheadings with the claims paragraphs that answer them immediately below. This can help you to stay organized, ensuring that like information is grouped together. You can then delete the questions themselves in the essay's final draft if you choose (Note that headings are used more frequently in APA than in MLA).

Let's look at the way that one of Grace's questions helped her create a subclaim and supporting paragraph. Remember that one of her questions was "What inspires these doctors and other volunteers to donate their time, money, and services, often in difficult and even dangerous situations?" As she researched, she discovered several reasons that they did so, and these answers gave her some of her subclaims. One subclaim paragraph appears below, with the actual subclaim sentence underlined. (An important reminder: we often find subclaim sentences, as in the example that follows, at the beginning of paragraphs. This helps readers to follow arguments easily and clearly. However, this placement is not always necessary. You can achieve interest and complexity by varying your paragraph structures, including the placement of subclaims).

> <u>Knowing that they are benefitting others and showing compassion while doing it are just two of the emotional rewards that come from doing this work</u>. Dr. Davinder Gill (2012), a surgeon who was twenty-six on his first Doctors Without Borders mission, stated, "I have a desire to do medicine for people who really need it. And that takes you to settings like this," (cited in Hopkins, 2012). One of the points that he is making is that MSF brought together his occupation and his passion to help others. While the job was strenuous at times, he was able to look at the grand perspective and see how he really was impacting and benefitting the world. Coinciding with this is the excitement that Morton (2013) shared during her interview about working in the

Philippines. Morton expressed the awesome feeling that came over her and the gratification that came from doing something to help these people that really depended on their organization. This feeling is not something that we experience every day, and it brings forth the revelation that you really are impacting lives when you are in the field working, she said (personal interview, April 28, 2013). I agree that many people never know how intense and great the feeling will be until they actually do something of this magnitude. By having these positive attitudes, they are benefitting their patients and everyone that witnesses how they represent the organization.

You can see the way that Grace's question drove her research and that, in answering the question, she was able to formulate a strong subclaim paragraph.

Paraphrasing, Summarizing, Quoting

Once you've answered your guiding questions with subclaims, you need to support those subclaims with evidence. This evidence may come from a variety of sources—evidence from your own life and experiences, evidence from primary research sources such as interviews, surveys, observations, and experiments, and evidence from secondary sources, including books, journal and magazine articles, internet sources, and even other, more esoteric sources such as films, music, works of art or theatre, etc. The kinds of evidence you put forth in support of your claims will depend largely on your topic and the level of formality expected by your professor. In very formal academic writing, you will select primarily peer-reviewed journal articles and books in support of your claims. Less formal writing may benefit, however, from the interest that non-academic sources (such as films, magazines, or web sites) add to your writing.

Once you've selected your sources, you will need to include specifics from those sources to support your claims. In the student example above, notice that Grace supported her claim with two separate sources: one a documentary film and the other a personal interview. In borrowing from these two sources to support her claim, Grace chose to quote from one and paraphrase from the other.

Quoting is the replication of information from a source word for word. All capitalization and punctuation must be preserved and quotation marks placed around the whole.

Paraphrasing is the restatement of a section from your source in your own words and sentence structure. It is as long or longer than the original and represents all the original ideas, but rephrased, using synonyms and alternate constructions. You must be very careful, when paraphrasing, not to reproduce phrases from the original unless you put them in quotation marks.

Summarizing, as we discussed in the last chapter, provides readers a condensed overview of the main points of a piece of writing. It, too, should be in your own words, and you must take care not to replicate phrases from the original without the use of quotation marks. However, a summary is much shorter than the original source. A single paragraph, or sometimes even a single sentence, that explains the main argument(s) of the original piece is sufficient for a summary.

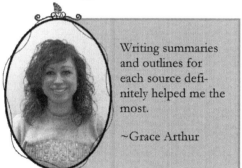

Writing summaries and outlines for each source definitely helped me the most.

~Grace Arthur

All three of these types of source use are important and should be used in your research writing. Summary can be useful when the central claim or primary finding of a piece of writing supports your claims, but when the individual details of that writing are not important to your argument. Paraphrases and quotes are useful when particular sections of the writing—subclaims that the author has made or particular pieces of evidence she or he has employed—are useful to you in the support of your own subclaims.

Quoting may seem to be the easiest method of incorporating source support into your writing, and I often get papers that quote almost exclusively. However, I want to caution you against this reliance on quotations. When you quote, you turn the rhetorical power of your writing over to someone else; you allow someone else's voice to take over for *your* voice. And while this is occasionally helpful, allowing you to borrow ethos, for example, or infuse your writing with the conversation of very adept writers, you don't want to turn too much of your power over to others. For this reason, paraphrases and summaries should outnumber quotes in your writing. In fact, in trying to decide whether you should paraphrase or quote a passage, ask yourself the following questions:

- Is the author of the source you are citing particularly famous so that readers will instantly recognize her or him?

    If yes, then you might think about quoting instead of paraphrasing as quoting very famous people gives your writing borrowed ethos.

- Is the section of writing you are aiming to reproduce so beautifully written that you would like others to see the loveliness of the writing?

    If yes, then you should consider quoting. The felicity of the original author's writing will lend beauty to your own prose.

- Is the section of writing you are looking at so specific that you would lose the meaning of the writing if you were to reproduce it in other words?

    If yes, then you should quote. You don't want to lose the impact of an important piece of information because there are inadequate synonyms to replicate the text's meaning.

In the absence of one of these three reasons, however, you should either paraphrase or summarize so as to maintain rhetorical power over your writing.

■ ■ ■ ■

Framing Your Sources

Regardless of which method of source support you are using—quoting, paraphrasing, or summarizing—you need to frame your sources. Frames accomplish several purposes: they make readers aware of where you began borrowing information and where you stopped, distinguishing your own ideas from those of your sources; they give a context for your source use by introducing the authors and stating their credentials; and they make it easy for readers to transition between your source use and your own ideas and claims.

To see what a good frame looks like, let's return to Grace's paper on medical volunteer organizations. After writing her subclaim, she then uses the following source to support that claim (frames are underlined):

> <u>Dr. Davinder Gill (2012), a surgeon who was twenty-six on his first Doctors Without Borders mission, stated</u>, "I have a desire to do medicine for people who really need it. And that takes you to settings like this," <u>(cited in Hopkins, 2012). One of the points that he is making is that MSF brought together his occupation and his passion to help others.</u>

Notice that Grace has framed this quotation with both an opening frame, and a closing frame. Let's look more closely at the opening, noting some of the features of good framing:

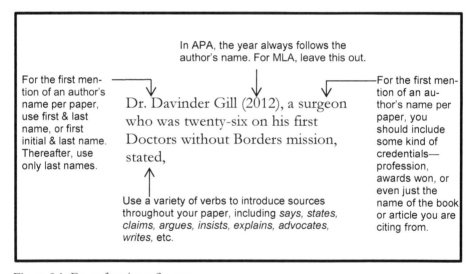

Figure 8.1: Front-framing a Source

The opening frame introduces the author and prepares readers to read the quote, paraphrase, or summary. The end frame then wraps up the source by placing the source in the context of the student's own argument:

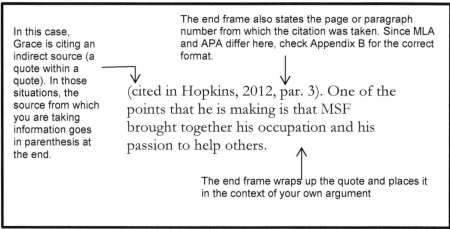

Figure 8.2: End-framing a Source

Of course, there are occasions when you will not frame your sources, but instead include source citations in parentheticals. For example,

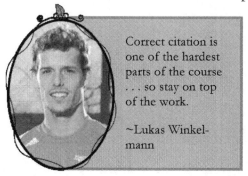

Grace might simply have written, "I have a desire to do medicine for people who really need it. And that takes you to settings like this," (Davinder Gill, cited in Hopkins, 2012, par. 3). However, you should limit the number of unframed sources in your paper, using this technique only occasionally or even not at all. It is important to note that some disciplines (notably psychology) use this kind of source citation more frequently than others. For most classes, however, framing is the recommended method of source inclusion.

Avoiding Plagiarism

The Tusculum College plagiarism statement reads, "Cheating and plagiarism are violations of our College's code of ethics and integrity. Plagiarism is a form of academic dishonesty. It consists of knowingly presenting in writing or in speech the intellectual or creative work of others as if it were one's own." *Knowlingly* claiming someone else's work as your own is clearly dishonest. Whether you've borrowed an essay from the internet or had your sister or roommate write it for you, you are obviously violating the ethical code of the College.

However, this is not the kind of plagiarism I see most often in my own classes. Most students I work with wouldn't cheat on purpose. But it's important for you to understand that you can also *unknowingly* or *unintentionally* plagiarize. In fact, this is the kind of plagiarism I see most often in my own classes.. This kind of plagiarism occurs when students fail to quote, paraphrase, or summarize correctly. The following are some of the most common types of unintentional plagiarism:

I felt that the most important thing I learned was to avoid plagiarism by citing sources correctly.

~Ignacio Collado

- Including ideas or interpretations from a source without proper acknowledgment of that source
- Including language in a paraphrase that is too close to the original source
- Improperly replicating quotations so that there are spelling or grammatical errors where there were originally none
- Even worse, improperly quoting, paraphrasing, or summarizing in such a way that the original source's meaning is altered
- Failing to put quotation marks around material that is directly replicated
- Quoting passages that are too long (copying two pages of an article directly, for example, even *with* quotation marks, is still unacceptable)
- Improperly framing or at least citing your sources so that readers can easily find them (e.g. leaving off page or paragraph numbers, dates where needed, etc.)
- Leaving cited sources off the Works Cited or References page
- Including photographs or other graphics without citing the sources from which they were borrowed.

Whether intentional or unintentional, plagiarism can have serious consequences, from the failure of an assignment or course, to expulsion from the College. For that reason, we encourage you to carefully study the sections above about correct source citation in quoting, paraphrasing, and summarizing, and follow these guidelines meticulously.

RETAINING RHETORICAL AUTHORITY

While it is vital that you support your claims with evidence from your sources, this is not enough to make a compelling argument. You must also argue from your own perspective, ideas, or experiences. You must retain *rhetorical authority* or ownership of the piece of writing. If your paper reads simply like a collection of sources, quote after quote and paraphrase after paraphrase, then your reader is likely to wonder why they are bothering to read *your* text rather than simply reading the sources themselves. To maintain rhetorical authority, then, you must include your own voice. Because this will look different for different disciplines, I will show you several ways to do so.

Including your own perspective is easiest when the topic is one with which you have a lot of familiarity. You can then include your own experiences. Take the following paragraph from a research paper by student Logan Hunter. He is writing about the importance of involved fathers, and he had a lot of personal experience to draw from in support of his claims:

> Involvement with a father who devotes his time and monetary support has a direct correlation on the behavior of the child. Carlson (2006) writes that, "Father Involvement also has a direct effect on delinquent behavior" (p. 148). Basically, Carlson is saying that if the father is *not* involved with the child's development, the child has a higher chance of becoming a delinquent. On the other hand, if a father has been deeply involved in a child's life and the child becomes a delinquent for some reason, the child is more likely to take his [father's] advice and change his act more quickly. When I was only six years old, I decided that it would be a great idea to steal a candy bar from a convenience mart while my father went in to buy gas. . . . I walked up to the counter with

my father and while they were both distracted, I reached out and grabbed a Hershey's bar from the bottom racks of the counter. I quickly stuck it into the front pocket of my sweatshirt. When I got to the car, I decided to put it into my back pack. When my dad looked back to see what I was doing, he asked me where I had gotten the candy bar. At this point, I knew I had been caught. I stared into his wide blue eyes, and I knew I was in deep trouble. I looked down and stared at the floorboard as I told him what I had done. He immediately turned the truck around and we started heading back to the store. He made me walk in with him, and he asked if he could talk to the manager. At this point, I was so scared I was about to cry because I thought I was going to go to jail for stealing a candy bar. I could see the manager walking towards us after just a few seconds. When he got right in front of us he politely asked my father what the problem was. My father looked at me and said, "Tell this man what you have done, Logan," in a stern and uninviting voice. I looked up at the man and explained to him that I had taken a candy bar without asking and started apologizing. . . . My father stopped a problem that could have escalated quickly by showing me how important it was to him that I was honest.

Logan makes all of the appropriate moves to create a good research-paper paragraph: he makes a claim (that a father's involvement in a child's life may help deter bad behavior); he supports that claim with research from a credible source (a quote from an article by Carlson); and finally, he contributes to the conversation, supporting his claim with his own experience and thus retaining rhetorical authority over his own argument.

Some of you will be writing papers about topics developed from field-working. You will be doing a lot of primary research, including observations and interviews, and then you will be combining these sources with your own ideas garnered as you observe the group or culture of your choice. In this case, what *you* contribute to the conversation is the perspective of an outsider. Take the following example from Jessica Marie Smith's paper, "Into the Light." Jessica argues that the Appalachian culture, often stereotyped as "old-fashioned" or "uncivilized," is actually a place of close and caring communities where art and beauty thrive. In one paragraph, she writes,

<u>The Appalachian culture has always been in my backyard; I, however, repeatedly chose to play in the front yard. I never embraced my heritage; thus, I was never exposed to the beautiful traditions and art of the culture.</u> Artist Jim Gray fell captive to the mountain's splendor and beauty and found them "enclosing...[and] comforting" (Amy McRary). The mountains seem to serve as a fence surrounding this community, creating a bond among all the people inside it. As I'm getting older, I am now realizing my place in that community and that I should take pride in my background. This topic intrigued me because I knew from the first moment I stepped into this subculture that I would face certain aspects of my past that I chose long ago to ignore. Afraid of subjecting myself to all the horribly negative criticisms of East Tennessee culture, I decided not to have any ties to that world. Now after researching and submitting myself to the allure of the culture, I am enthralled with the art, the culture, the love of family and traditions. I was fascinated by the sheer number of smiling faces and warm greetings that I encountered during my time there.

Although structured very differently from Logan's paragraph, Jessica also has the important elements of a good argument. She makes a claim (that Appalachia is a place of beautiful tradition and art); she supports it with a source (an interview she conducted with Jim Gray and a quote from feature writer Amy McRary); and she contributed her own observations taken from her interactions and formal observations of this cultural group.

Other topics, however, may be harder for you to contribute your own experiences or observations. If you are writing about historical subjects from a period before you were born, or about topics that, while interesting to you, take place outside the realm of your experience, you will not be able to contribute to the discussion in quite the same way. Moreover, if you are writing in the hard sciences or social sciences, personal experience is a kind of evidence largely discouraged. That does not mean that you are freed

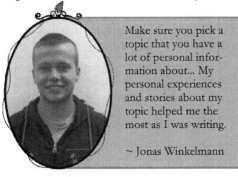

Make sure you pick a topic that you have a lot of personal information about... My personal experiences and stories about my topic helped me the most as I was writing.

~ Jonas Winkelmann

from the responsibility of adding your own voice and ideas to the paper, however, only that you will need to do so in a different way. After the research you have done, you should consider yourself qualified to add your own opinions on the topic and the reasons for those opinions. Alternatively, you might add even more clarification of the topic for your readers. You might add things you have seen in movies or read in fictional stories. You might develop analogies or metaphors to help your readers understand the topic better. The following paragraph, from a paper by English 111 student Ignacio Collado, is a good example of how to contribute your own ideas about a topic even when your personal experience is limited. In his paper, Ignacio argued that understanding our personalities, our individual strengths and weaknesses, could help us better choose careers that would make us happy and successful.

> Creativity is a value that guarantees success in nearly any discipline today. Kirkpatrick and Locke(1991) refer to this quality as one of the traits required to succeed professionally (p.56). I believe that creativity is becoming priceless in a society like ours that's evolving lightning-fast. Most people – including myself– only come up with painters, singers, or modern artists in general when they hear this term. However, creativity also involves originality, and it's extended to almost any field today. It's essential in everyday jobs, like a simple office job where an innovative idea could change the future of a corporation. Our society today craves fresh and groundbreaking ideas that could transform the way we run the world. One of the latest examples of how important creativity can be is the case of Mark Zuckerberg, the founder of the social network Facebook. A single revolutionizing idea became worth billions of dollars and transformed society.

Although Ignacio is not currently in the workplace, and thus has limited *personal* experience to share, he drew ideas from the world around him to contribute to his claim and support his sources. He both shares his opinion that creativity is becoming increasingly important in our fast-paced, technological age, and includes an observation from real life, that Mark Zuckerberg is a good example of the kind of creativity Ignacio is promoting.

Some disciplines demand a more objective-sounding approach. They do not encourage the use of personal experience *or* the use of the first person. This does not mean, however, that a writer in these disciplines has no responsibility to interject his or her own rhetorical authority. Such authorial interjections might include,

- Guiding your readers through an interpretation of the data
- Explaining the significance of your topic
- Comparing or contrasting the findings of your research with those of others
- Including observations you have made in support of your findings
- Describing hypothetical situations that would illustrate your claims
- Developing analogies or metaphors that help to clarify your topic
- Suggesting future research that might be done
- Predicting the future path of the current research

The following examples are taken from the article "Gesture's Role in Speaking, Learning, and Creating Language," by Susan Goldin-Meadow and Martha Wagner Alibali. It appeared in 2013 in *The Annual Review of Psychology*, and offers several good illustrations of the way an author might inject their own ideas and interpretations without using personal narrative experience.

Example One

> Although some argue that gesture plays little role in language comprehension (Krauss et al. 1995, 1996), there is a great deal of evidence that gesture can have an impact on language comprehension. Consider a speaker who says, "The man was wearing a hat," while moving her hand as though grasping the bill of a baseball cap. This gesture could help listeners understand that the man was wearing a hat, and it might even encourage them to infer that the hat was a baseball cap... (260)

In this example, the authors follow all of the conventions we have suggested to you thus far in this book. They make a claim (that some people argue that gestures aren't important in language communication); they back up this claim with a source (from Krauss et al.); and then they interject their own ideas, in this case, refuting this counter-argument and offering a hypothetical situation to illustrate the point they are making.

However, note that they did not use personal experience nor the first person pronoun "I."

Example 2

> To summarize thus far, gesture plays a role in both language production and comprehension. <u>One area that has received very little attention is individual differences</u> (but see Bergmann & Kopp 2010, Hostetter & Alibali 2007)—are there differences in the rate at which people gesture when they speak or in the reliance people put on gesture when they listen to the speech of others? We know little about what accounts for individual differences in gesture, or even how consistent those differences are across tasks and conversational partners. This is an area of research in gesture studies that is ripe for future examination.(262)

In this example, Goldin-Meadow and Alibali back up their claim (that there is an area related to their research that has not been much examined by other researchers) with two source citations and a list of questions that imply a direction for possible future research. This latter is an excellent way to guide readers through your own ideas without injecting language that is too personal for the sciences and social science.

However you do it, remember that your professor wants to hear *your* voice in combination with those of others. We do plenty of research of our own—we don't need you to simply rehash research we have likely already read. What we haven't heard, and are interested in hearing, is what *you* think, what *you* have experienced, and what *you* believe. All well-grounded, of course, in solid research.

Addressing Counter Claims

Of course, you will also find, over the course of your research, that you disagree with conclusions reached by other scholars. Or you may find that, in researching, you have come to disagree with commonly held beliefs that people around you hold. In either case, you need to address counter arguments in your paper to show that you have thoroughly thought through the implications of your argument. Representing counter arguments builds trust with your readers as well—they can feel assured that you have considered all angles before making your claims.

You need to be careful when presenting counter arguments, however, as there are several common pitfalls writers fall into. One of these is failing to make completely clear, from the first sentence of your paragraph, that what is to follow is not your own claim but a claim with which you disagree. The following example illustrates this flaw:

> "There are significant disadvantages to home schooling which outweigh the benefits," writes Matthew Tabor (para. 1). These include both cost and time—things which parents rarely take into consideration. Moreover, children that are homeschooled miss out on crucial interaction with other children and thus lack interpersonal and communication skills. Children who are homeschooled can often be identified by their lack of social skills. However, all of these reasons that Tabor lists are incorrect and reveal his bias. My own experience contradicts many of his concerns...

It seems from the beginning of the paragraph that the student writer agrees with Tabor's assessment of homeschooling. It's not until the end of the paragraph that the reader realizes that the student actually *disagrees* with her source. How much better it would have been if the student had alerted her readers to her own stance right from the beginning. Consider the improved version of this paragraph below:

> Despite the many advantages to homeschooling, there are still some who insist that the disadvantages are greater. Matthew Tabor, staff writer for *Education News*, is one such person. In an article entitled "Parents Must Consider Disadvantages Before Homeschooling," Tabor claims that "there are significant disadvantages to home schooling which outweigh the benefits." He then lists what he sees as these "disadvantages," including cost, time, and lack of social development. However, I believe that Tabor over-states the case. Certainly, there are costs associated with home schooling, including a lack of opportunity for social interaction. However, my own experience contradicts many of his concerns...

The student could then proceed to share her own experiences with home schooling, which will help readers to see why Tabor's concerns may not be entirely valid. This second example, in contrast to the first, alerts readers from the first sentence that a counter-argument is being addressed. Phrases like "some who insist," lets readers know that this is not the writer's own claim, but the claims of some other person or persons. Without such language, readers can become confused about the stance the writer is taking on the issue.

For some topics, particularly topics that are controversial in nature, finding counterarguments is easy. For these types of claims, there are clear opponents offering opposite points of view. For other topics, however, counterarguments are less direct and thus less easy to examine. Let's say, for example, that you are writing a paper on the benefits of recycling. There probably aren't many direct opponents who will say, "recycling is bad; don't do it." You will have a hard time finding these kinds of *adversarial* counterarguments. But if there are no counterarguments to recycling, then why isn't everyone doing it? That question generates quite a long list of possible opponents. People who find it inconvenient, for example, or who don't know where to take their recycling. Or people who don't really recognize or think about the benefits to recycling or the urgency with which it is needed. These *passive* opponents also need to be addressed in your writing. If you can't find direct opponents to your central claim, then, ask yourself the following questions:

- Are there people who don't know about my topic? And if so, why?
- Are there people who don't care about my topic? Why?
- Are there people who have misunderstood my topic? Why?
- Are there people offering alternate solutions to my topic? Who and what?

These are all potential opponents whose views need to be addressed. Take, for example, the following paragraph identifying an indirect counterclaim from English 111 student Jodee Giarratana's paper on teen suicide:

> Despite many people thinking they understand the dark constricting arms of suicide, there are many misconceptions out there. People have the mindset that suicide has a certain type of person it likes to claim for its victim. S. Gardner (1990), former weekly columnist for *The New York Times,* explains some common myths about suicide. She states, "One myth about suicide is

that there is a suicidal type or a suicidal personality." A lot of people assume the only person who will commit suicide is the kid who is the "loner" or the "over emotional" one who can't take a joke. This is beyond wrong. Suicide can claim anyone as its next victim.

Jodee didn't have a direct opponent to address here. She didn't have someone saying, "Ra, ra, ra, teen suicide!" Instead, she addresses the indirect opponents of misconception and ignorance. More often than not, these will be the kinds of counterarguments you will need to pay attention to and address in your paper.

Revising a Research Paper

As you begin revising your research paper, I encourage you to revisit chapter 3 of this book which is specifically dedicated to revision techniques. In addition to the general revision activities presented there, however, I'd like to discuss three other revision techniques that are particularly helpful on lengthy, research-based papers such as the one you are writing for English 111.

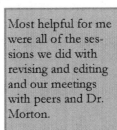

> Most helpful for me were all of the sessions we did with revising and editing and our meetings with peers and Dr. Morton.
>
> ~ Ashleigh Taylor

Revising with Questions

I've suggested several times throughout this book that inquiry should guide your research and your writing. It can also guide your revision. You began this process with a central research question. You also started with a list of questions that your central question naturally generated. These questions (hopefully) led you to make subclaims that would answer them. Having drafted your paper, it's time to see if your questions successfully guided you in constructing a logical, well-ordered paper.

First, find a friend or relative whose intellect you trust. Ask them to read over your paper and then write what they think the central research question was. This will help you to see what a reader, having finished your paper, thinks the paper *answers*.

Then ask yourself, How close is this question to your initial research question? If it's fairly close, then no worries. You've managed to maintain a coherent purpose throughout the writing process. If, however, it is quite different from your original question, then you need to consider the idea that your purpose actually changed over the course of the writing. With that in mind, go back through your paper and make certain that you don't have some paragraphs dedicated to answering the original question, while others are now answering the new research question. Focus on individual paragraphs and ask yourself, "Does this paragraph lend itself to my refined and current purpose?" If not, think about eliminating that paragraph or else revising it to more directly relate to your new research question.

Then ask your friend or relative to read over the paper once more, this time noting in the margin the question that each *paragraph* answers. For example, for a cause/effect paper, they might write, "Why is this issue happening?" "What are the historical reasons?" "What are the cultural reasons?" "What solutions can we offer?" "What predictions can we make about the future?" etc. For a compare contrast paper, they might write questions like "How is this similar to this other thing?" "How is it different?" and "What do we learn from this comparison?" Remember that you will likely have several paragraphs that answer each question (you may have four or five points of contrast, for example, each needing its own paragraph to explore fully). You will want to make sure that paragraphs that answer like questions are grouped together in a logical order, and that each paragraph answers the question you intended it to answer.

■ ■ ■ ■

Revising with Scissors

In his book *Writing with Power*, rhetorician and composition scholar Peter Elbow describes an activity he calls the "Cut and Paste Revision." In this activity, you will use scissors to literally cut your paper into separate paragraphs. From there, scramble your paragraphs so that the original order is lost. Next, read each individual paragraph carefully and ask yourself, "does this paragraph serve to help answer my central research question?" If it does, great. Put it in a "keep" pile. If it doesn't, if it is only tangentially related to your question, if it takes you on a little side trek, then put it in the "discard" pile. This may sound easy, but you'll be surprised just how hard it is for you to step back enough from your own writing, to emotionally divorce yourself from your creation to truly and critically decided which paragraphs may, in fact, not be necessary. For this reason, I advise students to find a friend willing to help them with this step.

I also advice students to reread each of the paragraphs in their "keep" stack (and here I will depart from Elbow a bit). Now, without thinking of the paper as a whole, concentrate on just the paragraph you are reading. Are there sentences or sections that are irrelevant to the subclaim? That are out of place or only loosely related? If so, cross those out or make a note to fix them so that they cohere with the rest of the paragraph.

Finally, as Elbow suggests, read through your revised "keep" stack and reorder your paragraphs, making sure that paragraphs on like topics are placed next to one another. In fact, I have my students write key words in the margin of each paragraph that summarize the main idea of the paragraph, and then try to match key words or at least place key words together that are closely related.

Once you have the paragraphs in their new order, tape them all back together. As you return to your computer, you can then cut and paste your paragraphs into the new order, adding transition sentences to help them flow into one another more logically, and eliminating those paragraphs you deemed irrelevant or tangential.

This is an excellent revision activity, and I've used it with success several times, but it is also a difficult one. It requires that writers be honest about their work and emotionally distance themselves from it enough to critically examine it as well as to physically assault it. With practice, however, you will come to see the value of the kind of emotional distancing this activity requires.

■ ■ ■ ■

Revising with Highlighters

For this revision activity, I am indebted to Boise State University Professor Bruce Ballenger, author of *The Curious Researcher*. I earlier noted the need to maintain rhetorical authority even as you create ethos by demonstrating your familiarity with and respect for the ideas of others. Striking this balance between your own voice and those of others is a crucial part of the success of your writing. To help you make certain that this balance is struck, Ballenger suggests that you turn to a random page in your draft and, using a highlighter, mark all of the borrowed text and ideas. These include all quotes, summaries, and paraphrases. Now, with a different color of highlighter, mark those passages that show your own thinking, including your interpretations and commentary, as well as personal experiences, observations, predictions, hypothetical situations, etc.

With these two colors contrasted on your page, you can assess the balance you have struck. Have you given sufficient space in your paper to other voices, showing that your writing is participating in a larger conversation? Or have you largely ignored these voices, backing up your own ideas with too few collaborating sources? By contrast, have you let your sources dominate, subordinating your own voice and ideas to theirs? Remember that balance is the key to success.

■ ■ ■ ■

Two Sample Student Research Papers

The following two examples come from students Aaron Wells and Jessica Drinnon. Aaron's class took place on the residential campus. Students began their research papers by reading the novel *Bud not Buddy*, selecting research topics from the novel, and developing central research questions from among those topics. Although Aaron's class actually used APA formatting, I have reformatted his paper using MLA so that you will have exemplary research papers in both styles.

By contrast, Jessica's class was taught in the Gateway program. Students were given a broad range of topics to choose from and asked to narrow those topics into specific research questions. All courses in Gateway use APA, so Jessica's paper will provide a good example of that kind of formatting. The different emphases of these two courses create research papers with considerably different structures. However, all of the guiding principles of good research discussed in this chapter are manifest in both papers.

Sample Student Research Paper 1

Aaron Wells

Dr. Sheila Morton

English 111

December 14, 2011

Note that in MLA format, the writer's information is placed on the first page on the left margin.

Hoovervilles and Dignity Villages: Helping the Homeless

Jesse Jackson was called the mayor of Hooverville. He was originally a lumberjack, but when the lumber industry fell through he lost his job, like so many others, and fell back on government relief. In a government funded relief shelter he was given a single meal that "resembled pig swill," and he wasn't even provided a blanket, not to mention a bed. He slept on the floor, under newspapers he had gathered earlier that day, not much better off than those on the street. Jesse, and many others, decided that they were better off on their own, so they left to "construct relief shelters of our own." In a few years this community snowballed into the largest shanty town of the Depression (286-293). Unlike Jackson, some homeless people prefer to stay on government support, but a surprising number reject the aid altogether. That government aid may have helped a great many unemployed and homeless get back on their feet, but there are far more homeless people than can be helped with the limited

Aaron begins his essay with a narrative. Though not a personal narrative, it still serves to draw readers in.

resources available in welfare and other such programs. <u>A lot of solutions to the homelessness problem have been proposed and implemented, but I believe that the most beneficial is to allow the homeless to band together in communities of their own, to help themselves get back on their feet.</u>

> His central claim is easily recognizable as the final sentence in the introduction.

But why should they help themselves? Aren't there systems in place to assist them? Well, yes, there are, but government aid to the homeless is often insufficient. That's the reason that Jackson, left to survive on his own in the first place, as he recalls, "One of the reasons we came [to Hooverville] was to get away from relief organizations" (293). In his eyes, the relief agencies of the Depression were worse than living in a shanty town. And he was quite right, I think. They were underfunded and overtaxed; there just wasn't enough help to go around.

> Remember that sometimes (though not too frequently) your subclaims may be in the form of questions.

Though to be fair, that was nearly eighty years ago, and during the worst depression in our nation's history. There can't possibly be as many homeless individuals today as there were during the Great Depression, right? According to Jonathon Lewin there were 111,223 homeless people in shelters in New York alone at the height of the Depression (66). Well, a recent statistic from 2010 given by the Coalition for the Homeless gives a number of 113,553 different homeless individuals currently in New York during the course of a year. Perhaps that's not the same as Lewin's snapshot, but it's still a great many people who have suffered from a lack of housing. And consider that this is only one state, that the whole country has homeless people in even greater numbers, and you can see why there isn't really enough money going around to help them all.

In this and succeeding paragraphs, Aaron does a nice job of using secondary sources to support his claims (in this case, he uses Lewin and the Coalition for the Homeless)

Sometimes, however, it's not that there's not enough aid, it's that the homeless don't want it. To some, government aid is humiliating, or else the individual is too proud to accept the help. As New York Times journalist, Christopher Gray says, "Then as now, there were many homeless people who refused to accept officially sanctioned help"(par. 15). He's referring to the Great Depression, and comparing the attitude of homeless people then with now. Back then, the relief aid was hurried and frantic with the sudden increase in need, and it was often dehumanizing. Nobody liked to be treated like they were just another problem and Jackson was not the only one to say "These conditions caused me to rebel against such a scheme of things" (286).

It wasn't always that the relief in particular was humiliating; sometimes it was just the fact that they were on relief that the homeless couldn't stand. There are always people who will do anything to avoid accepting help from the government.

They will try to make money in whatever way they can, be it scavenging waste and selling it to recycling companies, or maybe fishing on the side or selling fruit. Jackson observed the same behavior in his Hooverville, but remarked, "None of them realize very much from such enterprises, but they can hold their heads up and say 'I am not on relief'" (286). Just as Jackson is saying, it's often a matter of pride. There are some people who would rather work for their money than accept it from anybody, no matter what the circumstances. To them, it's an honest day's work that matters. The only problem is that they won't always be allowed to do their honest day's work. Often they'll be chased out, not even given a chance.

As Samuel Davis, an architect and writer describes, homelessness is criminalized rather than sympathized. Encampments of homeless people are cleared out by the police in most cities. They're sought out, woken from their night's rest and told that they have to leave. Sometimes, even after that, the area is power-washed, as if it were contaminated from the dirty homeless people who dared to camp there. Inevitably, Davis explains, a few days later the homeless men will come back (50). Of course they do, where else would they go? It's not like the homeless just disappear. The police and city offi-

The subclaim for this paragraph is actually given in the last sentence of the previous paragraph. This is an atypical placement, but if done only occasionally, it can lend interest and variety to your paper.

cials tell them "you can't be here," but don't offer an alternative.

The homeless are unwanted wherever they go, whether they can be gotten rid of or not. Jackson deplored this sentiment "They considered us a bunch of ne'er-do-well undesirables and wanted to get rid of us" (287). He's referring to the people of the community around his Hooverville who thought that the homeless must be delinquents or thieves. A lot of people thought that back when the Depression had first started, since the "American Dream" they had grown up with said that all it took to be successful was hard work. Obviously if they were out there, they hadn't worked hard enough. People still maintain this belief even now, as Paul Krugman ,Nobel Prize winner and teacher of economics at Princeton, points out. According to a survey Krugman mentions, 61 percent of Americans believe that "people get rewarded for their effort" (326). Krugman is pointing out the rather uncomfortable fact that we, as a country, still seem to believe in the American Dream, even though, as he later points out, it's not even remotely true. It's an unfortunate belief, but a lot of people in America still stand by it, and it's a little hard to look kindly on the homeless when all you see is a lazy person.

> Because of the nature of his topic, Aaron doesn't have personal experiences to share in corroboration of his sources. But this doesn't mean his voice is absent. Look at the way he comments on and interprets facts to make the paper his own (I've underlined his additions in this paragraph as a good example).

When the government won't help you, and people don't want you around, there's not much you can do. This leads to many of the nation's homeless being forced to turn to drifting. And this doesn't help the problem either. One city gets rid of them, but that doesn't mean that they're gone; they're just in another city that also wants to get rid of them. What's worse, when the homeless are wandering like that, what aid the government does give can't go to them. Not only is the government not able to do quite enough, but they are also, indirectly, exacerbating the problem. If there were just specific campgrounds, where homeless people were allowed to camp, to "squat" if you prefer, then they would already be a lot better off.

> Here, Aaron transitions readers from an explanation of the problem and its causes to the solution he is proposing.

It seems that, when properly organized and authorized, the homeless can help themselves quite well, with only a little support. Returning to an example from the 1930s, historian John Barnhill describes the self-sufficiency that the homeless often display: "In some of the larger Hoovervilles, the residents organized, chose a mayor, and established committees to deal with sanitation and other community matters" (839). Back in the Depression, some of these communities got so large that they needed to form a government of their own. I mentioned Jesse Jackson above, who came to be called the "mayor" of the Hooverville in Seattle. What's more, they took care of the is sues that the city would also deal with, like keeping the place clean and disease free, and trying to organize the shacks to make them easier to navigate. They're not the dirty homeless people that some assume; they tried to keep things clean too.

This isn't just something that can be seen in the past, there are communities just as complex in the modern world. Beth Slovic tells the story of one such community in Oregon. The city of Portland allowed a group of homeless people to camp in an unused area of public land, and the community has continued to thrive for ten years. It started as a camp of homeless people under a bridge in Portland. As usual, the city forced them to leave, so they moved on, as a group. They landed in a city owned tract of land and set up camp again, but then refused to leave. After they'd been living there four years already, the city deigned to designate the site a campground, making the residents' squatting legal, and also marking the first step toward their reentrance into society. Three years after this, the city started spending its own money on improving the community, now called Dignity Village. They spent over $180,000 upgrading the Village's tents into cheap wooden shacks. This may seem like an impressive amount of money, until you consider that it was spent on a large group of individuals, and that it took the city seven years to assist the Village. And what came of this?

> Here, Aaron seamlessly combines the summary of an article by Slovic with his own views on the narrative Slovic is relating.

Ten years after it started as a ragtag camp of homeless people, Dignity Village has become a largely self-sufficient community, with its own governing board and regulations (prohibiting violence, disturbing others and drugs and alcohol). The population is by no means static, for some Dignity Village acts as a waypoint, a place to stay between jobs. Many of the people who lived there for a time eventually moved out and moved on, back into mainstream society, usually now employed and living in a more traditional home. All this has been accomplished with minimal support and interference from the city of Portland. Now Dignity Village is its own non-profit organization, which handles its own fundraising and is allowed to continue existing as long as it follows certain regulations imposed by the city.

So the Homeless in these communities can govern themselves, and if they've gotten to that point then they must have already covered the basic necessities of human life. They managed to feed themselves by working together, demonstrated by Lewin's interesting story, "… each man was responsible for finding a specific ingredient for that night's stew" (66). He's telling of the people of the Hoovervilles and their surprising communal spirit. By pooling together what food they could manage to scrounge up, they could turn it into a stew that stretched each person's contribution even further, and fed them all more fully. The people of Dignity Village have gone a step beyond even this, as they grow their own vegetables on the land that they've been allowed to camp in. So they are better and more easily fed when banded together.

After the more pressing need of food, a human being needs shelter. A transient (which is to say, a homeless man who moves around) has to take refuge wherever he can manage when the weather gets bad. The people of Dignity Village, as of the Hoovervilles of the 1930's, had their own shelter. A little jerry rigged and ragtag, maybe, but shelter nonetheless. Dignity Village in particular has shown "how homes could be constructed using very inexpensive materials" (Duncan Campbell), even in modern times. Campbell goes on to say that Dignity Village has also shown that the ways in which we deal with the homeless aren't necessarily the only ones.

The problem is, this method requires, not assistance so much, but cooperation from the authorities, and even the public itself. As I've said, the homeless are often viewed in a negative light, making the acceptance of an entire community of homeless people seem so much more unsightly in the eyes of "hard working Americans." This may seem like a difficult hurdle to jump, but the problem actually resolves itself as long as the community is given a chance to exist. Gray reminds us of what hap-

After outlining two examples of the kind of solution he is advocating, Aaron addresses counter claims, or reasons that some might oppose his solution

pened with the Hoovervilles in the thirties, "As the depression set in, public sentiment became more sympathetic" (7). Once the Hooverites had been living alongside them for long enough, the public got a better look at them and saw that they were people, not just bums as they had feared before. Jackson also tells of how the business and people in the surrounding district came to know the people of his Hooverville. Once they saw who these people really were, they became much less hostile, and even helped in some ways (287). And Dignity Village was much the same way. They were originally forced to move, but by the end of it they were not only allowed to live on the land, but even granted official support.

    It's not that the government shouldn't help; indeed without the city's help Dignity Village would never have gotten where it is. Instead the government should change the way it deals with homeless people altogether. One of the most important changes that needs to be made is to completely rewrite vagrancy laws. How can the homeless get off the streets if they can't even stay one place for long without being removed by force? If campgrounds, like the one in Portland, that are specifically designated for the homeless were put up over the country, more communities like Dignity Village could exist, and the lots of thousands of homeless men, women and children could be improved.

How the homeless live may not seem like much of a problem to the average citizen, but it must be remembered that in these uncertain times anyone can suddenly lose everything. Among the residents of Dignity Village are such high class workers as laser optic technicians and electricians. People who can look back on "the time I had my sports car, my condo, and my jewelry" (Campbell). How many right now can claim these status symbols as it is? Are you just an accident, or a layoff away from being on the streets?

> His conclusion uses one of the introductory strategies mentioned earlier—a series of questions that keeps the reader thinking even after the paper is over.

Works Cited

Barnhill, John. H. "Bonus Army (1932)". *Revolts, Protests, Demonstrations, and Rebellions in American History: An Encyclopedia.* Ed. Steven. L. Danver. Santa Barbara, CA: ABC-CLIO, 2011. 829-846. *Ebrary.* Web. 3 December, 2012.

Campbell, Duncan. "America's Homeless Become New Small-Town Pioneers." *The Guardian* 23 October, 2003. Web. 3 December, 2012.

> For help formatting sources in MLA, please see Appendix C.

Coalition for the Homeless. Basic Facts about Homelessness. "Coalition for the Homeless." 2011. Web. 4 December, 2012.

Davis, Sam. *Designing for the Homeless: Architecture That Works.* Berkeley, CA: University of California Press, 2004.

Gray, Christopher. "Streetscapes: Central Park's 'Hooverville'; Life Along 'Depression Street'". *The New York Times.* 29 August, 1993: 7. *LexisNexis.* Web. 5 December, 2012.

Jackson, Jesse. "The Story of Seattle's Hooverville." *Social Trends in Seattle.* Ed. C. F. Schmid. Seattle, WA: University of Washington Press, 1944. 286-293. Print.

Krugman, Paul. "Confronting Inequality." *They Say/ I say.* Eds Gerald Graff, Kathy Birkenstein, and Russel Durst. New York, NY: W. W. Norton and Company, 2009. 322-341. Print

Lewin, Jonathan. "Keeping Up Appearances: Hooverville, 1931." *Big Town Big Time.* Ed. Jay Maeder. New York, NY: Sports Publishing LLC, 1998. 66. Print.

Slovic, Beth. "Portland's Dignity Village Homeless Camp Set to Get Another Year, At Least on City Land." *The Oregonian,* 7 June, 2011. Web. 3 December, 2012.

Sample Student Research Paper 2

Running Head: WHATEVER REMAINS   1

Whatever Remains: An Elementary Examination of How Sherlock Holmes Transformed Crime Scene Analysis

Jessica Drinnon

Tusculum College

Note that APA format requires a cover page. Please see Appendix A for more formatting help.

Author Note:

This paper was prepared for Dr. Anne Acker's English 111 class at Tusculum College.

Abstract

This paper undertakes an in depth examination of the popular fictional character, Sherlock Holmes and his revolutionary concepts of crime scene analysis, and investigational methods. In addition to an examination of Holmes and his methods, this paper casts an eye forward into history, identifies the link between Holmes' pioneering concepts, and elaborates on how they translated into major turning points in crime scene analysis. Through various sources such as peer reviewed journals, news articles, direct quotes, and documentaries, I cite evidence that supports my theory that Holmes did play a key role in revolutionizing crime scene investigations. Each part of the evidence sequences in scaffolding order, from base to most complex, and how real world investigators later introduced and employed Holmes methods and concepts.

> APA requires the writing of an abstract—a brief overview of the major arguments of the paper.

Whatever Remains: An Elementary Examination of How Sherlock Holmes Transformed Crime Scene Analysis

Whatever Remains

In the nineteenth and even the early twentieth centuries, when disorganization and superstition characterized many crime scenes, investigators had inadequate training and did not recognize the importance of evidence. When some unfortunate person discovered a lifeless body, for various reasons tension and emotions ran high, and officials often cast a mistrusting eye toward the most suspicious looking character in the immediate vicinity. Many times in the effort to uncover truth, investigators pushed aside potential evidence in favor of eyewitness testimony. Because dead men (or women) do not actually tell tales, investigators sought the statements and testimony of living eyewitness with little regard to the witness's possible prejudices, reliability, or observational skills; presence at the crime scene was often the sole qualifying requirement to testify against someone. The injustices that came from such top-heavy investigations were often the cause of public outcry.

Unfortunately, the masses who raised objections in favor of reform usually lack the power or influence to bring about the much-needed change; the individuals that did possess the resources to influence the system simply did not care.

> Notice that Jessica begins with one of the introductory techniques discussed in chapter 2: Beginning with a historical story or background. Notice, too, how she makes it intriguing so that readers will want to read on.

Sherlock Holmes could not have stepped into the limelight at a more opportune time. <u>The culmination of many factors opened the door, and many minds to the necessity of pioneering concepts and methods that Holmesian deduction and logic regularly employed.</u> To fully grasp the transformation, one must first understand where it came from, and what was before.

Victorian Crime and Punishment; a run-on sentence

The standard American way of thinking about our legal system is that justice is a basic God-given human right and should be blind and impartial. Unfortunately, true justice was not commonplace in many turn of the century English courtroom cases involving poor, working class citizens. <u>Some historic scholars may challenge the view that impoverished defendants were often deprived of proper legal defense and convicted based on false eye witness testimony</u>, but consider John Walker, who was sentenced to seven years in prison for stealing a bag of onions. (East of England Broadband Network, 2006) Fourteen year old, Henry Catlin found himself sentenced to fourteen years of hard labor in an Australian penal camp for stealing a pair of shoes and 17 pence (28¢). (East of England Broadband Network, 2006) In other words, many working class citizens identified with the necessity of criminal cases hinging on

Jessica's thesis statement (underlined) comes at the end of her introduction and provides a clear direction for the paper.

Notice the expert way Jessica addresses counterclaims. She first names her opponents (some historical scholars) and their views, and then gives specific reasons and examples to counter them.

unbiased, physical evidence instead of eyewitness testimony. Impoverished citizens were often denied the right to a fair, impartial trail because many could not afford good legal counsel, and consequently were doomed to lengthy jail sentences, prison colonies, or even death, based on faulty eyewitness testimony.

> She then steers the discussion back to her own claims. Very well done!

Crime Scene Investigation; Then and Now

While the English turn-of-the-century criminal justice system was not impartial, its flaws were made greater by the investigational methods of the same era. When it comes to the topic of the highly publicized "Jack the Ripper" case, most historical scholars will readily agree that there were many crucial factors contributing to Jack the Ripper's abilities to continually dodge Scotland Yard. Where this agreement usually ends, however, is on the question of which factor ultimately allowed a serial killer to evade authorities and continue his murderous rampage. Some are convinced that he got away with the murders, because of the poverty-stricken neighborhoods in which he committed the crimes. Along the same lines, others think that since there was a lack of streetlamps, it gave him the cover of darkness that helped him sidestep police. However, in *The Science of Sherlock Holmes*, author E.J. Wagner (2006) is convinced the reason he evaded

> Notice that Jessica follows the principles of good organization we discussed earelier. In this paragraph, for example, she gives us her subclaim (first sentence), then provides an example (Jack the Ripper), and backs up her claims with both secondardy source evidence and her own reflections..

authorities is that the crime scene was a "debacle." The crime scene and evidence were "...treated with an impressive lack of scientific organization" (p.81). It was general knowledge up until this point in time that the crime scene investigations were lax and mishandled, by authorities who made many speculations at, but never instituted, change. In *A Study in Scarlett,* (1887) Doyle's popular novel written the previous year, Holmes skillfully introduces the necessity of crime scene preservation as he uses deductive reasoning to unravel a mystery centered around a murderous lover bent on avenging the death of his sweetheart and her father. Holmes emphasizes the importance of immediately securing and preserving a crime scene upon arriving at the contaminated murder scene. It was Holmes opinion that, "If a herd of buffaloes had passed along there could not be a greater mess," and it echoed many scenarios of real life investigations of the day much like the Jack the Ripper case.

> Although not required, APA encourages the use of headings, which both help to divide the text into distinct sections and help readers transition between those sections.

Manual Field Labor

Historical scholars believe that it was an Austrian investigator, Hans Gross who, after reading *A Study in Scarlet* (1887) recognized the need for standard procedures and guidelines in crime-scene investigations. This led him to write, *Manual For Examining Magistrates*. The manual has been revised many times down through the years, but crime scene technicians today still widely

WHATEVER REMAINS

use this manual under the title, *Criminal Investigation* (1970). It has become a field manual, promoting standard operating procedures, and scientific principles similar to those of Holmes. This manual was innovative, making it possible for investigators to maximize gathered evidence and coordinate with all personnel involved. As a result, it reduced evidence contamination and gave investigators an opportunity to fully evaluate every aspect of the crime scene. Some historical authors support the controversial claim that Arthur Conan Doyle mimicked Gross with Sherlock Holmes, since the detectives' methods are so similar (R.Grassberger, 1957). However, that argument is simply not valid; one only has to look at the chronological timeline to put that argument to rest. *A Study in Scarlett* (Doyle, 1887) was published in 1887; it was not until 1893, a full six years later, that Gross published his manual.

Standing on Sherlock's shoulders

> While it is true that an isolated event does not give one a key role in history, Holmes' reach of influence stretches its fingers far beyond Gross. Crime scene and evidence preservation would be pointless without a reason for preservation. They are important because when unaltered, they are silent witnesses offering unchanging testimony—justice to silenced victims and freedom to innocent defendants.

Notice that Jessica often uses transition sentences between sections, a good way to steer readers through an argument.

In 1910, French criminologist and later the director of the Institute of Criminalistics, Dr. Edmond Locard fully understood the importance of trace evidence. He was fascinated with Holmes' ability to identify tobacco ashes (Powell, 2013) in the novel *A Study in Scarlet* (Doyle, 1887). Although tobacco ashes may seem trivial, Locard recognized that they are in fact crucial in terms of identifying a potential murderer. He went on to do extensive research of his own, examining tobacco ashes and afterward, publishing numerous papers about his findings. Locard authored many other papers and in the article, "The Analysis of Dust Traces" (1930) recommended that his students examine the logic behind how Holmes in the short story, "A Case of Identity" (Doyle, 1892) was able to identify a dirt speck on the cuff of pant leg in (Powell, 2013) (Berg, 1970). When asked about his inspiration for the scholarly article, Locard quickly credits Holmes saying, "Sherlock Holmes was the first to realize the importance of dust. I merely copied his methods" (Berg, 1970).

Locard demonstrated that he was a master of deductive reasoning and openly credited Holmes' methods for his inspiration for many of his pioneering techniques, such as the first police crime laboratory, and being the first to use the microscope to identify, classify, and catalogue hair and fiber samples.

> Jessica does a masterful job of making claims (last sentence on previous page) and then backing those claims with specific, historical examples such as this one about Locard.

(Berg, 1970 and Powell, 2013) In spite of the massive contributions Locard made to forensic science, none compare to his theory, later named Locard's Principle of Exchange, which states, "Any action of an individual, and obviously the violent action constituting a crime, cannot occur without leaving a trace." In short, Locard believed that a criminal, regardless of his location comes in contact with his surroundings and leaves trace evidence of himself such as fingerprints, hair, pieces of fiber from clothing, and skin cells and in turn carries away parts of his surroundings as well. To put it another way, Locard's exchange theory contributed to the field of forensic science in the same way that Einstein's theory of relativity contributed to the field of physics, and Locard was inspired by the methods of Sherlock Holmes.

He is the criminal type.
At first glance, the mountain of evidence that a typewritten document contains is not obvious to the average, untrained eye. From around the mid 1800's until the 1980's the typewriter was the standard mode of written communication, replacing handwritten notes and letters. Many people might assume that since type is not written by hand, typewritten communication is not personally identifiable. However, that is not entirely true; Holmes, in the short story "A Case of Identity," was the first,

known, and documented reference to describe the identification potential of typewriting (Crown, 1967). Holmes' author, Arthur Conan Doyle's diary dated, for the same time, also corroborated this fact. Holmes was the first to point out that no two typewriters are the same, even among the same brand and series. In fact, each typewriter has distinguishing features such as uneven wearing of certain letters, tilting characters, and the typefaces (fonts) of the characters (Crown, 1967).

In his article, "Landmarks in Typewriting Identification," postal document examiner for San Francisco and Criminologist, David Crown (1967) insists that details down to personally identifying the typist can be observed such as wearing based on the way the keys have been struck, repeated grammar and spelling errors, and error-and correction patterns, just to name a few. In 1996, using Holmes' theories of typewriter identification, the United States Federal Bureau of Investigation was able to positively identify domestic terrorist and criminal genius, Theodore Kaczynski, known as the Unabomber. Based on previously known documents Kaczynski typed, the Bureau linked him and his two vintage typewriters to threatening letters sent to the *Washington Post* and *The New York Times*. This was a crucial piece of evidence ultimately contributing to a conviction, because Kaczynski had ingeniously thrown investigators off track by planting false latent prints on bombs (Greeneburg J., Greenburg, C., Marx C., 1996).

A Jolly Good Fellow

Though I concede that Sherlock Holmes is a fictional character, I still insist that he is more than that. Some readers may challenge this view and only see Holmes as nothing more than a character on a page. Is it unrealistic to think that a fictional character can step out from between two covers and influence the surrounding culture? The prestigious, Royal Society of Chemistry does not think so. In 2002, the Royal Society of Chemistry in England awarded Holmes with an honorary Posthumous Fellowship for his contributions to fighting crime (Chemistry, 2002). This honor has been awarded in the past to many Nobel Laureates. When asked about the validity of the award, Dr. David Giachardi, secretary general of the Society said that the society wanted the world to know, "…Here was a great man who selflessly pursued bad people on behalf of the good, using science, courage, and crystal clear thought processes to achieve his goals." (McGourty, 2002)

> Though she has already addressed specific counterarguments several times, here and in the following section Jessica addresses general objections reader may have to her central claim.

Keep the Change

In the late 1800's, at the turn of the twentieth century, Holmes challenged many societal stereotypes about poverty and crime. Many modern-day celebrities use their celebrity status as a platform for championing their cause, and along the same lines, Arthur Conan Doyle used Holmes' character and popularity to champion the cause of the destitute and the defenseless. Holmes was very much like the American pioneers who began expanding west to discover new territory and search for nuggets of gold. Through logical reasoning and scientific deductions, Holmes rode his popularity on a journey to promote new ideas in crime scene investigations, and bring reform to English societal perceptions.

  Anyone familiar with present-day forms of media would agree that what we visually ingest does affect our mindset. Yet, is it true that a work of fictional literature could bring societal change? For those that might object, one might think about how the novel Jurassic Park (Crichton, 1991) introduced the science of genetic cloning in a radical way with implications that mainstream society had not previously entertained. Along the same lines, Holmes was able to introduce into mainstream Victorian society revolutionary ideas about applying scientific methods and concepts to crime scene investigations. Holmes' influence through literature tells us a great deal about influencing the masses and might make one take a second to consider the power of literature to bring about social change.

The Beginning of the End

Holmes did in fact play a key role in bringing about change in the field of crime scene investigation at the turn of the twentieth century. Even though some historians and scholars may dispute the argument, the evidence I present supports my initial claim. One of Holmes most quoted statements is, "When you have eliminated the impossible, whatever remains, however improbable, must be the truth" (Doyle, 1890). Given the evidence, it is impossible to see Holmes as anything but revolutionary. What remains is that he was influential.

In her conclusion, Jessica uses another of the concluding techniques I discussed in chapter 2—she ends with a famous quote. She also turns the quote to her topic in a clever and memorable way.

References

Berg, S. (1970). Sherlock Holmes: The father of scientific crime detection. *The Journal of Criminal Law, Criminology, and Police Science, 61,* 456-452. Retrieved from http://scholarlycommons.law.northwestern.edu/cgi/viewcontent.cgi?article=5674&context=jclc

For help in formatting sources on the References page in APA, please see appendix C

Crichton, M. (1991). *Jurassic park*. New York: Random House Publishers.

Crown, D. A. (1967). Landmarks in typewriting identification. *Journal Of Criminal Law, Criminology and Police Science, 58*(1), 105. Retrieved from LexisNexis.

Doyle, A. C. (1887). *A study in scarlet*.Retrieved from http://www.gutenberg.org/ebooks/244

Doyle, A. C. (1890). *The sign of sour*. Retrieved from http://www.gutenberg.org/ebooks/2097

Doyle, A. C. (1892). *A case of identity*. United Kingdom: George Newnes.

Doyle, A. C. (1894, October). The Stark Munroe letters. *Idler Magazine*. Retrieved from http://www.sshf.com/encyclopedia/index.php/The_Stark_Munro_Letters

East of England Broadband Network. (2006). Case study-John Walker. (E2Bn) Retrieved from *Victorian Crime and Punishment*: http://vcp.e2bn.org/prisoners/180-1-john-walker.html

East of England Broadband Network (2006). Case study-Henry Catlin, age 14 - Deported. Retrieved from *Victorian Crime and Punishment*: http://vcp.e2bn.org/case_studies/casestudy11208-henry-catlin-age-14-deported.html

Grassberger, R. (1957). Pioneers in criminology XIII--Hans Gross (1847-1915). *Journal of Criminal Law and Criminology*, *47*(4). Retrieved from http://scholarlycommons.law.northwestern.edu/cgi/viewcontent.cgi?article=4512&context=jclc

Greeneburg J., Greenburg, C., & Marx C. (1996, April 16). Typewriters may be critical clue. *Chicago Tribune*. Retrieved from http://articles.chicagotribune.com/1996-04-06/news/9604060122_1_unabomber-theodore-kaczynski-mail-bombs

Locard, E. (1930). The analysis of dust traces. *American Journal of Police Science*, *1* (3), 276-298. Retreived from http://0-www.jstor.org.library.acaweb.org/stable/1147154..

McGourty, C. (2002, October 16). Chemists honour Sherlock Holmes. *BBC World News*. Retrieved from http://news.bbc.co.uk/2/hi/science/nature/2331113.stm

Powell, T. (Producer), & Bernays, P. (Director). (2013). *How Sherlock changed the world*. [Motion Picture]. United States Of America: Public Broadcasting Service.

The Royal Society of Chemistry (2002, October 16). Sherlock Holmes honorary fellowship. *Press release*. Picadilly, London, UK. Retrieved from http://www.rsc.org/AboutUs/News/PressReleases/2005/Sherlock-holmes-rsc-fellowship.asp

Wagner, E. J. (2006). *The science of Sherlock Holmes; From Baskerville Hall to the Valley of Fear, the real forensics behind the great detective's greatest cases.* Hoboken, New Jersey: John Wiley & Sons, Inc.

Wolfe, A. (1932, Feburary 27). The debt of the police to detective fiction. *The Illustrated London News Historical Archive*, pp. 320, 328. Retrieved from Infotrac.

IV. Appendices

CITATION GUIDES:
The Extra Tools You Need

There are four common formatting styles that dictate source citation in the disciplines, and each is governed by a specific disciplinary body: MLA is the citation method used in literature and many of the humanities and is governed by the Modern Language Association; APA is used in psychology, most of the social sciences, education, and business and is the purview of the American Psychological Association; Chicago style is used in the fields of history and archeology and is governed by a board of scholars associated with the University of Chicago Press; and CSE is used in the hard sciences and is maintained by the Council of Science Educators. There are other, lesser-used formatting styles as well, but these four are used by the majority of disciplines. While all four are important, we find that MLA and APA are used in the vast majority of classes here at the College, and for that reason, we have included citation guides for those two formats. If your professor prefers one of the other citation methods, we recommend visiting Diana Hacker's excellent guide at www.dianahacker.com/resdoc

When people think of using a specific citation format, they generally think of formatting sources. However, these formatting styles also provide instructions on how to lay out a paper, giving direction on everything from where to put your name to how to structure your page numbers. So when a professors says, "Write this paper in MLA format," she isn't just talking about how to put together a works cited—she also has specific expectations for the appearance of the paper. Consequently, this citation guide is broken into three parts. The first, Appendix A, will show you the basic page-formatting for both APA and MLA. Appendix B explains how to format your sources in text. And Appendix C will give you the basic rules for organizing your reference sheet at the end of the paper.

Appendix A: Paper Formatting

Some General Rules for Formatting in APA

- APA style defines four major areas of a research paper: the title page, abstract, main body, and reference page.
- The APA also has font and margin requirements. You should use Times New Roman 12 point font with 1 inch margins. All text, including that on the title and reference pages should be double spaced.
- The title page should have a running head at the top. Page numbering begins on the title page and is visible in the top right corner.
- The title, writer's name, and institutional affiliation should be centered on three separate, double-spaced lines at approximately four inches from the top of the title page (this is my approximation; the APA does not dictate exact placement by inches).
- The APA encourages you to choose descriptive but succinct titles, limiting them to 12 or fewer words
- If the paper is written for a class (as opposed to being written for publication) you should include an author note at the bottom giving the course name and professor.
- The second page of your paper is the abstract page. The word "Abstract" should be centered at the top. An abstract is a concise summary of your paper. The APA advises you to keep your abstract to between 100 and 250 words.
- On the third page, you will begin the main body of your paper. In addition to the running head at the top (which should be on every page), you will also need to reprint your paper's title once more, centered and at the top of the page. Do not put it in larger font; do not underline, italicize, or in any other way alter the font size or appearance.
- Your introduction will then begin on the following line after the title.
- For the correct way to format your sources in the body of your text, please refer to Appendix B.
- The final section of your paper is your reference page. The word "References" should be centered at the top of the page. Again, do not alter the font size or appearance. Entries on the reference page are alphabetized by authors' last names. For help in formatting these entries correctly, please see Appendix C.

The following sample pages show you how to format according to the preceding guidelines.

Running Head: THE USE OF FIRST NAMES   1

The Use of First Names as a Vehicle for
Transmitting Parental Values
Sheila Morton
Illinois State University

Author Note

This paper was prepared for Dr. Mahide Demirci's English 341 class at Illinois State University

Abstract

Trends in naming over the last several decades have tended toward the unique over the common, emphasizing the individuality of the new baby over its place in the community. Much has been written about this trend and the parental values it communicates. However, other values are also communicated in this essential act of naming. This study examined the naming practices of 100 families, determined through a series of surveys and interviews distributed to Illinois State University students and drew some conclu-sion

The Use of First Names as a Vehicle for Transmitting Parental Values

"Don't stand chattering to yourself like that," Humpty Dumpty said, looking at her for the first time, "but tell me your name and your business."
"My name is Alice, but -- -"
"It's a stupid name enough!" Humpty Dumpty interrupted impatiently. "What does it mean?"
"Must a name mean something?" Alice asked doubtfully.
"Of course it must," Humpty Dumpty said with a short laugh: my name means the shape I am -- and a good handsome shape it is, too. With a name like yours, you might be any shape, almost."
~Lewis Carroll, Through the Looking Glass

A few years ago, a unique baby book came out; unlike those before it, this book didn't give the etymology of baby names. Instead, it described current attitudes toward first names taken from hundreds of surveys on the kind of person each name connotes. Many people would be startled, and some displeased,

References

Hook, J. N. (1991). *All those wonderful names*. New York: John Wiley & Sons.

Joubert, C.E. (1995). Relation of frequency to perception of gender-appropriateness in personal names. *Perceptual and Motor Skills, 80*, 331-335.

Kaleta, Z. (1995). Human values as reflected in Indo-European compound first names. *Onoma: Bibliographical & Information Bulletin, 32*, 83-94.

Lu, Z. & Millward, C. (1989). Chinese given names since the cultural revolution. *Names: a Journal of Onomastics, 37*, 265-280.

Reed, J.W. (1992). The process of name-giving. *Dissertation Abstracts International, 53*, 571B-72B.

Turner, N. S. (2000). Zulu names and indirect expression. *Names: a Journal of Onomastics, 48*, 127-37.

Willis, F.N., Willis, L.A. & Gier, J.A. (1982). Given names, social class, and professional achievement. *Psychological Reports, 51*, 543-49.

Some General Rules for Formatting in MLA

- For font requirements, the MLA asks only that you use a reasonable font and suggests Times New Roman or similar font style.
- All text, including that on the works cited, should be double spaced.
- Margins should be 1" on all sides.
- Page numbering should be in the top right, and page numbers should be preceded by the writer's last name.
- The MLA now suggests including the page number on the first page of text. However, in past editions of the MLA manual, they suggested suppressing the page number on the first page so ask your professor which style they prefer and follow that preference.
- The writer's name, instructor's name, course name, and date should be placed on four separate, double-spaced lines in the top left corner of the first page. IMPORTANT NOTE: Many students are placing this information in the header. Please DO NOT put this information in the header. It should be on the first page only and should be within the regular margins of the text.
- The paper's title should then be centered on the fifth line of text. Do not enlarge, italicize, underline, bold, or in any other way alter the font for the title.
- After one double space, begin the introduction of the paper, indenting the first line of this paragraph and every subsequent paragraph.
- The MLA now asks that writers use italics for emphasis and for long titles instead of underlining.
- For the correct way to format your sources in the body of your text, please refer to Appendix B.
- The final section of your paper contains your references. The phrase "Works Cited" should be centered at the top of the page. Again, do not alter the font size or appearance. Entries on the works cited page are alphabetized by authors' last names. For help in formatting these entries correctly, please see Appendix C.

The following sample pages show you how to format according to the above guidelines.

Sheila Morton

Dr. Lucia Getsi

English 403

May 2, 2006

Not Mine but Thine: The Subjection of the Lyric Self in the Poetry of

George Herbert

Barbara Harman, in her book *Costly Monuments*, writes, "One of the first things I am doing when I begin to speak is insisting, in a new way, upon the fact that I am present. . . and regardless of what else my words mean they almost always mean that" (41). Here, Harman is writing, not about actual *speech* but about the inevitability of authorial presence in poetry. Her ch[...]
more so th[...]
transition f[...]
poetry with[...]
obviously, [...]
me, I am n[...]
possible w[...]
simply stop[...]

Works Cited

Derrida, Jacques. *Of Grammatology*. Baltimore, MD: Johns Hopkins University Press, 1998. Print.

Fish, Stanley. *Self-Consuming Artifacts: The Experience of Seventeenth-Century Literature*. Pittsburgh, PA: Duquesne University Press, 1998. Print.

Harman, Barbara. *Costly Monuments: Representations of the Self in George Herbert's Poetry*. Cambridge, MA: Harvard University Press, 1982. Print.

Herbert, George. *The Complete English Poems*. Ed. John Tobin. London: Penguin Classic, 2004. Print.

The Holy Bible. New York, NY: American Bible Society, 1980. Print. King James Version.

"Lyric Poetry." *The New Princeton Encyclopedia of Poetry and Poetics*. Ed. Alex Preminger, Terry V.F. Brogan, and Frank J. Warnke. Princeton, NJ: Princeton University Press, 1993. Print.

Miller, Paul. *Lyric Texts and Lyric Consciousness: The Birth of a Genre from Archaic Greece to Augustan Rome*. New York, Routledge, 1994. Print.

Pindar. *The Extant Odes of Pindar*. Trans. Ernest Myers. London: MacMillan, 1892. Gutenberg.org. Web. March 11, 2006.

Appendix B: In-text Citation

In chapter seven, you learned the basic rules for introducing and citing a resource in the text of your paper. This appendix will give you the specific rules for formatting those citations in both APA and MLA. Please note: alone, this guide is incomplete; you will need to use it in conjunction with the rules and conventions laid out in chapter seven.

How to Use This Guide

First, read through the rules for a standard in-text citation (the first entry in the table below). Then, locate the rules for any sources you may have with special or unusual circumstances and make the necessary adjustments to the standard citation. The conventions for APA are laid out in the left column, for MLA in the right.

In-text citation rules for the following kinds of sources are provided:

- Basic format for an in-text citation
- Citing multiple authors
- Citing authors with the same last name
- Citing an unknown author
- Citing an organizational author
- Citing two or more works by the same author
- Citing a work in an edited book or anthology
- Citing a sacred text
- Citing a play or a poem
- Citing personally-conducted primary research
- Citing an indirect source
- Citing a source with missing information (such as author, year, or page number)

Style Guide 1

Basic Format for an In-text Citation

The majority of your source citations should mention the author's name in the signal phrase (please refer to chapter 8 for details). In addition. . .

- In APA, the year needs to follow the author's name the first time an author is mentioned *per paragraph*. If you mention the same author another time in the same paragraph, you may omit the year.
- If the quote you are citing is found on a single page, write "p." preceding the page number. Use "pp." for a piece of text that spans one or more pages.
- For web sources with no page numbers, you (may) use paragraph numbers preceded by "para." (see section on "Missing Information")
- Remember that APA generally does not use author's first names.

- In MLA, the first mention of an author's name per paper should include both first and last names. Subsequent uses of that author need only cite the last name.
- Page numbers are given as simple numerals; do not include p. or pg. or any other page designation.

G. Poitras (2008), one of the first scholars to study the impact of anime and manga in America, explains that many viewers of anime are surprised, and even offended, by its often adult content. However, he contends, "Once the audience puts aside the expectation that animation is either just for kids or just visually intriguing, and allows it to tell stories in the same manner as other media, elements like suffering or even death, including the death of innocents, is not as surprising" (p. 60).

Gilles Poitras, one of the first scholars to study the impact of anime and manga in America, explains that many viewers of anime are surprised, and even offended, by its often adult content. However, he contends, "Once the audience puts aside the expectation that animation is either just for kids or just visually intriguing, and allows it to tell stories in the same manner as other media, elements like suffering or even death, including the death of innocents, is not as surprising" (60).

Sometimes you will want to cite a source only in parentheticals, not in the signal phrase. Please note that you should use parenthetical citations far less often than signal phrases, though more often in APA than in MLA. In those few cases where you do choose parentheticals, observe the following rules:

- When citing the author's name in the parenthetical reference at the end of a quote, make sure that the year still follows the author's name
- Page numbers follow the year, separated by a comma

- Simply list author's name and page number(s)
- Do NOT use a comma to separate the author's name and page numbers, a common mistake.
- Parenthetical citation should be used very sparingly if at all.

"Once the audience puts aside the expectation that animation is either just for kids or just visually intriguing, and allows it to tell stories in the same manner as other media, elements like suffering or even death, including the death of innocents, is not as surprising" (Poitras, 2008, p. 60).

"Once the audience puts aside the expectation that animation is either just for kids or just visually intriguing, and allows it to tell stories in the same manner as other media, elements like suffering or even death, including the death of innocents, is not as surprising" (Poitrase 60).

Citing Multiple Authors

- When citing two authors in the signal phrase, separate their names with the word "and":

F. Ladd and H. Deneroff (2009), authors of the book *Astro Boy and Anime Come to the Americas*, claim that "teenagers routinely prefer anime to American-made cartoons" (pp. 189-190).

- However, when citing them in the parenthetical reference, separate names with an ampersand.

"Teenagers routinely prefer anime to American-made cartoons" (Ladd & Deneroff, 2009, pp. 189-190).

- Name all authors, regardless of number, either in the signal phrase or in the parenthetical reference, and use the word "and" to separate names in both formats.

Fred Ladd and Harvey Deneroff, authors of the book *Astro Boy and Anime Come to the Americas*, argue that "teenagers routinely prefer anime to American-made cartoons" (189-90).

"Teenagers routinely prefer anime to American-made cartoons" (Ladd and Deneroff 189-90).

Also

- For three to five authors, mention all authors the first time you use the source in your paper. In subsequent uses, mention only the first author's name followed by the words "et. al" meaning "and others."

First mention: As authors of the article "Manga and the Pirates" Gnestre, Marcu, Mayfield, and Mayfield (2000) argue, the market in Japan is so saturated with popular manga that there is little room for growth (p. 35).

Subsequent mentions: Gnestre et. al (2000) explain that before the manga industry alliance was formed, they were being undercut dramatically by media pirates, and that "the pirates wielded a high degree of power over the manga producers" (p. 38).

- For six or more authors, you need only name the first author followed by "et. al" in all in-text citations.

J. Wayne et. al (1996) ask, "Does material evidence form the basis of identity alone or, as with art, do methods of environmental manipulation control evolutionary development?" (p. 33).

As authors of the article "Manga and the Pirates" Gnestre, Marcu, Mayfield, and Mayfield argue, the market in Japan is so saturated with popular manga that there is little room for growth (35).

And

We might ask, "Does material evidence form the basis of identity alone or, as with art, do methods of environmental manipulation control evolutionary development" (Wayne, Siler, Anker, Clarke, Denes, Grey, Kavenoff, Kovachevich, Kremers, Newman, and Rich 33).

- However, using your own discretion, you may decide that a series of names is too long to include them all and choose instead to list only the first followed by "et. al":

June Wayne et. al ask, "Does material evidence form the basis of identity alone or, as with art, do methods of environmental manipulation control evolutionary development?" (33).

Citing Authors with the Same Last Name

- In the first and every subsequent use of the author's name, include the first initial.

In his article, "Anime Gives Kick in the Art," J. Smith (2006) insists that American animation, though

- In the first and every subsequent use of the author's name, include the first name.

In his article, "Anime Gives Kick in the Art," Jeremy Smith insists that American anima-

"more graceful," lacks the impact of Japanese anime (p. A10).

tion, though "more graceful," lacks the impact of Japanese anime (A10).

In her book, *A Brief Guide to Anime and Manga*, K. Smith (2011) details the history of anime in America.

In her book, *A Brief Guide to Anime and Manga*, Kaelyn Smith details the history of anime in America.

Citing a Text with an Unknown Author

- Simply give the title in either the signal phrase or parenthetical reference.

- Simply give the title in either the signal phrase or parenthetical reference.

According to the article "Eclectic: Japanese Manga" (1995) "Besides karaoke, this is the only modern art form in which Japan is a world leader" (p. 82).

According to the article "Eclectic: Japanese Manga," "Besides karaoke, this is the only modern art form in which Japan is a world leader" (82).

Citing a Text with an Organizational Author

- Simply name the organization in either the signal phrase or parenthetical reference.

- Simply name the organization in either the signal phrase or parenthetical reference

- Manga sales in the United States in 2010 reached nearly $180 million (US Department of State, 2012, para. 3).

- Manga sales in the United States in 2010 reached nearly $180 million (US Department of State).

Citing Two or More Works by the Same Author

- Because publication year is always included in APA in-text citations, distinguishing one work from the other, this is not usually a problem. However, if you are citing two works by the same author in the same year, simply add a small "a" and "b" after the year, with the "a" assigned to the title that comes first alphabetically.

- In the first and all subsequent uses of the sources, include both the author's name and the works' title, either in the signal phrase or the parenthetical reference.

D. Avallaro (2010a) likens visual novels to video games in the agency they afford readers/players.

Dani Avallaro, in his book *Anime And The Visual Novel* likens visual novels to video games in the agency they afford readers/players.

D. Avallaro (2010b) believes that "Japan's visual arts resemble the magical arts insofar as they engage with latent essential realities that evade rational scrutiny" (p. 4).

Dani Avallaro believes that "Japan's visual arts resemble the magical arts insofar as they engage with latent essential realities that evade rational scrutiny" (*Magic as Metaphor in Anime* 4).

Citing a Work in an Edited Book or Anthology.
Use Also for Introductions, Forewords, & Afterwords

- Cite the author of the shorter work, NOT the editor of the anthology or author of the book.

- Cite the author of the shorter work, NOT the editor of the anthology or author of the book.

Citing a Sacred Text

- Write the name of the sacred text as well as the version you used, if relevant. In parentheticals, identify the part cited (for example, chapter, verse, line).

- Write the name of the sacred text, the version you used (if relevant), and the part cited (for example, chapter, verse, line).

The world began when the two deities, His Augustness the Male-Who-Invites and Her Augustness the Female-Who-Invites, "standing upon the Floating Bridge of Heaven pushed down the jeweled spear and stirred with it, whereupon, when they had stirred the brine till it went curdle-curdle, and drew the spear up, the brine that dripped down from the end of the spear was piled up and became an island" (The Holy Kojiki part 1).

The world began when the two deities, His Augustness the Male-Who-Invites and Her Augustness the Female-Who-Invites, "standing upon the Floating Bridge of Heaven pushed down the jeweled spear and stirred with it, whereupon, when they had stirred the brine till it went curdle-curdle, and drew the spear up, the brine that dripped down from the end of the spear was piled up and became an island" (The Holy Kojiki part 1).

Citing Old Texts in Reprint

- Put the year of the original printing followed by a slash and the year of the reprinting

(Jihei, 1713/1992)

- No special citation format is needed. Cite as any other source, using the current reprint year.

Citing Plays

- For verse plays, give act, scene, and line numbers. If the play is not a verse play, simply use page numbers. For passages of three or more lines, treat as a block quote.

Because of Sukeroku, a quarreling son, a mother's life is black.
Because of Sukeroku, my quarreling lover, my life, too,
Is black. How pitiful is woman's fate (Jihei, 1713/1992, 1.1.181-183).

- For verse plays, give act, scene, and line numbers. If the play is not a verse play, simply use page numbers. For passages of three or more lines, treat as a block quote.

Because of Sukeroku, a quarreling son, a mother's life is black.
Because of Sukeroku, my quarreling lover, my life, too,
Is black. How pitiful is woman's fate (Jihei 1.1.181-183)

Citing Poems

- For poems, give part, stanza, and line numbers. If there are no separate parts or stanzas, just use line numbers preceded by the word "lines."

In her poem "In Childhood," K. Hahn (2002) creates a haunting image of the way that children perceive (or fail to perceive) death:
> things don't die or remain damaged
> but return: stumps grow back hands,
> a head reconnects to a neck,
> a whole corpse rises blushing and newly elastic (lines 1-4).

- For poems, give part, stanza, and line numbers. If there are no separate parts or stanzas, just use line numbers preceded by the word "lines."

In her poem "In Childhood," Kamiko Hahn creates a haunting image of the way that children perceive (or fail to perceive) death:
> things don't die or remain damaged
> but return: stumps grow back hands,
> a head reconnects to a neck,
> a whole corpse rises blushing and newly elastic (lines 1-4).

Citing Primary Research

- Cite personally conducted primary research by naming the kind of research in the parenthetical citation. If citing an interview or email, name the interviewee or correspondent as well.

Of the 120 Tusculum College students surveyed, 98, or approximately 82%, said that they had viewed some form of anime within the last week (personal survey, June 10-24, 2012).

"I watch anime because it reminds me of being a kid, watching cartoons, but with adult themes and ideas," said Brandon Davis (personal interview, June 10, 2012).

- Cite personally conducted primary research by naming the kind of research in the parenthetical citation. If citing an interview or email, name the interviewee or correspondent as well.

Of the 120 Tusculum College students surveyed, 98, or approximately 82%, said that they had viewed some form of anime within the last week (personal survey).

"I watch anime because it reminds me of being a kid, watching cartoons, but with adult themes and ideas," said Brandon Davis (personal interview).

Citing a Source Indirectly (from another source)

- If you are citing a source that is quoted in another source, cite the original author in your text with the author of the secondary book or article in which the quote appears in the parenthetical citation.

Nakazawa and Nakazawa claim that because of the complexity of Japanese manga, both textual and visual literacy among teens who view manga have increased (as cited in Toku, 2001, p. 14).

- In this case, Toku is the source you actually have and the one that will appear on your reference page. Toku has cited Nakazawa and Nakazawa in his article,

If you are citing a source that is quoted in another source, cite the original author in your text, with the author of the secondary book or article in which the quote appears in the parenthetical citation.

Nakazawa and Nakazawa claim that because of the complexity of Japanese manga, both textual and visual literacy among teens who view manga have increased (qtd. in Toku 14).

- In this case, Toku is the source you actually have and the one that will appear on your works cited page. Toku has cited Nakazawa and Nakazawa in his article,

and you would like to cite them as well. Nakazawa and Nakazawa will not, however, appear on your reference page.	and you would like to cite them as well. They will not, however, appear on your works cited.

Some Final Notes: What to Do if You Are Missing Information

- If, after doing absolutely everything in your power to find the year of publication, you still cannot do so, you may use (n.d.) in place of the year.
- If you have a source with no author, simply use the source title for all in-text citations.
- If you have a web source that does not have page numbers but does have paragraph numbers, you should cite the paragraph number using "para." preceding the numeral.
- When the web page has neither page nor paragraph numbers, things become a bit murkier. The APA says that you may either leave this information out altogether, or you may number the paragraphs yourself. Several professors at the stated that they would like you to number the paragraphs. However, you should ask your professor for her or his preference before proceeding.

Rabkin et. al (2001) describe the characteristics of anime: "Huge eyes, brightly colored hair, well-endowed female characters, and exaggerated emotional expressions and gestures are typical of anime style" (para. 5).

- If, after doing absolutely everything in your power to find the year of publication, you still cannot do so, you may use (n.d.) in place of the year.
- If you have a source with no author, simply use the source title for all in-text citations.
- If you have a web source that does not have page numbers but does have paragraph numbers, you should cite the paragraph number, using "par." preceding the numeral.
- When the web page has neither page nor paragraph numbers, the MLA instructs you to simply leave this information out.

Rabkin et. al describe the characteristics of anime: "Huge eyes, brightly colored hair, well-endowed female characters, and exaggerated emotional expressions and gestures are typical of anime style."

Appendix C: Bibliography

How to Use This Guide

The guide is divided into two columns, APA on the left, MLA on the right. Use the style that your professor and/or discipline requires.

The first several pages lists various kinds of authors. Locate the type of author appropriate to the text you are trying to cite and format that part of the entry. Then, locate the source *type* in the pages that follow and finish the entry. The different types of source listed in this guide include,

Author Types
- Single Author   258
- Multiple Authors   258
- More Than One Work by the Same Author   259
- Editor but No Author   259
- Author and Editor, Translator, or Illustrator   260
- Organizational Author   260
- Author and Government or University Organization   260
- Unknown Author   260
- Author Using a Pseudonym   261

Source Types
- Standard Book   261
- Introduction, Preface, Foreword or Afterword   261
- Sacred Book   262
- Ebook   262
- Article or Work in an Edited Book or Anthology   263
- Article from a Reference Book   263
- Standard Journal Article   264
- Magazine Article   264
- Newspaper Article   264
- Editorial or Letter to the Editor   264
- Book or Film Review   265

- Article from a Database — 265
- Article in Online Magazine or Newspaper — 266
- Journal Article Republished on a Website — 266
- Standard Web Page — 266
- Entire Web Site — 267
- Blog — 267
- Discussion Board — 268
- Email — 268
- Published Interview — 268
- Movie, Television Series, or Video File — 269
- Audio File — 270
- Work of Art — 270
- Speech or Lecture — 271
- Personal Primary Research — 271

Style Guide 2

Some General Rules

- In APA, you will not list authors' first names, only first initials.
- With multiple authors, preserve the order listed.
- The year always follows authors' names.
- Dates are formatted by year, month, and day. Also, months are fully spelled out.
- Short titles are NOT in quotation marks ON THE REFERENCE PAGE ONLY.
- Only periodical titles are capitalized normally on the reference page. For all other titles, capitalize only the first word, the first word after a colon, and proper nouns.
- Alphabetize all entries on the reference page.

- In MLA, use author's first and last names.
- With multiple authors, preserve the order listed.
- Dates are formatted by day, month, year. Also, months are abbreviated, not fully spelled out.
- Preserve all standard punctuation and capitalization rules on the works cited page.
- Do not use full URLs either in text or in the works cited page.
- Don't forget to name the medium on ALL entries (e.g. print, web, CD, film, etc.).
- Alphabetize all entries on the works cited page.

Single Author

Brenner, R. E. (2007). [Title of Work; See Rules Below].

Brenner, Robin E. [Title of Work; See Rules Below].

Multiple Authors

- For two to seven authors, list them all, last names first in all cases, and the final name separated by an ampersand. Preserve original order.

- Regardless of the number of authors, list them all in the order listed in original text. The first author is listed with last name first. Sub-sequent authors are listed by first then last name.

Frey, N. & Fisher, D. (2004). [Title of Work; See Rules Below].

Frey, Nancy and Douglas Fisher. [Title of Work; See Rules Below].

258

- For more than seven authors, list the first six followed by ellipses and the final author's name.

- Even for long lists of authors, include all

Wayne, J., Siler, T. Anker, S., Clarke, K, Denes, A., Grey, M. J. . . .Rich, M. R. (1996). [Title of Work; See Rules Below].

Wayne, June, Todd Siler, Suzanne Anker, Kevin Clarke, Agnes Denes, Michael Joaquin Grey, Ruth Kavenoff, Thomas Kovachevich, David Kremers, John Newman, and Marvin R. Rich. [Title of Work; See Rules Below].

More Than One Work by the Same Author

- List sources chronologically.

- Alphabetize works by title. For the second and sub-sequent entries, substitute author's name with --.

Napier, S. J. (2005). [Title of Work, etc.].
Napier, S. J. (2006). [Title of Work, etc.].

- If sources were written in the same year, add "a" and "b."

Napier, S. J. (2005a). [Title of Work; See Rules Below].
Napier, S. J. (2005b). [Title of Work; See Rules Below].

Napier, Susan J. "Matter out of Place: Carnival, Containment, and Cultural Recovery in Miyazaki's 'Spirited Away.'" *Journal of Japanese Studies* 32.2 (2006): 287-310. JStor. Web. 22 June, 2012.

---. The Problem of Existence in Japanese Animation. *Proceedings of the American Philosophical Society*. 149.1 (2005): 72-79. JStor. Web. 22 June 2012.

Editor but no Author

- Begin with the editors' names, followed by (Ed.) or (Eds.)

- Begin with the editors' names, followed by ed. or eds.

MacWilliams, M. W. (Ed.) (2008). [Title of Work; See Rules Below].

MacWilliams, Mark W., ed. [Title of Work; See Rules Below].

Author & Editor, Translator, or Illustrator

- Begin with the author; put editor(s) (Ed. or Eds.), translator (Trans.), or illustrator (Illus.) after book title.

Tezuka, O. (2002). *Astro boy*. Fredrick L.Schodt (Trans.). Milwaukee, WI: Dark Horse.

- Begin with the author; put editor(s) (Ed.), translator (Trans.), or illustrator (Illus.) after book title.

Tezuka, Osamu. *Astro Boy*. Trans. Fredrick L. Schodt. Milwaukee, WI: Dark Horse, 2002. Print.

Organizational Author

- If there is no single author but is an organizational author, begin with them.

Federal Bureau of Investigations (2011). [Title of Work, etc. See Rules Below].

- If there is no single author but is an organizational author, begin with them.

Federal Bureau of Investigations (2011). [Title of Work, etc. See Rules Below].

Author & Government or University Organization

- Put author's name first, followed by title, with organization in the "Retrieved from" section of information

Izawa, E.(1995). *What are manga and anime?*. Retrieved from Massachusetts Institute of Technology website: http://www.mit.edu/~rei/Expl.html

- Put author's name first, followed by title and then organization.

Izawa, Eri. "What are Manga and Anime?" *Massachusetts Institute of Technology*. MIT, 1995. Web. 14 Nov. 2013.

Unknown Author

- If there is no author, simply begin with the title of the work.

- If there is no author, simply begin with the title of the work.

Eclectic: Japanese manga (1995, December 16). *The Economist*, pp. 82-3. Retrieved from *General OneFile*.

"Eclectic: Japanese Manga." *The Economist* 16 Dec. 1995: 82-83. Web. 14 Nov. 2013.

Author Using a Pseudonym

- Just use the pseudonym—there's no need to include the author's real name. If the pseudonym is not in the form of "First name, last name" but is, instead, a specialized name, preserve original order.

- Begin with the pseudonym followed by author's real name (if known) in brackets.

Dr. Seuss. (1985). [Title of work, etc. See rules below].

Dr. Seuss [Theodor Seuss Geisel]. [Title of work, etc. See rules below].

Standard Format for a Book

- List in the following order: Author, year, title, place of publication, and publisher.

- List in the following order: Author, title, place of publication, publisher, year, and format.

Ladd, F. & Deneroff, H. (2009). Astro Boy *and anime come to the Americas*. Jefferson, NC: McFarland.

Ladd, Fred and Harvey Deneroff. Astro Boy *and Anime Come to the Americas*. Jefferson, NC: McFarland, 2009. Print.

Introduction, Preface, Foreword, or Afterword

- Begin with the author of the introduction, preface, foreword, or afterword, followed by the author and title of the major work.

- Begin with the author of the introduction, preface, foreword, or afterword followed by the title and author of the major work.

Kawakita, M. (1993). Introduction. In K. Hokusai, *Hokusai manga; The sketchbooks of Hokusai* (pp. x-xxi). New York, NY: Weatherhill.

Kawakita, Michiaki. Introduction. *Hokusai Manga: the Sketchbooks of Hokusai*. By Katsushika Hokusai. New York, NY: Weatherhill, 1993. x-xxi. Print.

Sacred Book

- There is no need to cite sacred texts such as the *Bible*, *Qur'an*, *Kojiki*, etc. in your reference page, only in your text.

- Start with the title of the sacred text. Then put any of the following information available in this order: editor, translator, publication information, medium, and version.

The Holy Kojiki, Including the Yengishiki. New York, NY: Cosimo, 2007. Print.

Books in Multiple Volumes

- List the volume used in parentheses after the title.

- Place volume number you are using before publication information. Put total number of volumes at the end.

Arakawa, H. (2005). *Full metal alchemist*. (Vol. 1). San Francisco, CA: VIZ Media.

Arakawa, Hiromu. *Full Metal Alchemist*. Vol. 1. San Francisco, CA: VIZ Media, 2005. Print. 27 vols.

E-Book

- If the book comes from one of the library's databases of ebooks, list this information at the end.

- If the book comes from one of the library's databases of ebooks, list this information at the end.

Brenner, R. E. (2007). *Understanding manga and anime*. Westport, CN: Libraries Unlimited. Retrieved from *NetLibrary*.

Brenner, Robin. E. *Understanding Manga and Anime*. Westport, CN: Libraries Unlimited, 2007. *NetLibrary*. Web. 23 June 2012.

- If the book is online, list the URL at the end and omit publication information.

- For online books, list the title of the website and the sponsoring organization (if there is one), following the publication information. Then the year the work was uploaded or updated, followed by the date retrieved.

Lent, J.A. (1999). *Themes and issues in Asian cartooning: Cute, cheap, mad, and sexy.* Retrieved from http://www.questia.com/PM.qst?a=o&d=102541499

Lent, John A. *Themes and Issues in Asian Cartooning: Cute, Cheap, Mad, and Sexy.* Bowling Green, OH: Bowling Green State University Popular Press, 1999. Questia.com. Web. 23 June 2012.

Article or Work in an Edited Book or Anthology

- Begin with the author and title of the shorter work followed by the editor and title of the book. Article titles are not in quotes on the reference page.

- Begin with the author and title of the shorter work followed by the title of the book or anthology and then the editor.

Poitras, G. (2008). Contemporary anime in Japanese pop culture. In M. W. MacWilliams (Ed.) *Japanese visual culture: Explorations in the world of manga and anime* (pp. 48-67). Armonke, NY: M.E .Sharpe. Retrieved from Ebrary.

Poitras, Gilles. "Contemporary Anime in Japanese Pop Culture." *Japanese Visual Culture: Explorations in the World of Manga and Anime.* Ed. Mark W. MacWilliams. Armonke, NY: M.E. Sharpe, 2008. 48-67. *Ebrary.* Web. 24 June 2012.

Article from a Reference Book

- List as any article in a book except add the volume and page numbers after reference book title.

- List author (if there is one), title of entry & reference work, edition, and format (print or web). Do NOT include editors or volume and page numbers.

Mizumura, A. (2011). Manga: Slow opening to women cartoonists. In Mary Zeiss Stange, Carol K. Oyster, and Jane E. Sloan (Eds.), *The encyclopaedia of women in today's world* (Vol. 2, pp. 891-893). Thousand Oaks, CA: Sage Reference. Retrieved from Gale Virtual Reference Library.

Mizumura, Ayako. "Manga: Slow Opening to Women Cartoonists." *The Encyclopaedia of Women in Today's World.* 1st ed. 2011. Gale Virtual Reference. Web. 15 Nov. 2013.

Standard Journal Article

- The following is the standard format for a *print* article. For articles from databases, see additional instructions below.

Toku, M. (2001). What is manga?: The influence of pop culture in adolescent art. *Art Education, 54*, 11-17.

- The following is the standard format for a *print* article. For articles from databases, see additional instructions below.

Toku, Masami. "What is Manga? The Influence of Pop Culture in Adolescent Art." *Art Education* 54.2 (2001): 11-17. Print.

Magazine Article

- Treat the same as a journal article except add the month after the year.

Mad about manga. (2006, November). *Chickadee, 28*(9), 12-15.

- Treat as a journal article except replace the volume number with the month and year.

"Mad About Manga." *Chickadee* Nov. 2006: 12-15. Print.

Newspaper Article

- Treat as a journal except give the year, month, and day, and include p. or pp. before page numbers.

Adams, M. (2003, July 8). Manga. *The Roanoke Times*, p. 1.

- Treat as a journal article except give the day, month, and year instead of volume number.

Adams, Mason. "Manga." *Roanoke Times* 8 July 2003: 1. Print.

Editorial or Letter to the Editor

- Treat as a journal or magazine article except include [Editorial] or [Letter to the editor] in between the article and periodical titles.

- Treat as a journal or magazine article except include Editorial or Letter in between the article and periodical titles.

Creel, S. L. (2008, August). Graphic novels and manga and manwha...Oh my!. [Editorial]. *Voice of Youth Advocates, 31*, 197.

Creel, Stacy L. "Graphic Novels and Manga and Manwha...Oh My!." Editorial. *Voice of Youth Advocates* Aug. 2008: 197. Print.

Book or Film Review

- Begin with the author and title (if any) of the review. In brackets, give the author and title of the work being reviewed; then proceed to periodical information.

- Begin with the author and title (if any) of the review. Follow this with "Review of" and the title and author of the work being reviewed, then the periodical information.

Theroux, M. (January 2005). The road to anime. [Review of the book *Wrong about Japan: A father's journey with his son* by P. Carey]. *New York Times Book Review*, p. 8.

Theroux, Marcel. "The Road to Anime." Review of *Wrong about Japan: A Father's Journey with His Son*, Peter Carey. *New York Times Book Review.* Jan. 2005: 8. Print.

Article from a Database

- If your article comes from a database (as most here at the College will), list the doi number at the end of the entry. If no doi number is available, list the stable URL or database name.

- If your article comes from a database (as most here at the College will), list the database information and date accessed at the end of the entry.

Ito, K. (2005). A history of manga in the context of Japanese culture and society. *Journal of Popular Culture, 38*, 456-475. doi: 10.1111/j.0022-3840.2005.00123.x

Ito, Kinko. "A History of Manga in the Context of Japanese Culture and Society." *Journal of Popular Culture* 38 (2005): 456-475. *General OneFile.* Web. 25 June 2012.

Ito, K. (2005). A history of manga in the context of Japanese culture and society. *Journal of Popular Culture, 38*, 456-475. Retrieved from General OneFile

Article in an Online Magazine or Newspaper

- Treat the same as a print magazine or newspaper article, adding the URL at the end.

- Treat as a magazine or newspaper article, adding the sponsoring organization (if there is one) in between the periodical title and the year published, and adding the access date at the end.

Mastri, M. (2011, January 15). Reflection on Sotoshi Kon's *Paranoia agent*. *Senpai Magazine*. Retrieved from http://www.senpaimagazine.com/pdf/sample_mag.pdf

Mastri, Mike. "Reflection on Sotoshi Kon's *Paranoia Agent*." *Senpai Magazine*. Anitopia LLC. 15, Jan. 2011. Web. 25 June 2012.

Journal or Magazine Article Republished on a Website

- Cite original publication information followed by the source and URL where accessed in the "retrieved from" section.

- Cite publication information for the original document, followed by the website you located it on.

Exhibit examines the 'many faces of manga,' (2009, January 15). *Nichi Bei Times*. Retrieved from Discover Nikkei: Japanese Migrants and Their Descendants at http://www.discovernikkei.org/en/journal/2009/1/30/2843/

"Exhibit Examines the 'Many Faces of Manga.'" *Nichi Bei Times*. 15 Jan. 2009. *Discover Nikkei: Japanese Migrants and Their Descendants*. Web. 15 Nov. 2013.

Webpage

- List, in the following order, as many of these pieces of information as possible: author, date of publication (n.d. if none), title of document (in italics), and the words "Retrieved from" followed by the URL

- List, in the following order, as many of these pieces of information as possible: author, title of page, title of site, sponsoring organization (if it's a personal website, relist author), date last updated (or n.d. if none listed), and finally, the word "Web" and the date accessed.

Rabkin, E., Bonifeld, B., Goldberg, E., Kerr, B., Lee, J., & Sharer, L. (2001). *Introduction to anime: Everything you ever wanted to know about Japanese cartoons, but were afraid to ask*. Retrieved from http://www.umich.edu/~anime/intro.html

Rabkin, Eric, Bonnie Bonifeld, Eric Goldberg, Brian Kerr, Jeff Lee, and Lianna Sharer. "Introduction to Anime: Everything You Ever Wanted to Know about Japanese Cartoons, but Were Afraid to Ask." *That Anime Project*. University of Michigan, 2001. Web. 25 June 2013.

Entire Website

- The APA discourages the listing of entire websites (such as "Tusculum.edu"). Instead, list the individual pages referenced as separate entries.

- List, in the following order, as many of these pieces of information as possible: author, title of site, sponsoring organization (if it's a personal website, relist author), date last updated (or n.d. if none listed), and finally, the word "Web" and the date accessed.

Rabkin, Eric, Bonnie Bonifeld, Eric Goldberg, Brian Kerr, Jeff Lee, and Lianna Sharer. *That Anime Project*. University of Michigan, 2001. Web. 25 June 2013.

Blog

- List the author of the blog and the date and subject. Then write "Web log post," and give the URL.

- List the author, title of post (if none, write "Web log entry,") title of blog, date created, the word "Web," and the date accessed.

Cassidy, K. (2011, July 27). Using anime soundtracks to introduce anime itself [Web log post]. Retrieved from http://animeyourway.blogspot.com/2011/07/using-anime-soundtracks-to-introduce.html

Cassidy, Kevin. "Using Anime Soundtracks to Introduce Anime Itself." *Anime Your Way*, 27 July 2011. Web. 26 June 2012.

Discussion Board

- Give the name of the poster (if available) and the date posted, followed by the title of the post and the phrase "Discussion Board Post" in brackets. Finish with URL.

- Give author's name (if available), followed by title of post, the name of the discussion board, the sponsor, date the post was created, the word "Web," and the access date.

Anime/manga that helps with your education (2012, June 27). [Discussion Board Post]. Retrieved from http:// my-animelist.net/forum/ ?topicid=457015

"Anime/Manga That Helps with your Education." *MyAnimeList.net*. CraveOnline Media, 27 June, 2012. Web. 28 June 2012.

Email

- There is no need to cite email communications on the reference page, only in text.

- Give the author's name and subject line, followed by the phrase "Message to. . ." and the name of the recipient. Then give the date of the message and the word "E-mail."

Nielson, Miles. "Re: Why Do You Watch Anime?" Message to the author. 20 June 2012. E-mail.

Published Interview

- Begin with the person being interviewed followed by the date of the interview. List title if any, then "Interview by. . ." in brackets. Then add the remainder of the publication information depending on type (see previous types including journals, newspapers, webpages, etc.).

- Begin with the name of the person being interviewed, followed by the name of the interviewer. Then list title of interview and publication information depending on type (see previous types including journals, magazines, newspapers, webpages, etc.).

Gaiman, N.. (2005, July 25). Talking manga with Neil Gaiman [Interview by C Reid]. *Publishers Weekly, 252*, 16. Retrieved from *General OneFile*.

Gaiman, Neil. Interview by Calvien Reid. "Talking Manga with neil Gaiman." *Publishers Weekly* 25 July 2005: 16. *General OneFile*. Web. 26 June 2012.

Movies, Television Series, & Video Files

- Begin with the name of the director, producer, writer and/or other relevant contributor (whomever you are citing in your paper. If in doubt, choose director) followed in parenthesis by that title.
- Next list the date of release and the title.
- Then, in brackets, put the kind of video file it is (e.g. motion picture, documentary, television episode, video file, etc.).
- For television series, list the name of the producer and the series next.
- For all, if there is a movie studio or network available, list that information next.
- Finally, if the video is an online file, list the URL.

- Start with the name of the film, television episode, or television series (if citing the whole series).
- If citing a single television episode, include the name of the series next, in italics.
- In all cases, follow with the director and major performers if relevant, preceded by Dir. for director and Perf. for performers.
- Next, list the distributor (for movies) network (for Television Series) or website (for online videos).
- Finally, include the release date, the medium (i.e. "Film," "Television Episode," "Television Series," or "Web"), and for online videos, the date accessed.

Schaffel, A. & Hadley, D. (Writers, Directors, Producers). (2006, December 20). *An introduction to anime through science fiction*. [Video File]. Retrieved from http://www.youtube.com/watch?v=kqSj6liMWwI

An Intoruction to Anime Through Science Fiction. Dirs. Schaffel, Arlin and Dan Hadley. Perf. Arlin Schaffel and Dan Hadley. *YouTube*. 20 Dec. 2006. Web. 26 June 2013

Jun'ichi, S. (Director). (1992). Punish them! The house of fortune is the monster mansion [Television series episode]. In Andy Hayward (Executive producer), *Sailor Moon*. Tokyo, TV Asahi.

"Punish Them! The House of Fortune is the Monster Mansion." *Sailor Moon*. Dir. Satô Jun'ichi. TV Asahi, Tokyo. 14 March 1992. Television Episode.

Miyazaki, H. (Director). (1999, November 26). *Princess Mononoke*. [Animated Motion Picture]. Dentsu.

Princess Mononoke. Dir. Miyazaki, Hayao. Perf. Yôji Matsuda, Yuriko Ishida, and Yûko Tanaka. Dentsu. 1999. Film

Audio File

- Begin with the name of the recording artist followed by the date and title. If the audio is from an album of multiple audio files, include the name of the album. Next include the file type (e.g. CD, MP3, or Audio file) in brackets, the place of publication and publisher if there is one, and the URL if the file is online.

- Begin with the name of the person you are citing (e.g. composer, performer, conductor, etc.), followed by the name of the work (for songs, use quotation marks, for long works—like symphonies or scores—use italics). If the song comes from a larger album, include that title next, italicized. This is followed by the names of the performers, the orchestra, and conductor if relevant. Finally, include the manufacturer, the date created, and the file type (e.g. CD, MP3, Audio File, etc.).

The New Japan Philharmonic Orchestra. (2008). A road to somewhere. *Spirited away: The soundtrack*. [MP3]. Los Angeles, CA: Milan Records. Retrieved from http://www.amazon.com/Spirited-Away-Joe-Hisaishi/dp/B00006HCT7

The New Japan Philharmonic Orchestra. "A Road to Somewhere." *Spirited Away: The Soundtrack*. Milan Records, 2008. MP3.

Work of Art

- Begin with the artist's name and year, followed by the work in italics. If the work is in a museum, give the name and place of the museum; if online, give the name of the website and the URL.

- Begin with the artist's name, the title of the work, and the date. If you have access to the artwork in real life, give the medium (e.g. Photograph, Oil on Canvas, Watercolor, etc) and the location. If it is online, put the name of the web site (and location if applicable), the word "Web," and the date of access.

Kojima, G. (1970). *Lone wolf and cub.* Cartoon Art Museum, San Francisco, CA. Retrieved from http://cartoonart.org/2010/01/drawing-the-sword-samurai-in-manga-and-anime/

Kojima, Goseki. *Lone Wolf and Cub.* 1970. Cartoon Art Museum, San Francisco, CA. Web. 26 June 2012.

Speech or Lecture

- After author and year, give the name of the speech or lecture in italics, followed by the type of presentation it was, the name of the conference (if any), and the place of presentation.

- Begin with the speaker's name followed by the title of the speech or lecture. Then put the name of the meeting or conference (if there is one), the location, and the date. Finally, give the type of presentation it is.

Davis, C. (2013). *Using Graphic Novels in the Classroom.* Conference Presentation, ACA Summit, Knoxville, TN.

Davis, Charles. "Using Graphic Novels in the Classroom." ACA Summit, Knoxville, TN, 17 Oct. 2013. Conference Presentation.

Personal Primary Research

- There is no need to cite personal interviews, surveys, experiments, or observations on the reference page, only in text.

- For interviews, begin with the name of the person interviewed, followed by the phrase "Personal Interview" and the date.

Davis, Brandon. Personal Interview. 10 June 2012.

- While the MLA does not specifically address citing personal surveys, experiments, or observations, these are similar in essence to the personal interview, so we suggest following that format, using yourself as author, and naming your participant pool in the title.

Morton, Sheila. Personal Survey of Tusculum College Students. 10-24 June 2012.

Works Cited
(By Chapter)

Chapter 1

Cioffi, Frank L. *The Imaginative Argument: A Practical Manifesto for Writers.* Princeton, NJ: Princeton University Press, 2005.

Dunn, Patricia. *Talking, Sketching, Moving: Multiple Literacies in the Teaching of Writing.* Portsmouth, NH : Heinemann, 2001. Print.

Elbow, Peter. *Writing with Power: Techniques for Mastering the Writing Process.* London, UK: Oxford University Press, 1998. Print.

Meyers, Walter Dean. *Monster.* New York, NY: Amistad, 2004. Print.

Potok, Chaim. *The Chosen.* New York, NY: Ballantine, 1967. Print.

Chapter 2

"Anew Clinical Absolute Even Multi-Tone Skin Corrector." *Avon.* 2014. Web. 31 Mar. 2014.

Berry, Jason. "Cancer Alley: The Poisoning of the American South." Photog. Richard Misrach. *Aperture* 162 (2001): 30-41. Web. 3 Jan. 2012.

Berry, Wendell. "The Pleasures of Eating." *What Are People For?: Essays.* New York, NY: Farrar, Straus and Giroux, 1990. *Organic Gardening.* Web. 15 Sept. 2011.

Buckingham, David. "Childhood in the Age of Global Media." *Children's Geographies* 5.2 (2007): 43-54. *Academia.edu.* Web. 4 Feb. 2012.

Carter, Stephen L. "The Insufficiency of Honesty." *Atlantic Monthly*, Feb. 1996: 74-76. *California State University, Northridge.* Web. 15 Dec. 2012.

Draut, Tamara. "The Growing College Gap." *Inequality Matters: The Growing Economic Divide in America and its Poisonous Consequences*. Eds. James Lardner and David Smith. New York, NY: New Press, 2006. 89-101. Print.

Friedman, Thomas. *The World is Flat: A Brief History of the Twenty-first Century*. New York, NY: Farrar, Strauss, Giroux, 2005. Print.

Greene, Stuart and April Lidinsky. *From Inquiry to Academic Writing*. Boston, MA: Bedford/St. Martins, 2011. Print.

Hamill, Pete. "Crack and the Box." *Piecework: Writings on Men and Women, Fools and Heroes, Lost Cities, Vanished Cities, Small Pleasures, Large Calamities, and How the Weather Was*. Boston, MA: Little, Brown, and Company, 1996. Print.

Harris, Sam. *The Moral Landscape: How Science Can Determine Human Values*. New York, NY: Free Press, 2010.

"Is College for Everyone?" *Yahoo Voices*. 25 Apr. 2007. Web. 2 Feb. 2012.

Kimmel, Michael S. "Gender, Class and Terrorism." *The Chronicle of Higher Education* 48.2 (2002): B11-B12. *Proquest*. Web. 10 Jan. 2012.

Lorber, Judith. "Believing is Seeing: Biology as Ideology." *Gender and Society* 7 (1993): 568-581. *JStor*. Web. 3 Jan. 2012.

"Lysol Disinfectant Spray." *Lysol*. 2013. Web. 3 Mar. 2014.

Matherly, Desirae. "Wagering Pressures." *Lake Effect: A Journal for the Literary Arts*. 13 (2009): 51-66. Print.

Muller, Richard. *Physics for Future Presidents: The Science Behind the Headlines*. New York, NY: Norton, 2008. Print.

Obama, Barack. "A More Perfect Union." Philadelphia, PA, 18 Mar. 2008. Speech. *Huffington Post* 17, Nov. 2008. Web. 8 Feb. 2012.

Postman, Neil. *Amusing Ourselves to Death: Public Discourse in the Age of Show Business*. New York, NY: Penguin, 2005. Print.

Reardon, Sean F. "No Rich Child Left Behind." *New York Times* 28 Apr. 2013: SR1. *LexisNexis*. Web. 2 Dec. 2011.

∎ ∎ ∎ ∎

Chapter 3

Morton, Sheila. Personal Survey of Tusculum College Students in English 111. 12-14 Dec. 2011.

Sommers, Nancy. "Revision Strategies of Student Writers and Experienced Adult Writers." *College Composition and Communication*. 31.4 (1980): 378-388. *JStor*. Web. 28 Mar. 2012.

Thomas, Nancy. "Peer Review." Handout. Tusculum College. Greeneville, TN.

Strunk, William. *The Elements of Style*. New York, NY: Macmillan, 1951. Print.

∎ ∎ ∎ ∎

Chapter 4

Aristotle. *Rhetoric*. Ed. W. Rhy Roberts. Mineola, NY: Dover, 2004. Print.

Arkes, Hadley. "Statement of Hadley Arkes, Edward Ney Professor of Jurisprudence and American Institutions, Amherst College." *Defense of Marriage Act: Hearing Before the Subcommittee on the Constitution of the Committee on the Judiciary, House of Representatives, One Hundred Fourth Congress, Second Session, On HR. 3396, Defense of Marriage Act, May 15, 1996*. 15 May 1996. Web. 5 Apr. 2013.

Arnhart, Larry. "Why Males Rule." Review of *King of the Mountain: The Nature of Political Leadership*, Arnold M. Ludwig. *Claremont Review of Books* 3.4 (2003): 64-65. *Academic OneFile*. Web. 10 Aug. 2012.

Bartless, Neil. Review of *Vested Interests: Cross Dressing and Cultural Anxiety*, Margery Gerber. *American Theatre* 9.4 (1992): 44. *Academic OneFile*. Web. 10 Aug. 2012.

Browne, Harry. *How I found Freedom in an Unfree World.* New York, NY: Avon Books, 1974. Print.

Burnham, Bo. "Love Is." *Love Is (Live).* Comedy Central Records, 2009. MP3.

Bush, George. "Address to a Joint Session of Congress and the American People." Washington, D.C., 20 Sept. 2001. Speech. *Whitehouse*. Web. 1 Sept. 2012.

Cameron, David. "There Are Five Million People on Benefits in Britain. How Do We Stop Them Turning into Karen Matthews?" *The Daily Mail*, 8 Dec. 2008. Web. 10 Oct. 2012.

Carroll, Marilyn E. "Primate Model of Drug Abuse: Intervention Strategies." *National Institute of Health Research Reporting Portfolio Online Reporting Tools.* University of Minnesota and National Institute on Drug Abuse, 2011. Web. 18 Mar. 2013.

Clinton, Hillary. Interview by Dan Rather. *CBS Evening News*. 13 Sept. 2001. *YouTube*. Web. 1 Sept. 2012.

Crane, Stephen. *Red Badge of Courage.* 1895. Mineola, NY: Dover, 1990. Print.

Dakss, Brian. "I Need Everything." *CBS News,* 6 Sept. 2005. Web. 18 Nov. 2012.

Engel, S. Morris. *Fallacies and Pitfalls of Language: The Language Trap.* Mineola, NY: Dover, 1994. Print.

Freston, Kathy. "Vegetarian is the New Prius." *Huffington Post* 18 Jan. 2007. Web. 2 Sept. 2012.

Garcia Marquez, Gabriel. *Living to Tell the Tale.* Trans. Edith Grossman. New York, NY: Vintage, 2004. Print.

Goudreau, Jenna. "Why Men and Women Get Married." *Forbes*, 27 May 2010. Web. 1 Sept. 2012.

Greene, L. D. "Pathos." *Encyclopedia of Rhetoric*. 1st ed. Oxford, UK: Oxford University Press, 2001. Print.

Guider, Margaret Eletta. "She Who Serves." Review of *An Argument for the Restoration of the Female Diaconate in the Catholic Church*, Phyllis Zagano. *America* 182.21 (2000): 31. *Academic OneFile*. Web. 12 Aug. 2012.

Harris, Sam. *Letter to a Christian Nation*. New York: Borzoi, 2006. Print.

Lakoff, George and Mark Johnson. *Metaphors We Live By*. Chicago, IL: University of Chicago Press, 1980. Print.

Little, Paul E. *Know Why You Believe*. Downers Grove, IL: Intervarsity Press, 2000. Print.

Mackey, Robert. "Bloggers Cherry-Pick from Social Media to Cast Trayvon Martin as a Menace." *New York Times Blog: The Lede*. 29 Mar. 2012. Web. 2 Apr. 2013.

Morrison, Toni. *Tar Baby*. New York, NY: Signet, 1983. Print.

Obama, Barack. "Inaugural Address." Washington, D.C., 20 Jan. 2009. Speech. *Whitehouse*. Web. 1 Sept. 2012.

O'Neill, Molly. "A Growing Movement Fights Diets Instead of Fat." *The New York Times*, 12 Apr. 1992. Web. 2 Apr. 2013.

Paul, Rand. "Sen. Paul Addresses 40th Annual Conservative Political Action Conference." National Harbor, MD, 14 Mar. 2013. Speech. *CPAC*. Web. 18 Mar. 2013.

Quindlen, Anna. *Loud and Clear*. New York, NY: Ballantine, 2004. Print.

Roosevelt, Franklin D. "First Inaugural Address." Washington, D. C., 4 Mar. 1933. Speech. *Bartleby*. Web. 1 Sept. 2012.

Salinitri, Rose Ann. "Bill Clinton: A Man You Can Trust?" *Conservative News and Views* 6 Sept. 2012. Web. 8 Sept. 2012.

Sanders, Scott Russell. "Under the Influence: Paying the Price of My Father's Booze." *Harpers*, Nov. 1989. Web. 10 Nov. 2012.

"Trayvon Suspended Three Times for 'Drugs, Truancy, Graffiti and Carrying Burglary Tool' and Did He Attack Bus Driver Too? New Picture Emerges of Victim as Parents Claim it's All a Smear." *The Daily Mail*, 26 Mar. 2012. Web. 2 Apr. 2013

The White House Working Group on the Family. *The Family: Preserving America's Future*. Washington, D.C.: The Working Group, 1986. *Hathi Trust Digital Library*. Web. 4 Sept. 2012.

■ ■ ■ ■

Chapter 5

Ballenger, Bruce. *The Curious Researcher*. New York: Longman, 2009. Print.

Lunsford, Andrea A, and John Ruszkiewicz. *Everything's an Argument*. Boston, MA: Bedford/St. Martin's, 2010. Print.

Matherly, Desirae. Personal Interview. 17 Jan. 2013.

Pagnucci, Gian. "The Tyranny of Argument: Rethinking the Work of Composition." Conference on College Composition and Communication, Las Vegas, NV, 15, Mar. 2013. Conference Presentation.

"Sample Size: How Many Survey Participants Do I Need?" *Science Buddies*, 2014. Web. 9 May, 2014.

Sunstein, Bonnie Stone and Elizabeth Chiseri-Strater. *Fieldworking: Reading and Writing Research*. Boston, MA: Bedford/St. Martins, 2007. Print.

Toulmin, Stephen E. *The Uses of Argument*. 1958. Cambridge, UK: Cambridge University Press, 2003.

Young, Richard, Alton Becker, and Kenneth Pike. *Rhetoric, Discovery and Change*. San Diego, CA: Harcourt, 1970. Print.

■ ■ ■ ■

Chapter 6

Burke, Kenneth. *The Philosophy of Literary Form*. Berkeley, CA: University of California Press, 1941. Print.

Crovitz, Darren and W. Scott Smoot. "Wikipedia: Friend, Not Foe." *The English Journal* 98 (2009): 91-97. *JStor*. Web. 20 Mar. 2012.

■ ■ ■ ■

Chapter 7

Bodary, Michael. "Annotated Bibliographies." Handout. Tusculum College. Greeneville, TN.

Bremer, Sidney H. "Home in Harlem, New York: Lessons from the Harlem Renaissance Writers." *PMLA* 105(1990): 47-56. *JStor*. Web. 15 Apr. 2013.

Association of American Publishers. "Learn More About Scholarly Information." *AAP*, 2014. Web. 9 May 2014.

Thomas, Susan. "Primary vs. Secondary Sources." *BMCC Library*, 14 Apr. 2014. Web. 9 May, 2014.

■ ■ ■ ■

Chapter 8

Ballenger, Bruce. *The Curious Researcher*. New York: Longman, 2009. Print.

Elbow, Peter. *Writing with Power: Techniques for Mastering the Writing Process*. London, UK: Oxford University Press, 1998. Print.

Goldin-Meadow and Martha Wagner Alibali. "Gesture's Role in Speaking, Learning, and Creating Language." *The Annual Review of Psy-*

chology 64(2013): 257-283. *EBSCO: Psychology and Behavior Sciences Collection* Web. 30 Dec. 2013.

Tabor, Matthew. "Parents Must Consider Disadvantages Before Home Schooling." *Education News* 12 June 2009. Web. 18 Dec. 2013.

Tusculum College. "Plagiarism Policy." Syllabi Handout. Tusculum College. Greeneville, TN.

■   ■   ■   ■

Made in the USA
San Bernardino, CA
14 August 2016